Consuming

Media

Consuming

Media

Communication,

Shopping

and

Everyday

Life

Johan Fornäs
Karin Becker
Erling Bjurström
Hillevi Ganetz

Oxford • New York

English edition
First published in 2007 by
Berg
Editorial offices:
First Floor, Angel Court, 81 St Clements Street, Oxford OX4 1AW, UK
175 Fifth Avenue, New York, NY 10010, USA

© Johan Fornäs, Karin Becker, Erling Bjurström and Hillevi Ganetz 2007

Berg is the imprint of Oxford International Publishers Ltd.

Library of Congress Cataloging-in-Publication Data
Consuming media : communication, shopping, and everyday life / Johan
Fornäs ... [et al.].
    p. cm.
Includes bibliographical references and index.
ISBN-13: 978-1-84520-759-5 (cloth)
ISBN-10: 1-84520-759-9 (cloth)
ISBN-13: 978-1-84520-760-1 (pbk.)
ISBN-10: 1-84520-760-2 (pbk.)
 1. Mass media—Social aspects. 2. Communication—Social aspects.
3. Consumption (Economics)—Social aspects. I. Fornäs, Johan, 1952-

HM1206.C67 2007
302.2301—dc22   2007007417

British Library Cataloguing-in-Publication Data
A catalogue record for this book is available from the British Library.

ISBN   978 1 84520 759 5 (Cloth)
       978 1 84520 760 1 (Paper)

Typeset by Avocet Typeset, Chilton, Aylesbury, Bucks
Printed in the United Kingdom by Biddles Ltd, King's Lynn.

www.bergpublishers.com

Published with support from the
Bank of Sweden Tercentenary Foundation.

CONTENTS

ACKNOWLEDGEMENTS

This book has been written by four authors in a collective fashion, with Johan Fornäs bringing it all together at the end. All the other co-researchers who in various periods and functions worked with the Passages project have delivered invaluable material, ideas and other inputs: Åsa Bäckström, Göran Bolin, Leonor Camauër, Lena Gemzöe, Nanna Gillberg, Anette Göthlund, Martin Gustavsson, Hasse Huss, Lars Kaijser, Sonia Kalmering, Martina Ladendorf, Karin Lövgren and Love Nordenmark. A reference group has been in support with important feedback: Bosse Bergman, Dag Björkegren, Ulf Boëthius, Peter Dahlgren, Kirsten Drotner, Pierre Guillet de Monthoux, Orsi Husz, André Jansson, Lisbeth Larsson, Marianne Liliequist, Ulf Lindberg, Orvar Löfgren, Bo Reimer and Ove Sernhede. We are grateful to them all, as well as to the scholars and institutions who have shown an interest in our work at different universities in Sweden and internationally, including colleagues at the Department of Culture Studies, Linköping University; Orvar Löfgren, Tom O'Dell and other ethnologists at Lund University; Jonathan Schroeder at the School of Business and Economics, University of Exeter; Magnus Mörck and his crew at the Centre for Consumer Science, Göteborg University; Roger Odin *et al.* at Nouvelle Sorbonne in Paris, France; Sonia Livingstone, Nick Couldry, Don Slater *et al.* at the London School of Economics, UK; Daniel Miller at University of Central London, UK; Mica Nava and colleagues at the University of East London, UK; David Morley *et al.* at Goldsmiths College, London University, UK; Ien Ang and her team at the University of Western Sydney, Australia; Meaghan Morris and her colleagues at Lingnan University in Hong Kong, China; Kuan-Hsing Chen and others at three universities in and near Taipeh, Taiwan. We also send warm thanks to all our helpers in the ethnographic work, including visitors, customers, salespersons, civil servants and managers at all levels. The project as well as the publication of this book were generously funded by the Bank of Sweden Tercentenary Foundation. It was hosted first by the Department of Journalism, Media and Communication at Stockholm University, and then by the National Institute of Working Life in Norrköping, Sweden. Its first four volumes are published in Swedish by the publisher Nya Doxa, and this volume makes free use of elements from these previous ones. Finally, through their encouragement and support, Tristan Palmer and his colleagues at Berg Publishers have made this last Passages book become reality in a most wonderful way.

THE AUTHORS

JOHAN FORNÄS is Professor at the Department of Culture and Society at Campus Norrköping of Linköping University, where he is also Director of the national centre for interdisciplinary cultural research called the Advanced Cultural Studies Institute of Sweden (ACSIS). His background is in musicology, and media and communication studies, and he has done extensive research on popular music, youth culture and media culture. He has also published widely in English, with articles in journals like *Black Renaissance*; *Convergence*; *Cultural Studies*; *European Journal of Cultural Studies*; *New Formations*; *Nordicom-Review*; *Popular Music*; *Popular Music and Society*; *Social Science Information*; *Theory, Culture and Society*; and *Young: Nordic Journal of Youth Research*. His nearly thirty published books and anthologies include *Moves in Modernity* (A&W International, 1992), *Cultural Theory and Late Modernity* (Sage, 1995), *Youth Culture in Late Modernity* (Sage, 1995), *In Garageland: Rock, Youth and Modernity* (Routledge, 1995), and *Digital Borderlands: Cultural Studies of Identity and Interactivity on the Internet* (Peter Lang, 2002).

KARIN BECKER is Professor at the Department of Culture and Society, Campus Norrköping of Linköping University, and the Department of Journalism, Media and Communication, Stockholm University. She began her career in the mass communication and journalism programs at Indiana University and the University of Iowa, specializing in documentary photography and photojournalism, and moved to Sweden in the mid 1980s. She has also worked as Professor at the National College of Art, Craft and Design (Konstfack) in Stockholm. Her research focuses on cultural histories and contemporary contexts of visual media practices, in the press, in museums, in private settings and in ethnographic research. Her English publications include *Dorothea Lange and the Documentary Tradition* (Louisiana State University Press, 1980), *The Strip: An American Place* (University of Nebraska Press, 1985) and *Picturing Politics. Visual and Textual Formations of Modernity in the Swedish Press* (JMK/Stockholm University, 2000), as well as numerous journal articles and anthology contributions.

ERLING BJURSTRÖM is Professor at the Department of Culture and Society, Campus Norrköping of Linköping University. He has a background in sociology, and media and communication studies. His previous research includes studies on youth culture, media culture, advertising, popular music and ethnicity. He has published seventeen books and contributed to over sixty anthologies in Swedish, and also published English articles on advertising and consumer research, cultural studies, cultural policy and ethnicity. His Swedish publications include the extensive volume on youth culture, *Högt och lågt. Smak och stil i ungdomskulturen* (*High and Low: Taste and Style in Youth Culture*, Boréa, 1997), and among his English publications, *Children and Television Advertising: A Critical Study of International Research Concerning the Effects of TV-commercials on Children* (The National Swedish Board For Consumer Policies, 1994).

HILLEVI GANETZ is Associate Professor at the Centre for Gender Studies, Uppsala University. Her background is in media and communication studies and literature – fields that she combined in her dissertation on Swedish female rock lyrics. Her research interests are popular culture, consumption, young women, popular literature and music, feminist theory and cultural studies. She has co-edited several books in Swedish concerning youth culture, young women, feminism and Marxism, and most recently, media and consumption. She is currently conducting research on how nature, culture, gender and sexuality are represented in wildlife films and how gender and sexuality is constructed in a TV docu-soap depicting sixteen young music artists on their way to fame. Her English publications include: 'The female body, the soul and modernity: A dichotomy reflected in a poem and a rock text', *Young*, 3/1994; 'The shop, the home and femininity as a masquerade', Fornäs and Bolin (eds): *Youth Culture in Late Modernity* (Sage 1995); 'Her Voices: Mediated Female Texts in a Cultural Perspective', *Nordicom Review*, 1/1998; 'Diving in the river or being it: Nature, gender and rock lyrics', Toru Mitsui (ed.): *Popular Music: Intercultural Interpretations* (1998); 'The happiness of being sad, or What is melancholic rock lyrics?', Tarja Hautamäki and Helmi Järviluoma (eds): *Music on Show: Issues of Performance* (1998); 'Familiar Beasts: Nature, Culture and Gender in Wildlife Films on Television', *Nordicom Review*, 25:1–2 (2004).

TABLES AND FIGURES

1. LOCATING MEDIA PRACTICES

Media transgress borders. This is their main purpose and function: to put people in contact with someone or something that would otherwise be beyond reach in time or space – like an image from the past or a voice from far away. Communication implies the crossing of borders – historically across *time*, geographically across *space*, socially between *people*, and culturally between *texts* within various symbolic forms and genres. Media use belongs to the core of human activities in late modern societies, reconfirming that human beings are transgressing animals. For Georg Simmel, 'the human being is the connecting creature who must always separate and cannot connect without separating' and 'the bordering creature who has no border'.[1]

There is in world history, in the modern era, and most particularly in its current late-modern phase, an accelerating growth, spread, diversification and interlacing of communications media across the globe. Media use constitutes increasingly greater parts of everyday life for a growing number of people around the world. This historical process of mediatization draws a widening range of activities into the sphere of media, making mediation an inreasingly key feature of society and everyday life. All contemporary major social and cultural issues directly implicate uses of media. Debates on war, science, ethics, ecology, gender identities, ethnic communities, generation gaps and socialization – all immediately raise questions of media power. Media no longer form a distinct sector, but are fully integrated in human life. This paradoxically means that their enormous influence can never be adequately 'measured', since there is no media-free zone with which to compare their effects.

The compression of time and space brought on by digital network technologies is one aspect of this process of mediatization. Never before have so much information and so many kinds of symbolic forms been transmitted across such great distances, stored and preserved for future generations, and shared by so many people for such multifarious purposes. Digitalization has also made possible an unprecedented convergence of media branches (institutions), genres (symbolic modes) and uses (practices), which blurs traditional distinctions.[2] Media thus not only move across time and space, but also transgress their own traditional classifications. The very concept of media is diffuse and contested, calling for more integrated forms of investigating. It is increasingly difficult to distinguish communication media technologies from other artefacts and to draw clear lines between main types of media. Mediation is everywhere, media technologies are today integrated into almost all other technologies and all social practices, and media forms tend to mix and blend in increasingly complex ways. This pervasive presence and heterogeneous hybridity of media invites an open investigation of how people meet and deal with all kinds of media, and a renewed reflection on the basic ways in which communication is mediated in the contemporary world of late modernity.

However, while communication media cross borders, they do not erase them. Media practices are always situated in time and space. This is rarely adequately reflected in media research. Media use is always spatially and temporally located, while simultaneously both representing and shaping space and time. Mediated communication both takes time and makes time, and it both takes place and makes place. Localizing mediated communication in temporal and spatial settings makes it possible to discern connections and distinctions that are easily forgotten. A cultural studies perspective on media use focuses how meanings, identities and power are produced and implied in practices that are simultaneously interactive and textual, both localized and globalized. The acquisition and use of media are embedded in everyday lifeworlds where people interact using multiple technologies as tools of communication. These have essential time-space co-ordinates. Recent transformations of communication and consumption processes through mediatization, aestheticization, digitalization, hybridization and globalization have necessitated new and better ways of understanding the uses of media in everyday life, in at least three respects.

1. First, the widening forms of mediation and their mutual interdependence due to dense intermedial transactions necessitate a broader concept of media and a focus on the interplay between different media circuits. Media studies need to respond to media expansion by including a wider range of communication technologies: traditional mass media as well as interpersonal and interactive media. And as a response to media convergence, one must investigate numerous ways in which different kinds of media interrelate.
2. Second, it is crucial to restore the full temporal process of consumption, through the four main phases from selection and purchase to use and disposal. The communicative encounters between people and media form extended and varied processes of interlaced consumption chains, which the traditional division of consumption and reception studies usually bifurcates. The combinatory ways in which various kinds of media circuits are selected, bought, utilized and resold, thrown or given away typically differ, depending on the duration, setting and character of each such phase. And these processes look different when media are immediately consumed, hoarded and collected, loaned or used as gifts.
3. Third, processes of consumption and communication have to be contextualized in space and time. All media are used in specific places. Until recently, media research has tended to make the spaces of media practices invisible, depicting communication and media reception as if they happened anywhere. There is now a growing

interest in the geographies of communication, in line with a more general effort to situate cultural processes.[3]

Localizing media consumption in physical and social space and time makes visible connections and distinctions that are otherwise neglected. This book explores what can be learnt from a consistently localizing approach to media practices. It starts from a specific site rather than from specific kinds of media or specific audiences. A shopping centre offers a context for studying late-modern consumption typical in the sense that most kinds of people and media flow through such a space. Investigating how media are sold, bought and used by people in such a centre, a wide range of interactions between people and media are discerned. Based on solid ethnographic research, this book offers a unique and comprehensive presentation of late-modern media practices in their full complexity, cutting across boundaries such as those between production and consumption or between various kinds of media. It thus enables a transgression of the prevailing borders that otherwise hampers a critical understanding of how different localities, media, people and practices are interconnected in a mediatized world. It highlights how people consume media, and how media in a sense also consume people, mediating and shaping their interrelations, actions and thoughts. It thereby indicates how deeply intertwined communication and shopping are in everyday life of today.

PARIS 1800 – BERLIN 1900 – STOCKHOLM 2000

This approach moves not only translocally between contemporary spaces of media consumption across the globe, but also across temporal distances. Each time-space has links to other ones – through historical memory and through anticipatory imagination. One particularly fruitful move leaves our present location in Stockholm at the threshold of the twenty-first century and follows the German cultural critic Walter Benjamin (1892–1940) back to early twentieth century Berlin, continuing in his company back to the Paris of the early and mid nineteenth century. Benjamin's work offers an historical backdrop as well as a methodological influence. His unfinished *Passagen-Werk*, written in the 1930s, posthumously published in German in 1982 and in English in 1999 as *The Arcades Project*, was an admirable effort to depict the fluidity and incongruence of the modern world by studying all the people and commodities that flowed through the commercial urban spaces of the nineteenth-century Paris shopping galleries.[4] As a critical historical materialist on the fringe of the dissident early Frankfurt school, with both Jewish and Marxist philosophical affinities, Benjamin developed ideas about modern mediatized society that still remain valid and useful. There are innovative traits to be taken up from his specific analyses of modern times and media, from his consciously ambiguous position combining sensual fascination and sharp critique, and from his labyrinthine, winding and multifarious writing style, creating a montage of voices from theoretical as well as popular sources.

Passages of consumption transgress times as well as space. Our study juxtaposes early, high and late modernity, as well as the European locations of Paris, Berlin and

Stockholm. Such double movements highlight historical and spatial specificities, but also establish continuities across chronological sequences or geographical maps. It is not only cultural analysts who choose to juxtapose times and spaces in order better to understand their differences. Urban shopping spaces themselves also make such juxtapositions, not least by using media of communication to construct memories and interactions through superimposing distant and past images onto the local and the present. Media assist other human artefacts in preserving and reworking the past within the present, and they also aid other transportation technologies in overcoming physical distance. Media are cultural tools that compress, juxtapose and define time and space. Media texts and technologies are integral to the production of experiences, of memories and of dream images – and thus of the identities of individuals, collectivities and sites.

Media play key roles in Benjamin's texts. One influential example is his idea that mass reproduction eroded the quasi-sacred 'aura' of art – the unique sense of presence in time and space that was profaned by print, posters, photographs and phonographs.[5] But his phenomenological analyses of everyday life were also filled with references to advertising images and texts that in papers and signs expressed the fantasies and dreams of consuming collectives, and to the practices of people who encounter and use a large range of media, as collectors, flâneurs or ordinary city dwellers, consumers and citizens. His interest in arcade 'passages' was not arbitrary. They offered a chance to study the fleeting transitions and contradictions, ambiguities and ambivalences inherent in modern urban life, where the dichotomies of house/street, inside/outside, private/public, commerce/culture and consumption/communication were repeatedly deconstructed and reconstituted. His writings are exemplary in their understanding of media culture in terms of dynamic processes, flows, transitions and mediations rather than in stiff and static categories. These passages run through urban spaces as well as temporal phases, indicating a non-linear historical dimension where dream-like utopias and nostalgic memories intersect with the fleeting present, resulting in the unstable uncontemporaneities that define modernity itself.

Benjamin used historic inquiry to search for hidden tendencies beneath the surface of official culture. Like an archaeologist or genealogist, he traced the criss-crossing roots of contemporary phenomena, but also looked for repressed memories of past brutalities and forgotten dreams of a better life.[6] In *The Arcades Project*, Paris after 1800 was the frame within which he placed an exuberant series of fragments trying to come to grips with how modern life was formed in urban constructions and media texts of all kinds. The classical arcades were arched passages, covered walks lined with shops. The winding, arched passageway is frequently used as a metaphor for individual processes of communication and consumption, and in the contemporary media world, such arcs are woven together into extremely intricate paths along which people and media move and interact.

The past lives on in the present, in surviving traces, documents and monuments that are continually engaged in collective and individual identity constructions.[7] The future resides in the past and present, in those moments of anticipation where people dream of new worlds. Many such dreams remain imaginary; others are transformed into realities, often in unintended and sometimes even catastrophic ways – as witnessed by victims of regimes like that of the Khmer Rouge. The distant is also present in the nearby, through images and voices that carry experiences across space. Shopping spaces and practices of media use are filled with references to the foreign and the past, made to reinforce impressions of intimacy and urgency. This is typical of the modern epoch. Benjamin defined the 'modern' not as just everything new, but rather as 'the new in the context of what has always already been there'.[8]

> Corresponding to the form of the new means of production, which in the beginning is still ruled by the form of the old (Marx), are images in the collective consciousness in which the old and the new interpenetrate. These images are wish images; in them the collective seeks both to overcome and to transfigure the immaturity of the social product and the inadequacies in the social organization of production. At the same time, what emerges in these wish images is the resolute effort to distance oneself from all that is antiquated – which includes however, the recent past. These tendencies deflect the imagination (which is given impetus by the new) back upon the primal past. In the dream in which each epoch entertains images of its successor, the latter appears wedded to elements of primal history (*Urgeschichte*) – that is, to elements of a classless society. And the experiences of such a society – as stored in the unconscious of the collective – engender, through interpenetration with what is new, the utopia that has left its trace in a thousand configurations of life, from enduring edifices to passing fashions.[9]

Benjamin's view of the modern as a peculiar hybrid of the new and the archaic is a much more complex idea than those one-dimensional 'postmodernist' reductions of modernity to linear progress alone. Romanticism, nostalgia and primitivism are as akin to modernity as are futurism, classicism and abstract functionalism – and they all, in one way or another, attack the recent past in the name of the future but by connecting back to some kind of primal past, be it located in history or in nature. In a similar vein, more recent modernity theorists like Paul Gilroy and Zygmunt Bauman have suggested the historical presence of countercultures within modernity, so that the modern is not homogenous but dichotomous, or rather polyphonic.[10] There is an inherent ambiguity in the modern and its dialectical 'dream images', in which the past, present and future are overlaid.

> But precisely the modern, *la modernité*, is always citing primal history. Here, this occurs through the ambiguity peculiar to the social relations and products of this epoch. Ambiguity is the manifest imaging of dialectic, the law of dialectics at a standstill. This standstill is utopia and the dialectical image, therefore, dream image. Such an image is afforded by the commodity per se: as fetish. Such an image is presented by the arcades, which are house no less than street.[11]

The shopping arcades are themselves dream images, in Benjamin's sense, but they are also filled with a wealth of other such images, in the form of commodities with symbolic uses. Benjamin argues that fashion offers 'extraordinary anticipations', having a constant and precise contact with the emerging, due to the exceptional scent of the female collective for what awaits in the future. In its newest creations, each season offers some secret semaphore of coming events. The one who could read them would know in advance not only of new currents in art but also of new codes of law, wars and revolutions. – Herein lies no doubt the greatest incitement of fashion, but also the difficulty in making it productive.[12]

This is true for fashion, but crucial also for the popular culture of the media that flow through shopping centres.

ECONOMY AS CULTURE

Benjamin argues that:

> today arcades dot the metropolitan landscape like caves containing the fossil remains of a vanished monster: the consumer of the pre-imperial era of capitalism, the last dinosaur of Europe. On the walls of these caverns their immemorial flora, the commodity, luxuriates and enters, like cancerous tissue, into the most irregular combinations. A world of secret affinities opens up within: palm tree and feather duster, hairdryer and Venus de Milo, prostheses and letter-writing manuals.[13]

The economic world of commerce asks for cultural interpretation: 'These items on display are a rebus', and can be read if one discovers its secret codes.

It is this challenge that the field of cultural studies takes seriously for contemporary times. There is often said to exist an ongoing culturalization or aestheticization of the economy, parallel to an economization or commercialization of culture. The confluence of these two trends necessitates renewed discussions of the strained relations between the market, the state and a life world split between public and private spheres. Studying places where communication and consumption intertwine is one option. 'Marx lays bare the causal connection between economy and culture. For us, what matters is the thread of expression. It is not the economic origins of culture that will be presented, but the expression of the economy in its culture.'[14] Benjamin's ambition to connect a phenomenology of inner, personal experiences with material and political-economic structures remains a key task for today's cultural studies of consumption.

Marketplaces have always been sites of ambivalence and ambiguity. In *The Politics and Poetics of Transgression*, Stallybrass and White describe the marketplace as at once a bounded closure and a site of open commerce, 'both the imagined centre of an urban community and its structural interconnection with the networks of goods, commodities, markets, sites of commerce and places of production which sustain it'. The market is the epitome of local identity even as the trade and traffic of goods from elsewhere unsettle that identity. Their description of pre-capitalist fairs applies well to contemporary consumption sites: 'At the market centre of the polis we discover a commingling of categories usually kept separate and opposed: centre and periphery, inside and outside, stranger and local, commerce and festivity, high and low.' Stallybrass and White regard the market square and the fair as a hybrid place', situated at the intersection or crossroad of economic and cultural forces, goods and travellers. In sites of consumption, dichotomies of inside/outside and commerce/culture are systematically displaced, blurring cultural identities. Fairs and carnivals challenged prevailing orders in two ways: by opposing them from below, with profane pleasures that undermined the high and serene, and from without, through the intruding globalizing flows of foreign goods and merchants that disturbed local structures and introduced 'a certain cosmopolitanism, arousing desires and excitements for exotic and strange commodities'.[15] Benjamin found such desires in Paris and Berlin, and they seem to persist in today's world as well.

This connects to Hardt and Negri's critique in *Empire* of the localist position that wants to resist global capital through strictly localized struggles. Privileging the local is based on a false dichotomy between the global and the local, and easily devolves into 'a kind of primordialism that fixes and romanticizes social relations and identities'. Hardt and Negri instead advocate a focus on 'the *production of locality*, that is, the social machines that create and recreate the identities and differences that are understood as the local'. The most consequential tension is not between strictly local subaltern communities and global capital, but rather between forms of globalization. 'Globalization, like localization, should be understood instead as a *regime* of the production of identity and difference, or really of homogenization and heterogenization.'[16]

In the early twentieth-century department store, Mica Nava has found traits of a commercial Orientalism, which offered women in particular potentially liberating public spaces where identification with ethnic others was invited. Commercial discourses necessitated positive representations of the distant Other, making commodities from foreign cultures attractive for the Western consumer. 'Desire for the other, for something different, is also about the desire for merger *with* the other, about the desire to *become* different.'[17] Nava argues that foreign fashions transformed the intimate spheres of the body and penetrated the home. As incorporated into the culture, they signalled fusion and identification in a process leading to a destabilization of identities and a domestication or 'normalization of difference' that is part of the spread of a 'dialogic imagination'.[18]

There were many who saw shopping spaces such as department stores as key symbols of modern urban life and privileged spaces of contemporary experience in capitalist society. Among them were Émile Zola in his novel *Ladies Paradise* (*Au Bonheur des Dames*, 1883), as well as Swedish authors like Sigfrid Siewertz in *The Big Department Store* (*Det stora varuhuset*, 1923) and Karin Boye in *Astarte* (1931). All of them had a department store as a prismatic focus, and used fashion and the modern media including magazines and records as keys to understanding the ambivalences of gendered identity constructions and power relations in capitalist modernity.

Through history, there has been a continuous development and accumulation of new forms of shopping. To the early peddlers, fairs, shops and bazaars were added arcades around 1800, department stores in the 1850s and shopping centres after 1950. Old forms survived but were affected by or integrated into the more recent ones, resulting in a complex mix of sales forms side by side or overlapping each other. The department store, with the Paris Bon Marché of 1852 as the first example, had low and fixed prices, goods that were spectacularly displayed in an impersonal way that allowed customers an apparently free access.[19] The modern shopping centre or mall was born in response to limitations of the previous forms and combined elements from them all, in particular mixing traits from the arcade and the department store.

Benjamin's take on the theme of commercial space was related to critical discourses of the 1920s and 1930s, inspired by the unfinished programme for critical theory and cultural research developed by the Frankfurt *Institut für Sozialforschung*. Today, accelerating modernization processes have modified the conditions and tasks for such critical cultural studies of media, culture and consumption. The resources of consumption as well as of communication have multiplied, but the combination of shopping spaces and media use remain an exemplary prism to highlight modern life. Benjamin shed light on his own time and space – 1930s Germany – by analysing how the early modern French arcades in their turn connected to prior epochs and more distant places. Such superimpositions have multiplied since then. Our own past also includes Benjamin's high modern age, and each current setting of media consumption refers back to a series of historical layers. Such sites also contain seeds of different possible futures, accessible only through critical interpretations.[20]

A striking characteristic of contemporary sites of consumption – and of urban spaces in general – is their conspicuous level of mediatization, in several senses. Mediated texts and technologies for communication are everywhere. They fill every corner of any shopping centre, which cannot function without them. Media forms were also salient in nineteenth- century arcades. Benjamin and his colleagues in the Frankfurt school gave media phenomena a prominent place in their thinking about modern life. In later chapters, we will return to some of his influential interpretations of such phenomena, for instance on the loss of aura of the work of art in the age of reproduction. At that time it was still possible to depict metropolitan culture at large as a combination of people and built environment, with media entering only at specific points. Approaching a shopping centre today immediately places a vast complex of media forms in focus, in a much more intense and complex manner than ever before.

A contemporary shopping centre is like a prism through which urgent issues are broken: a magic entrance to a series of dialectical processes typical of our time, such as those between culture and economy, private and public, the past and the present, or the local and the global. It is both a meaning-making text to interpret and a functional machine to be mapped out. It is at once house and street, a delimited room and an open passageway between built structures, a place and a non-place, a local unity and a crossroads for currents of goods and people. It must remain safe as well as exciting, a home for its visitors as well as a place for thrilling events. This balance between efficiency and attraction had repercussions on the scope of culture in this environment, too, and testified to the existence of definite limits for the much-discussed tendencies towards the aestheticization of the marketplace and the 'experience economy' in general. There certainly are trends for culture and economy to be conflated, through the joint processes of culturalization and commercialization. But the boundaries between these spheres are also repeatedly reconstructed by practices and discourses that confirm that commerce and culture need a certain separation in time and space. Understanding such dialectics demand critical hermeneutic work that is able to register and uphold *ambivalence,* by oscillating between contradictory moments, as well as the *ambiguity* of polysemic or oppositional meanings in the same text or phenomenon.

THE PASSAGES PROJECT

The convergence of consumption and communication runs both ways. In order to understand media and communications in the commodified society of today, it is necessary to see their commercial aspects. Studying the media and their uses in terms of processes of consumption highlights important patterns and interconnections that tend to get lost in traditional media research. Locating a media study in a shopping centre turns out to be an excellent path towards a full picture of the multiple interconnections and border-crossings of various kinds of media practices.

This is the goal of this book. It is based on a long-term collective and ethnographic research project in a contemporary Swedish shopping centre. It has long been common in media studies to focus on a single mass *medium,* genre or text at a time, such as television news or the soap opera. Others have instead chosen to study one particular social category of *people* or group of media users, such as families or teenage peer groups. Starting instead with a specific social and physical *place* brings to light other aspects. A shopping centre is a relatively well-defined and manageable framework, but it is also large and complex enough to include a great variety of both media and people. Studying such a centre illuminates how the stages of consumption are intertwined, how people and media intersect, and how this is related to communicative processes. This makes it possible to dissolve some calcified categories, for instance of media genres or social groups. It enables an extension of the media concept to include all technically organized vehicles for communication; breaking out of the press/television confines that too often hamper media research even within the dominant cultural studies tradition.

Urban spaces are passages through which material objects, bodies and symbols move. Some of these spaces have more of a threshold character than others; some even grow into extensive borderlands. Consumption spaces are particularly marked by thresholds. Their external limits are often somewhat blurred, in order to make the entrance easier for potential customers. 'These gateways – the entrances to the arcades – are thresholds,' says Benjamin.[21] A shopping centre can be outlined on a map and treated like a fairly well-defined building, but is as such more permeable than many other kind of structure. There is also a certain lack of overview, control and structure in its interior, so that it is often easy to get lost there. Benjamin often states that arcades are ambivalent places: both buildings and streets, houses and passages. 'Arcades are houses or passages having no outside – like the dream.'[22] While this stimulates sales, it also nourishes unconscious impulses and communicative practices that are not so easily channelled into commodity consumption only.

The design of the *Passages* project was inspired by Benjamin's work.[23] The core idea was to study the multifarious ways in which a broad spectrum of media are circulated by a broad spectrum of people in and around such a space of consumption, thereby exploring key forms of the contradictory interlacing of consumption and communication. An ethnographic investigation of a shopping centre as a place where people encounter, buy and use media is a particularly fruitful way to approach a series of central issues concerning media consumption in general, since such a centre is an accessible and reasonably well-defined site through which most kinds of people and media pass, and where key social processes take place – a most suitable entrance to the world of late-modern media consumption!

Media use today is globalized, but is also always localized. Shopping centres have many different shapes in various world regions, but generally contain a series of individually run shops organized within a common frame together with restaurants and other services. The centre studied by the Passages project exemplified the city centre model, which usually contains a wide range of facilities. Other kinds of centre are located outside the municipal areas (external centres), or have a more limited range of stores covering the immediate needs of a smaller living area (local centres), or a more thematically specialized profile in larger inner cities (niche gallerias).

We chose one of Sweden's largest centres, Solna Centre north of Stockholm. It is in many ways an 'average', 'ordinary' Swedish place, with important similarities with corresponding sites in other parts of the world, but of course it is also in obvious ways characteristically different from elsewhere. Sweden is the largest of the Nordic countries, with 9 million citizens and with major media and cultural industries, notably in telephones (Ericsson), publishing, film and music. Stockholm is the capital, with nearly two million inhabitants, its fragmented archipelago facing the Baltic Sea. Since 1943, Solna has been established as a small city of its own, with roughly 60,000 inhabitants today. However, it is only some ten minutes north of Stockholm city, and so well connected to the capital that it for all practical purposes serves as one of its close suburbs. Solna is in many ways a typical Swedish town. The social composition of its population in terms of ethnicity, class and age is close to the Swedish and Stockholm average. It was the historical cradle of Swedish cinema. The industrial spaces, remnants of the golden age, where Greta Garbo and Ingmar Bergman once worked, are now being transformed for new purposes, not far from its centre. Another cultural highlight is the successful soccer team AIK with one of its particularly noisy supporter groups 'Black Army'. A third is the preserved home of the popular naivist painter, Olle Olsson-Hagalund.

The city centre of Solna was formed in 1965 in order to integrate the dispersed parts of the town. Some eighty shops, a town hall and a library were built around its main square. This town centre was gradually redeveloped into a shopping centre, and finally, its central square and streets were covered with a glass roof. In 1985, a nationally oper-ating real estate company called Piren bought all the buildings around the square, except for the public services. After extensive reconstructions, Solna Centre opened in 1989, transformed into a closed shopping centre, with rental space of more than 80,000 square metres. Today, its more than 100 shops, twenty-five eateries and one hotel annually attract some 9 million visitors – as many as the whole Swedish popula-tion, as the management proudly boasts, cunningly playing with statistics. There are also offices and flats in the buildings. In 2000, the Dutch company Rodamco CE acquired Piren and thus became the multinational owner of Solna Centre. Within this centre, a wide range of media commodities are sold and used by an equally wide range of people. Its specificities offer insights into increasingly global processes of space-bound media practices. The particular Swedish welfare state and the broader social history of Scandinavia supply conditions that are different from elsewhere. But each site is also specific, and the specificities of this one turn out to be both fascinating and instructive for the general themes to be developed here.

Solna Centre shares with other shopping centres all over the world many basic aspects of media consumption spaces, including the interplay among malls, chains and stores, as well as that among management, staff, customers and other visitors. Video rentals and photo shops, libraries and bookshops, mobile phones and records, journals and posters – none of these phenomena are unique to Solna or Sweden. Solna Centre could in important respects be almost anywhere in the world. But it also has its own specific context and history that make it particularly interesting to have a closer look at. Its specific combination of public and private space offers particularly enlightening insights into some of the contradictions of modern soci-eties. Further, the rapid privatization and commercialization of major parts of the Swedish welfare state structures also point to certain global trends.

This was our conviction when forming the Passages project. Our passages through the labyrinths of media consumption explored superimposed layers of meaning and power around the media commodities that were circulated, sold and used in a contemporary shopping centre. The research has proceeded in a series of steps. The first step was a theoretical overview of cultural perspectives on consumption and media use. In a second step, we explored the shopping centre as a general media space: its architecture, design and marketing, its visual display and aural soundscape, its internal organization and the movements of its visitors. The third step led us into its specific media shops, to see how they structured and sold their goods, and how customers made choices and used what they bought there. In a fourth step, the research group reflected upon methodological issues of collective media ethnog-raphy.[24] This in brief is the unique collective process that made this book possible.

AMBIGUOUS SPACES

Shopping spaces have an intermediary character between the public and the private. In contrast to the intimate familial sphere, they are relatively open and accessible arenas, even as they are strictly controlled and regulated by private owners and managers. As spaces of sales and consumption, the main orientation of such centres is towards the market system, but they are also to an important extent regulated by the administrative and judicial systems of the state. In this chapter we introduce Solna Centre as a specific place, with its different and competing histories, and the methodological issues it raises. The epistemological and political issues of location are central to understanding the encounters between people and media that take place in and through this environment. In our efforts to examine simultaneously the aestheticization of the economy and the commercialization of culture, we have found a rich source in the mediatized space of Solna Centre.[25] What dream images, ambiguities and contradictions arise in the commercial spaces of today? How are we to study these spaces and understand the meanings they have in everyday life?

Solna Centre was chosen because it is one of the largest in the region, containing all the basic kinds of media shops of today, and visited by customers from all social and ethnic groups. It is a particularly ambiguous place. Like Benjamin's Paris Arcades, it is simultaneously 'house and street', in having a glass roof and doors closing at night, yet open during the day and retaining street signs reminiscent of an old city centre. It is also in fact the centre of Solna City, and as both a city centre and a shopping centre, is a peculiar mixture of public and commercial space. In addition to commercial shops, Solna Centre includes public services of the city library and the town hall within its walls. And in the actual practices within the centre, various interests intersect and compete, including activities by NGOs, associations, peer groups and families that make this a highly contested space. Heated debates have arisen between the centre management and political parties or NGOs over the right to use the space as a forum (agora) for information, meetings and so on. Visitors to Solna Centre in fact use the space in many ways: some come to shop, others just pass through, visit the public library, sit on a bench with a newspaper or watch people over a cup of coffee – contrary to the mall manager's and shop owners' desperate attempts to maximize sales and profits.

Benjamin's reflections on the nature of consumption in such a place, and his concern for how new media and forms of advertising interpolated what was being offered to passers-by, provided a springboard for our own investigations. Confronted with a 'dream world' of mass culture, Benjamin strove to untie its inherent contradictions. Modes of production which, while privileging the private sphere and the concept of the subject as individual, had at the same time given rise to forms of social existence that engendered conformity and the absence of social solidarity and commonality. In order to dispel this dream world, Benjamin drew on a concept of history in a dialectical relationship to present experience. History, or rather our experience of it, does not follow a linear developmental sequence, according to Benjamin, but must be understood as made up of discontinuous events and impressions. Our access to the past occurs only through small windows, 'dream images' as he called them, which arise suddenly in response to something we see or experience that evokes a sudden memory. 'The true picture of the past flits by. The past can be seized only as an image which flashes up at the instant when it can be recognized and is never seen again,' writes Benjamin.[26] The discontinuity and transitory qualities of these individual experiences prevent us from weaving dream images together into a coherent picture of a common mythic past. Instead, they can become the basis for a critical, dialectical form of historical knowledge.[27]

The dream image becomes dialectical in the instant that we recognize it as a glimpse of the past in the present. Benjamin is careful to point out an important distinction: what we experience is not the temporal relationship of the past casting its light on the present, nor the present seen in light of the past. The image is rather an instance of what-has-been coming together 'in a flash' with the now to form a constellation. He writes of 'rescuing' these fleeting images from the past (and here he includes objects that evoke the image), ripping them out of a narrative of historical development in order to make each one accessible to critical analysis 'in the now of its recognizability'.[28]

> The relation of what-has-been to the now is dialectical: not temporal in nature but figural. Only dialectical images are genuinely historical … images. The image that is read – which is to say, the image in the now of its recognizability – bears to the highest degree the imprint of the perilous critical moment on which all reading is founded.[29]

In Benjamin's footsteps, Michel de Certeau has argued that city practices open up 'an 'anthropological', poetic and mythic experience of space'. James Donald adds 'the city we actually live in is poetic', and 'there is no possibility of defining clear-cut boundaries between reality and imagination'.[30] Benjamin's understanding of history as non-linear and constructed out of sudden conjunctions between dream images of the past and the present carries important implications for the study of this contemporary environment that is a labyrinth of passages, images and stories. The various and contradictory impressions, descriptions and histories of Solna Centre are also a labyrinth of interconnected meanings that offer a continual challenge to methodological clarity. In the pages that follow we look more closely at how conflicts between these various histories play out in the ambiguous construction of Solna Centre as a space that is simultaneously public and private. These apparent contradictions can be traced to the interplay between on the one hand the political and economic histories inscribed on the place, and, on the other, the ways that people today use it. A further complication is the transient relationship many people have to the place, at the same time that there are multiple references to other places that tie Solna Centre and its visitors to other localities. This complexity carried methodological implications for each phase of our study. While many of the problems we faced are common to any ethnographically based study of a late-nineteenth-century phenomenon, we managed to develop new ways of addressing many of them, largely through the efforts of a cross-disciplinary group of researchers intent on exploring media consumption through a collective research process.

CONFLICTING HISTORIES OF PLACE

Solna Centre's basic structure stems from 1965 when the original shopping centre was built. At one end the pedestrian main street opens toward Solna Square (Solna torg) and the subway station. At the other end it is connected to the City Hall (Stadshuset) with the municipal administration and services, including at the time of our study, the city's employment offices. Major renovations in 1989 including a glass roof over the central shopping complex marked the transformation of Solna's city centre from a city street to an indoor shopping environment. The glass roof was extended in 2001 to enclose the Hotel Street (Hotellgatan) that leads into Solna Square and continues to the hotel entrance. In this most recent renovation, the shops along Hotel Street received new glass fronts, and a broad majestic staircase was added leading up and out to an adjacent park.

Solna's local history has been another important ingredient in the construction of the shopping centre. The architect's vision when he redesigned the centre in 1989 included many references to the history and culture of the region, and specifically the city of Solna. Paintings on the walls refer to the adjacent soccer stadium, to the home team that is sometimes a contender for the national league pennant, to Solna's history of film production and to Greta Garbo's aura. Over the years these murals have become overshadowed by the trademarks and signs of the stores along the main passages. The major sports store's logo and Nike's oversized banners of international sports icons Carl Lewis and Tiger Woods tower over the pastel-coloured wall painting of an anonymous line of soccer players. And Garbo's familiar face is nearly hidden by an elevator shaft.

The main feature of Library Square (Bibliotekstorget) is the Hollywood Stairs (Hollywoodtrappan), an additional reference to Solna's old film studios, and linking them to the Hollywood dream factory. The architect further mixed rituals of high and popular culture by using the Hollywood Stairs to refer as well to the majestic staircase in Stockholm's City Hall, where Nobel laureates join the nation's political, economic and cultural elite for the annual banquet. At the top of the Hollywood Stairs are several stores and cafés around a 'Piazza', according to the sign hanging among the painted clouds. High on one wall a mural portrays a Solna landmark, the idyllic late-nineteenth-century house that once belonged to a popular local artist and is now the city's art museum. New apartment buildings tower over the house, a visual commentary on the urban renewal project that replaced the traditional buildings and culture of the nearby neighbourhood. The mural, with its complex visual display and associations, is the backdrop for business signs on the Piazza – clothing stores, a telecommunications shop and the 'Hollywood café' featuring a 'Sushi bar' with a neon image of a sumo wrestler.

Throughout the mall there are similar conflicting references to different pasts and different cultures, many far removed from the city of Solna. The long corridor of Postal Walk (Postgången) for example, was inspired by the Paris Arcades. The architect conceptualized this narrow passageway as a 'street by night' with hanging lamps modelled after the gaslights that hung from the ceiling of the Panorama Arcade in

Paris a century ago. The shops are angled toward the passage, creating shadowy alley-ways intended to create a sense of secrecy. The stylized pillars and glass roof imitate the popular iron constructions that held up glass ceilings in the late nineteenth century, and that so fascinated Benjamin:

> The first structures made of iron served transitory purposes: covered markets, railroad stations, exhibitions. Iron is thus immediately allied with functional moments in the life of the economy. What was once functional and transitory, however, begins today, at an altered tempo, to seem formal and stable.[31]

This architectural style embodies a sense of liminality, as Jon Goss noted, and has been quite common in shopping malls, especially in the 1990s. A decade later, the hypermodern and minimalist abstractness seems to be a more trendy transnational style of shopping-mall architecture, but even that is replete with implicit or open historical references – for instance to the 1920s' functionalism of Le Corbusier. Decades after Benjamin made his observation, the narrow corridor through Solna Centre represents a fictive past, using history decoratively as a 'sequence of style'.[32] Solna's late-twentieth-century reference to the Paris Arcades reconstructs the form of a commercial space that once embodied a new relationship between consumer and goods, as Benjamin argues, creating a visual display that is both intimate and public.

This second kind of 'history' rewrites the specifics of locality within a frame of popular culture and nostalgia, as a timeless past where Hollywood, celebrity and the dim light from *faux* gas lamps are visually inscribed onto the local. Solna Centre, like many other shopping centres around the globe, is filled with objects that stand synec-dochically for other periods and places. Global electronic media and tourism have vastly expanded the stock of place imagery in the consumer's *musée imaginaire,* creating a fount of 'real and fictitious elsewheres'.[33] When these images refer to the past, they articulate 'an ideology of nostalgia', generating what Susan Stewart calls the 'desire for desire', a fitting motif for a space for consumption.[34]

Many theorists argue that these display forms, signifying the past as a heritage culture industry, exploit nostalgia for real places and historic roots.[35] However, people with a long personal history of Solna Centre undeniably see it as a very real place. They recall events that have taken place there and businesses that have been replaced by new enterprises. Many people recount aspects of the shopping centre's history, such as the short-lived ice-skating rink that used to be on the lower level. These accounts have the character of oral tradition, a received history that is not always based in the individual's own experience. Several people mentioned that horse-drawn carriages once used the very street that now runs through the centre of the mall. These narratives, constructed from a received mythical past, are quite unlike the references to community history the architect wove into the shopping centre's design.

There is also the political economic history of Solna Centre with roots dating back to the 1960s, when the first shops were joined together around the town square. In 1985 the Solna city council and a large Swedish investment company signed an agreement that laid the foundation for the company's purchase and rebuilding of all the real estate on the town square, with exception of the city hall and the library. Office space and apartments were added, and by 1989 the new Solna Centre stood completed. This followed a trend: Solna Centre was one of ten old city centres in the Stockholm region that was renovated or rebuilt as a shopping centre between 1985 and 1995. These shopping centres often included community services, such as the post office, employment offices and library, a form of cooperation less common in the United States than in Europe.[36] The political and financial decisions which paved the way for corporate ownership of major parts of Solna's city centre led in turn to its purchase in 2000 by Rodamco, a multinational corporation with headquarters in the Netherlands. The shopping centre continues to expand, as adjoining streets and passageways are closed off to traffic and glassed in, linking the centre to a large hotel and with plans to eventually include the stadium.

The political economic history is often formulated as a success story, told and retold by the mall manager, the mayor and chairman of the city council, and the CEO for the Swedish division of Rodamco. This history lacks the visual specificity of the signs of local history and fictive pasts the architect built into the centre. It is more instrumental than the memories recounted by long-term residents and visitors to the mall. Yet, in photographs, speeches and documents in the city's archives, a history emerges that holds up Solna as a model of cooperation between the political and private sectors to develop a modern expansive city environment, and Solna Centre as the outstanding example of what this cooperation has accomplished. In this narrative, Solna Centre is the result of a tight and consistent cooperation between political and commercial interests that tie the place and its architects to global economic developments.

PUBLIC FOR WHOM?

The growing body of work on the politics of place was an important impetus for our research on Solna Centre, in particular how questions of power and authority are actualized when private commercial interests take over public arenas.[37] The contemporary shopping centre is often described as the 'main street' of contemporary urban life, referring implicitly to the street as a public forum where all citizens are free to participate in an open exchange of ideas.[38] Conceptualized as an idealized space of free information exchange, the street works as a metaphor for the public sphere.[39] Referring to the shopping centre as 'main street' evokes a sense of loss over the decline of the city street as a centre for the flow of a shared public (and American) social life. It is an ideal that has formed conceptions of the shopping centre, extending far beyond US borders, and including the shopping centre in Solna.

Entering Solna Centre, the visitor encounters the usual mix of stores, restaurants, commercial office space and services found in any middle-sized Swedish city, including, in addition, the library and city administration buildings, the post office and state liquor store. The atmosphere of the street is underscored by visual references to outdoor urban environments. Street signs and place names are set up on corners and intersections. Large sections of the tile floor through the mall are laid in a size and shape resembling the pattern of a city sidewalk. The soundscape was also important to the architect's concept of an urban environment, and he minimized features that would muffle the sound of footsteps, voices, and other noise that is natural to a city. His ideal was not the ambiance of the small town square or the city park that are other common 'themes' in contemporary mall design, but an urban milieu where commerce is integrated into the life of the street.[40] The rhythms of commerce also follow roughly those of the street, from early morning deliveries (arriving around 9 a.m.) and the first elderly shoppers, to the more rapid tempo of mid-morning shopping, peaking in the mix of employees and shoppers over lunchtime, followed by a second peak starting at mid afternoon as young people get out of school and people come through to shop on their way home from work.

It is, however, a street without the inconveniences of dirt and traffic, protected from the weather. On a dark November afternoon, Solna Centre's warm, light atmosphere of cheery hustle and bustle offers a welcoming respite from the cold and wet weather outside. It is, in other words, a typical mall environment where 'time of year, time of day, regional location are all hidden, available only through the activities going on in the mall'.[41] The visual reminders of time and season follow the material customs of seasonal decor and consumption – the Swedish customary Easter witches hanging from the ceiling in March, banks of red poinsettias at Christmas, spring clothing fashions in April – rather than exterior conditions of weather and climate. It is never winter in Solna Centre.

Peter Jackson has described the contemporary retail environment, the shopping mall, as a successful attempt to tame or 'domesticate' the street.[42] The danger of crime in the contemporary urban street is frequently cited as a reason for creating more easily regulated indoor shopping environments. Privatizing and enclosing urban space is part of this process of domestication, of 'making a "home" or familiar place from what was previously foreign or hostile territory'.[43] Solna Centre's history and its slogan 'Feel at home in Solna Centre' stand in contrast to the city street. In the 'feel at home' campaign, posters and ads for Solna Centre featured an image of a young couple and child sitting cosily on a sofa placed in the middle of the shopping space. The image, with its dislocation of domesticity, blurs the border between public and private, at the same time that it makes deliberate use of the surprise effect created by joining of these two disparate spheres. If the distinction between the home and the shopping mall were not evident to most people, the image would be pointless.

The 'domestication' of the shopping space includes an only slightly veiled reference to woman as consumer, and must be viewed against the longer history of the department store. That early predecessor to the shopping mall appealed directly to women, as a number of researchers have pointed out.[44] The department store served as a social and public space that was nevertheless safe for the middle-class woman. It addresses the woman as consumer, simultaneously acknowledging her economic power and cultural influence as arbiter of taste. Solna Centre's statistics show that seven out of ten of its visitors are women, a figure that fits with Miller's studies of two

British shopping centres (where 68.4 per cent and 71.7 per cent of the visitors were women).[45] These figures confirm the historical pattern of the retail environment as a public space that continues to attract and appeal to the woman consumer.

There are many strategies for maintaining the safety and security of an indoor shopping centre. Surveillance cameras are perhaps the first to come to mind, yet these are not part of Solna Centre's security system. Although cameras are mounted in many of the shops, there are none focused on the walks or other general areas of the shopping centre. Instead, the mall is patrolled by plain-clothes security guards who are called upon whenever trouble arises. The many reflective surfaces throughout the shopping centre also serve a surveillance function. Surrounded by mirrors, on the walls, posts, even ceilings, one has the feeling of being watched. But who and what are these strategies primarily designed to protect? In this case, protecting property and preventing theft seems to have a higher priority than preventing crimes against people.

Many activities that are routine for the street are strictly prohibited in the mall. These include panhandling and buskering, political demonstrations, roller-skating and skateboarding. Posters, flyers and other forms of advertising that do not support the merchants' interests are not permitted. A 'speakers' corner' that had been proposed during the early planning for Solna Centre was rejected, and political parties cannot campaign in the mall.[46] During one period of our research, the management removed many of the shopping centre's benches that were located along the passages and in the open squares, convinced that they encouraged loiterers who in turn would discourage shoppers. This provoked controversy, particularly among the many retired people who visit Solna Centre on a daily basis, and eventually many of the benches were returned. The benches continue to serve as signifiers of a space that is both public and domestic. They invite visitors to sit and watch the flow of passers-by, consistent with the slogan 'Feel at home in Solna Centre'.

Another controversy arose when a request by the local church to rent space in Solna Centre was turned down by the company that owns the mall. The refusal was seen as an additional sign that public space was becoming increasingly closed to non-commercial activities. A public debate was organized, and in the local press coverage it was noted that whereas the church formerly held a self-evident place in the village centre, today the central gathering place for town residents is a shopping centre, and the church is excluded.[47] The use of the church as a symbol in this controversy over public space is particularly noteworthy given the secularization of Swedish society and the fact that the former state church (which had requested use of the space) is generally considered marginal to social and political life.

The many restrictions on this space remain hidden until a conflict arises. Few people notice the list of prohibited activities at the mall entrance. The mall success-fully maintains its appearance as a public space, eliding its dependence on private and corporate ownership, planning and strict control. The social services available here, the library and the city hall, carry symbolic value that malls in other cities have made major concessions to obtain.[48] The ebb and flow of people through Solna Centre is essential to blurring the boundary between public and private space in this urban environment where consumption is the norm.

A TRANSLOCAL FIELD

Most visitors and employees in Solna Centre live in the surrounding area. According to the manager, the average mall visitor comes three times a week. A third of them drive, a third come by bus or subway and a third of them walk. The demographics of Solna correspond quite closely to the Swedish population as a whole, given age, income and ethnicity.

This relatively stable set of facts does not, however, tell us very much about how people relate to this place, to the people they encounter here nor the meanings it has for them. In late modernity, we can no longer assume that people ground their identities first and foremost in relation to a geographic place. As media increasingly refer to other places, and as people's own experiences of other localities broadens, cultural theorists have developed new concepts to account for identity processes that no longer depend on face-to-face communication within a group. Benedict Anderson developed the concept of 'imagined communities' to account for the ways that a sense of national identity is spread via media.[49] Arjun Appadurai's research on public culture and global cultural flows is based on analyses of how human mobility and the rise of new media forms intersect in the process of constructing cultural identities. Aspects of local culture are combined with experiences, many of them mediated, from other places.[50] This gives rise to what Johan Durham Peters has characterized as 'bifocality' as people learn to shift focus between local and global phenomena within their field of experience.[51] These and other ways of understanding the meaning of space, place and identity will be further developed in Chapter 9.

The cross-currents created through these encounters between people, other localities and media also affect the character of Solna Centre. Its histories and conflicts, and the experiences of its visitors and employees, include continual references to other places and events. Politically, economically, culturally it exists in a dynamic relationship with regional, national, transnational and global developments, a phenomenon continually reflected in the ways media are used and in the cross-currents between different media. This means that it is not only the people we meet in this place whose culture is shaped by their translocal experience. Solna Centre itself is a translocal place, where meanings cannot be fully understood in isolation from other locales, both near and far, in both time and space.

This has methodological implications for how we designated the 'field' of our study, that is, in concrete terms, where we carried out the research. To what extent are we able to keep the translocality of Solna Centre in focus, at the same time that we concentrated our efforts on a specific place? The question of locating the 'field' has been of increasing concern for social anthropology, where our study of Solna Centre drew much of its methodological inspiration. There have been many challenges to the anthropological paradigm, most stridently from within the discipline, which pictures the anthropologist heading off to spend an extended time in the 'field', a geographically isolated and culturally bounded location. Certain character-izations of the field persist, however, and continue to have consequences for the ways ethnographers think and work. Akthil Gupta and James Ferguson describe, for example, the value that continues to be placed on detailed description and contin-uous face-to-face interaction. These are factors that depend on a particular kind of place and a group of people with a common culture who inhabit it. This in turn generates a concept of what constitutes a field, a concept that privileges certain kinds of knowledge and obscures others. Ethnographic knowledge, as Gupta and Ferguson note, is highly dependent on the presence and experience of the participant observer, securely grounded in a local setting.[52]

In the meantime, anthropologists have struggled with the growing multiplicity of locations of the phenomena they study, and many address the dilemma through 'multilocal' fieldwork, for example in studies of professionals who work internation-ally.[53] In migration studies, anthropologists often carried out fieldwork in at least two sites, long before the concept of multilocal fieldwork was established. Hannerz has suggested the alternative term 'translocal' to describe the character of these studies, in order to emphasize not only that the fieldwork is carried out in several different loca-tions but also that the places are structurally related to each other.[54] Another research model is to select a place that can simultaneously provide access to a number of different sites, in order to employ a translocal perspective with a single strategically chosen location as the point of departure.[55] This is in effect the strategy we were using when we selected Solna Centre for a broader study of media consumption. At the same time, it landed us in the middle of a paradox. On the one hand, it was all too clear that Solna Centre, like many other significant sites of late modernity, is a far cry from the traditional anthropological ideal of a small community, isolated from the surrounding world, where people share a common, autonomous culture. Indeed the characteristics that distinguish Solna Centre from this ideal are precisely the reasons we were drawn to the place. On the other hand, many of our research methods seemed to demand a kind of contact that was for the most part unattain-able there. The transitory and translocal phenomena we were studying were difficult to capture, no matter how much time we spent in the shopping centre or how many interviews we did there.[56] We addressed the problem continually, if implicitly, through the forms our collaboration took and the methods we developed.

INTERSECTIONAL ETHNOGRAPHY

The task of investigating contemporary and spatially situated media practices demanded methodological innovation. We could for instance not rely on established models of audience or reception research. Three main cues guided our work. First, it was necessary to approach our complex field collectively, not by just adding indi-vidual studies, but by developing a tight interaction between the researchers involved. Each could only capture certain aspects and parts of the media practices in the centre, but in close dialogue with each other, we had to cultivate a shared knowledge. Second, our work had to be inter- or cross-disciplinary, making use of a wide set of competencies and putting them in joint motion. We needed specific capacities for deciphering specific media circuits, and we also needed combinations of historical, social and aesthetic perspectives. Third, we had to go against the grain of standard divisions in media research between producers, texts and publics. We knew that we had to deconstruct the strict line between production and consumption, as well as that between text and context.

All this was a great methodological challenge, forcing us to elaborate an innovative 'intersectional ethnography'. The current discourses on intersectional identity formations emphasize how dimensions like class, gender, sexuality, ethnicity, nationality, age and generation co-constitute each other and are always interlinked. We shared that perspective and expanded it onto other dimensions as well. Our intersectional ethnography was thus devised to overcome the common isolation of production from consumption, of media texts from spatial contexts, of media circuits from each other, of archival research from field studies, of social categories, and of academic disciplines. This could not be done by just lumping everything together, but had to be carefully engineered to make the resulting insights really useful.

We drew inspiration for this collective, cross-disciplinary effort from several sources. One was the classical Frankfurt School of critical theory, where dialogic forms of inquiry were crucial. Another was cultural studies, where the Centre for Contemporary Cultural Studies in Birmingham in the 1960s and 1970s developed collaborative research in working groups that crossed and combined perspectives from a range of disciplines. A third strand of inspiration was even closer at hand, namely the Nordic tradition of alternative or popular education, including study circles at various levels, but also the Nordic Summer University, which since its foundation in 1950 has offered young academics an alternative public sphere for pioneering projects and discussions. As individuals, we could all add our own experiences of collaborative research work.

We built a reference group of respected researchers serving as a sounding board at the project's annual seminars, and added co-researchers to supplement the competences of the initial research group with specialists from media and cultural studies, comparative literature, economic history, ethnology, social anthropology and ethnomusicology. We expected these disciplinary perspectives to complement each other and, more importantly, to contribute to a synthesis of new methodological and theoretical insights, relevant to the place and phenomenon we were studying. Whereas multidisciplinary research assumes an additive model of research collaboration, we had as our goal to challenge the borders between our respective disciplines and in so doing develop new perspectives and syntheses between the fields we represented. Rather than a summation of knowledge from our respective backgrounds, we aimed to develop something new in the 'crossover' spaces between the collaborating areas of work. In order to stimulate these trans- or interdisciplinary syntheses, we held monthly meetings to discuss the research and texts we were reading and writing, and made our research materials available to each other. All field notes, interviews and images went into a common 'bank' of information to which we all had access.

With its emphasis on ethnographic methods, the Passages project can be seen as a continuation of the 'ethnographic turn' in media and cultural studies from the late 1980s, when reception studies began to use ethnographic interviews to explore media use and interpretation as expressions of cultural identity.[57] By selecting a specific place as the location of the study, we had also created a context or 'field' that demanded, in addition to interviews, other forms of observation and documentation. It seemed at the time a natural choice to integrate participant observation, interviews and photography among our research tools. Many, but not all, of us had previous experience doing fieldwork using ethnographic methods.

Ethnographic research is, however, rarely conducted as a collective process. In this sense, the Passages project is unusual in its ethnographic approach to its field. Fieldwork was collective; even if a researcher made an individual trip to the field, the field notes and photographs were shared and often discussed with the research group as a whole. We developed a common set of practices for transcribing and cataloguing field notes and interviews in order to make them mutually accessible, and made suggestions from our own observations that would complement, or sometimes contradict a colleague's experience from the field. We planned routines and strategies together, discussed problems we had encountered of both practical and ethical nature, compared our maps of the shopping centre, and occasionally made field visits together. This intense collaboration was not without its problems, many of a practical nature, such as coordinating busy schedules, or sharing the extensive photographic documentation, which proved far more difficult than exchanging field notes.

Collective efforts also extended into the interpretation and analysis of the material. We drew on each other's field notes and interviews in our writing and discussions, and shared literature. We found common threads and contradictions that we realized carried meaning for the relationships and connections between different levels of analysis. The regular meetings and the often lively discussions that arose were instrumental for tying specific observations from the field into larger analytical structures, and vice versa, for finding specific examples that supported or contradicted the theoretical framework we were building. Again, there were inescapable problems. Some voices tended to weigh more than others in the group, and it would be naïve to claim the collaboration was non-hierarchical. In practice, one can see a parallel in the distinction between multi- and cross-disciplinary research in the nature of the collaboration within the Passages project. On the one hand, each researcher made specific and clearly defined contributions to the project, at the same time that the results were in many cases a synthesis of insights from several members of the group. Through a process of research triangulation, the project produced a body of shared experience, knowledge and texts.

In retrospect, we can trace the fluctuating geographical boundaries of our field in a series of steps, corresponding roughly to the project's three main phases. During the first background stage, we visited other malls in the Stockholm area, writing field descriptions and photographing them, which cast light on the research we later did in Solna. Field visits to local shopping centres were complemented by observations from other cities in Europe and the US, ranging from the classic old arcades of

Budapest and Paris, to large new shopping complexes, including Minneapolis and Lisbon, which we visited throughout the course of the project.

In the project's second phase, we focused on Solna Centre, with the goal of attaining an *overview* of the place itself and its relation to its immediate surroundings. We traced people as they walked through the mall, to see what they did, where they shopped, whom they met. We collected the local advertising papers, visited the home page, and interviewed the architect, the manager and a selection of mall visitors. We gave cameras to a small group of informants and asked them to document *their* Solna Centre. We also began to construct a history of the shopping centre and its relationship to the city of Solna, using archive materials, and gathered information about its demographics.

In the third phase, the focus was on specific media circuits, involving fieldwork in various shops and in the library, that is, the places where media selections were made. The aim was to conduct participant observation and interviews with employees and customers in order to trace media into the contexts of everyday use. We soon realized, however, that the informants with whom we would have the most regular contact were shop managers and employees. Customers, on the other hand, came and went, a fleeting population with whom we could at best exchange a few words or ask a couple of questions. We were confronted with the contradictions between this particular field as a translocal place and the traditional ideal of fieldwork based on extended face-to-face interaction with a consistent group of informants. Few of us were able to build our study of media use on sustained contact with a range of informants. This had several significant consequences for the project and also led to several innovative tactics for solving the problem. One consequence was that the shops and their personnel became more central to our study than we had first envisioned. Another tactic was to reach consumers through the Internet, through specific chat groups. Some of us based our analysis of media consumption on one or two key informants. We also used various means of locating informants who had a connection to Solna, even though we had not encountered them in Solna Centre. A majority of these tactics, at the same time that they solved the practical problem of finding informants with relevant experience, also took account of Solna Centre's translocality. They also contributed to what Lena Gemzöe described as the centrifugal character of our research process.[58]

SHOPPING IN THE FIELD

Solna Centre was a familiar place to us, even before we began our research there. Although some of us had never been to this particular shopping centre, we had all been in similar environments. We had different attitudes toward the place; whereas some of us felt immediately at home among the shops and shoppers, others in the research group had tried to avoid this kind of place, preferring to do their shopping elsewhere. Yet we were all familiar with the goods and services available, the basic structure of a shopping mall and how to move through this space. We were doing research in an environment that was not only close to home; it was also part of our own cultural experience.

The cultural knowledge one has of the field has the potential for being a valuable source of insight. The problem is that this kind of knowledge and experience is typically taken for granted. This background knowledge must be brought to the foreground before the researcher can gain access to it and use it. This requires establishing a distance or a point of view from which one's position and perspective can be examined, a challenge that can be experienced as a conflict, in particular between different roles. Perhaps the first conflict we experienced during our fieldwork was the urge to shop. Walking through the mall, notepad in hand, we frequently saw items we wanted to buy. We would wait until we had finished with the day's fieldwork, then return to take a closer look at the desired item. We also used trips to the field as an opportunity, for example, to post a package, or buy a birthday card or a bottle of wine for dinner.

Initially we experienced this as a conflict between two incompatible roles. It was a problem to remain focused on fieldwork when we were pulled away by a desire to make a purchase – to consume. Some of us viewed this desire as a sign of weakness or a sense of inadequacy about our seriousness as researchers. It was the women researchers who first discussed this issue and the problem of working in an environment where one was constantly being addressed as consumer. We began to reflect critically upon what this meant, which lead us toward insights about shopping and consumption as gendered activities. We learned to regard these glimpses into our own desire to consume, not as distractions from what we were really there to do, but as useful insights into the phenomenon we were studying. They contributed to a subjective and dialectical understanding of the field, corresponding to Benjamin's vision of a historical knowledge.

ARCADES, CIRCUITS, NETWORKS

In Solna Centre we encountered the myriad of forms and practices that constitute media consumption today. Within the specific environment of a shopping centre, we observed and interrogated media consumption as a process that on the one hand anchors people to local histories at the same time that it connects them to transnational flows of goods, services and ideas, as well as to other people and places. Broadening the concept of media to include, in addition to mass media, other communication forms and processes that mediate between people and between people and the environments that they pass through in their daily lives, brought to light a dynamic and complex web of relationships. Many of the implications of this broad approach were not evident at the outset, but emerged as the research developed. The centrality of place, and the ways the concept of place became problematized by our choice of a shopping centre, and Solna Centre in particular, proved significant for the kinds of interactions we studied. For example, the sheer omnipresence of media in this place, including media technologies, images and sounds, with their multiple references to other media and other places, convinced us of the need to conceptualize media consumption in broad terms. Another example was the significance of the media's materiality, which we realized in the analyses of individual media circuits (which we present in the next section) that take their point of departure in the selection and purchase of specific media products *as goods*. There is, in other words, a strong material basis in media consumption, grounded in the meanings and values people attribute to media objects and artefacts. Our study goes beyond an interest in media hardware and technology per se by interpreting these objects in the extended cultural context of exchange and use, stimulated by cultural anthropologists' work in theories of exchange within and between cultures and across time and space.[59] This can be seen as a chain of events, practices and meanings that extends media consumption in the shopping centre to other places of media use. The relationship between people and media is given the added dimension of media technologies' material form and physical presence in everyday life.[60]

These examples illustrate the distinction between our research and the vast majority of studies of media use that focus on media content and reception. The interaction between media and people cannot be contained within an act of consumption conceived of as the reception of a media text. Instead of referring to this interaction as media use, it is more appropriate to describe it as part of a broader media experience.[61] The individual act of media consumption always occurs within the context of an entire life where the presence of media has a continuing, significant and ever-changing role as one moves from place to place. Within Solna Centre, we found intersecting crosscurrents that are typically difficult to locate and examine simultaneously. Questions involving tensions between centre and periphery, between local and global, between outsider and insider, between public and private, between culture and commerce, and between subjective experience and the structures of political economy, could be kept in focus, if not all at once, in varying degrees and at various times, guided by the perspectives of our respective disciplines, the collective research process we had developed and actualized by the events and practices we observed in the field.

The following chapters cut through the arcades, circuits and networks of media consumption in a series of ways. We begin with a sequence of photographs made and gathered during the course of our research, in order to provide a visual overview of Solna Centre. In the text that follows we then develop basic concepts of media use and consumption, identify distinctive mechanisms of the main media circuits, and finally put the picture together and see how they interrelate to shape time and space.

Chapter 2, 'Consumption and Communication', highlights important aspects of the concepts of media, media use and consumption, thereby reproducing the necessary skeleton of the media arcades through which the investigation will then pass. The chapter challenges widely accepted notions of media and consumption by asking 'what is consumption?' and 'what is a medium?' thereby establishing new links between two otherwise rarely juxtaposed lines of thought. Whereas studies of consumption usually focus on shopping and the acquisition of commodities, and rarely deal with media commodities, studies of media use tend to emphasize reception – that is, the ways people read, watch and listen to mediated messages, while ignoring the ways they find, select and purchase media. Here the whole process of consumption is reconstructed, offering refreshing ways to rethink foundational definitions of media and media use. Distinctions are finally drawn between economic, political and symbolic power, making use of contemporary social and critical theory, in order to understand how media are embedded in multidimensional relations of power and resistance.

The next four chapters look more closely at four media circuits found in the shopping centre: texts (books, magazines and journals), pictures (photos, posters and postcards), audiovisual media (CD, radio, television and video) and media hardware (involved in most kinds of media, including hi-fi as well as computer media). Each chapter focuses on what is specific for each of them but also points out intermediary, overlapping and interlacing factors and forms, resulting from continuous dialectics of stabilization and mobilization. These media circuits are no logical necessities but rather provisional and localized conventions in the ways in which media circulate in a shopping centre. They have much in common, but each of them offers privileged insights into different aspects of media use in general. Three aspects are gradually developed through all these chapters: (1) the *spatial contexts*, locations and settings of media consumption, (2) the *temporal processes* of those same practices, and (3) the *intermedial relations* and intersections between different media circuits. This group of four chapters begins with the most traditional and discrete media forms and moves toward increasingly multi-modal media with the aim of providing an overview of the increasing complexity of media consumption. Through the process we also encounter the increasing difficulty of defining specific media and their circuits, thus pointing to a central characteristic of contemporary media.

Chapter 3, 'Print Media', deals with books, newspapers and magazines, which are found in bookstores, press shops and the local library. This media group actualizes issues of how place-bound identities are shaped by reading magazines and newspapers, and how social bonds are created by owning and giving away books. Chapter 4, 'Media Images', is devoted to the photographic goods, posters and cards that are sold and used in the shopping centre. It investigates the generic categories people develop in their use of these image forms, their relationship to mass-media images, and the ways these image practices are used to document and express personal history, identity and social relations. Chapter 5, 'Sound and Motion', studies the sale and use of films, videos, records and digital disks. The spatial and social settings of the media shops are depicted, but also how these media forms come to play in a broader range of activities, including musical performance and the functions and forms of collecting. Chapter 6, 'Hardware Machines', takes its point of departure in the machines that are a necessary component in the consumption of certain media texts: television sets, hi-fi equipment, cameras, cellular phones and computers. An analysis of these media machines and their place in media consumption leads to a consideration of issues of access, power over space and time, and cultural citizenship.

Following this overview, the specific media circuits are again combined in order to analyse the overarching networks of the media world at large. Chapter 7, 'Intermedial Crossings', summarizes overarching aspects and dimensions of media consumption, with an emphasis on intermedial passages between different media. At the same time as it critically deconstructs the very idea of fixed and distinct types of media, it nevertheless distinguishes some main differentiations made by media users, and discerns key forms of intermedial connection, proposing a model of how media circuits are produced and interrelated in our age of convergence and digitalization.

Chapter 8, 'Layers of Time', examines how media are used to construct time, memories and identities. It scrutinizes the ways in which media consumption is both located in time and constructs time, and it includes a section on collecting that also connects to Benjamin's analyses. Chapter 9, 'Translocal Spaces', deals with mobility and spatiality, analysing how media and people move across national and geographic boundaries while simultaneously reconstructing localities, bridging and dividing places and geographic regions.

Finally, Chapter 10, 'Communicative Power', develops a critical perspective on forms of power and resistance involved in communicative practices, based on our ethnographic findings. Political, economic and cultural front lines are investigated. An analysis is made of options and forms of resistance in everyday life and of the politics of media consumption, accounting for dialectical and multidimensional tensions between institutions and texts, structures and agencies, private and public, communication and consumption. The chapter ends with discussing issues of cultural citizenship and communicative rights, and finally summarizes the accomplishments of this whole study.

PICTURES OF PASSAGES

For Walter Benjamin, the culture of consumption that emerged in Europe during the nineteenth century was intertwined with two phenomena: the spread of photography and the new shopping arcades. Benjamin's entire Arcades project is marked by a fascination for the relationships being established there between new technologies and new ways of seeing. Throughout his investigation of new forms of consumption runs his sharp interest for the meeting points between people and pictures, and in particular the desire aroused through the possibilities of mass-produced images. In his 'Exposé' of 1935, he writes:

> For its part, photography greatly extends the sphere of commodity exchange, from mid-century onward, by flooding the market with countless images of figures, landscapes, and events which had previously been available either not at all or only as pictures for individual consumers. To increase turnover, it renewed its subject matter through modish variations in camera technique – innovations that will determine the subsequent history of photography.[62]

Photography changed ways of seeing. To regard one's environment as filled with things to look at, offering a wealth of objects to be consumed with the eyes was, according to Benjamin distinctly new. The architecture, display windows and signs of the Paris Arcades had radically altered the conditions for visual representation, as goods and people met in a constant and ever-changing flow of impressions.

Against this background, it is no accident that a book about passages through a contemporary shopping centre includes photographs, providing an overview of this visual environment. The sources of inspiration for the research group included the well-known tradition within sociology and anthropology of incorporating photography into ethnographic methods. In environments where cultural meaning is expressed in visual symbolic forms, the camera is a self-evident tool for documentation and interpretation.[63] Within the framework of the Passages project, we received permission from the shopping centre to take photographs as a part of our fieldwork.[64] In addition to our own photographs, we gathered other material where Solna Centre is visually represented. The visual space of the shopping centre extends beyond its geographic location, and we therefore included images, for example, from advertising campaigns and the centre's home page.

The pictures that follow are selected to represent that which we identify as typical for Solna Centre during the period we were carrying out our research. They are specific and concrete, all from a specific location and made between 1999 and 2002. Nevertheless, they must also be seen as abstractions. The still photograph can only ever isolate an instant; it can never represent the truth of how something always is. The 'here and now' that the photograph is witness to is already a thing of the past. This sense of looking into the disappearing past is certainly a primary reason that photographs continue to hold such fascination.

The image the photograph provides of the past is further related to what Benjamin referred to as the 'optical unconscious': 'Evidently a different nature opens itself to the camera than opens to the naked eye – if only because an unconsciously penetrated space is substituted for a space consciously explored.'[65] Through a photograph one can see or recognize things that are part of a past experience, including aspects of that experience one was not aware of at the time. Therein lies a paradox of photography. On the one hand, the photograph can reveal that which is no longer visible or has previously been unknown. However it can also transform that which was assumed to be well known and familiar into something strange and new.

The photograph's ability to 'make strange' what is familiar and known has clear advantages when exploring an everyday environment such as a shopping centre. The easily recognized mixture of objects and people that coexist in that space re-emerge in a new light. One notices details that one had not previously seen and discovers relationships between different phenomena of which one had been unaware. For the researcher, the photograph's ability to 'make strange' one's own perspective on a familiar environment can lead to a more nuanced and reflexive analysis of the field. The photographs we have selected hopefully support a more thorough understanding of the encounters between people and media that occur there. For the reader who is already familiar with Solna Centre, the photographs can offer a new perspective. For the majority of readers who have never visited Solna, or for that matter may never have been in Sweden, there is still much that will look strange yet also strangely familiar, recognizable from other shopping centres in other parts of the world. These photographs, for all their specificity of time and place, portray phenomena that are global.

FIGS 1.1 and 1.2. Inspired by Benjamin's Arcades project and visits to Paris, the architect modelled this passage through Solna Centre (above) after Passage des Panoramas (see over).

FIG. I.2. Passage des Panoramas, Paris.

FIG. 1.3. The shopping centre's slogan invites visitors to 'feel at home' in this place.

FIG. 1.4. It requires an ongoing effort to keep advertising to a minimum in front of the City Hall. The façade is considered a 'free zone' for the city's public art.

FIG. 1.5. The benches nearest the subway entrance are a common meeting point.

FIG. 1.6. Surrounded by blue clouds above the Hollywood Stairs is this nostalgic portrayal of Solna's cultural past.

FIG. 1.7. The Hollywood Stairs lead to the upper level of the mall. Their name and design refer to the 'dream factory' and to Solna's history of film production.

FIG. 1.8. Åke Ericzon in his usual spot in front of a bank and photography shop. His intermedial palette draws from a range of models, including Curt Cobain, Tina Turner, Renaissance painting and family photographs.

FIG. 1.9. One of Solna Centre's several shops for media 'hardware'.

FIG. 1.10. The AIK sports shop in Solna Centre is conveniently near the home team's arena.

FIG. 1.11. The shopping centre's largest sporting goods store has successfully negotiated a prominent display of its transnational brands on the façade, where they now overshadow an earlier wall painting of several anonymous soccer players.

FIG. 1.12. Visitors report that they often get disoriented and lose their way in the labyrinth of passageways through the mall.

FIG. 1.13. A lost child has found his way to the information desk with the help of an employee.

FIG. 1.14. In February 2000, Solna Centre's recently launched home page provided an overview of upcoming events, special offers and a couple of games for the virtual visitor.

FIG. 1.15. Greta Garbo, who played one of her earliest roles in Solna's 'Film City', is commemorated in a discrete wall painting near the elevator.

FIG. 1.16. The small cinema, Sagittarius, shares its entrance with one of the mall's bookstores.

FIG. 1.17. The bank window displays the latest information from stock exchanges in Stockholm, New York, London and Tokyo.

FIG. 1.18. In the library, people sit and read newspapers from 'home', whether that might be in other parts of Sweden or on the opposite side of the globe.

FIG. 1.19. A popular café, in front of the card and poster shop.

FIG. 1.20. The mall entrance, Solna Square, on a November evening.

2. CONSUMPTION AND COMMUNICATION

Throughout history, mass consumption and mass media have been intimately inter-connected – in practice as well as in cultural discourses. For more than a century, print, audio-visual and visual media have depended economically on advertising, while business and industry have needed media to reach their customers. But the media are themselves also marketed products; consumers select, buy, use and eventually dispose of their newspapers, magazines, books, videos, television sets, phonograms, etc. Media circulate primarily as commodities. Acts of communication are therefore typically formed as acts of consumption and embedded in market systems. This does not mean that 'media' can be reduced to specific technologies sold on a market. Consumption and communication are two different phenomena, but they overlap considerably in modern capitalist societies. *Consumption* is that specific kind of interaction whereby people exchange money for goods in an act of purchase, and then use these acquired goods. *Communication* is based on intersubjective acts of interpretation whereby people make meaning out of shared textual artefacts – be they transient, such as conversation or gestures, or relatively fixed, like books or houses. Consumption and communication are densely interwoven, but the balance between commerce and culture is far from harmonious. The use of space and time for combining these two overlapping processes gives rise to various power struggles. The shopping centre and the processes of media consumption share a borderland character by linking commerce to culture and consumption to communication in highly ambiguous and contested ways.

Though one obviously may consume things other than communication media, consumption is increasingly mediatized in two main ways. First, media commodities occupy a growing share of total consumption. Second, they are more frequently being used as tools in an expanding range of consuming practices – from mail order and telephone sales to Internet-based e-commerce. At the same time, the media are increasingly commercialized, in that communication more and more is shaped according to the forms of consumption in late modernity, characterized by the buying and selling of market commodities. Some forms of communication still remain outside the commodity sphere. Greeting a neighbour does not necessitate the purchase or sale of anything and is therefore hard to analyse as a kind of commodity consumption. But a growing number of communicative processes are drawn into that personal sphere, as media products sold as commodities are integrated into an endless number of contexts, and as ads and shopping-oriented activities occupy more and more of the time and space of everyday media use. This process is mirrored in an ongoing intimization of the media sphere at large.

Regarding *consumption as communication* highlights the interpretive aspects of shopping. In the reverse direction, viewing *communication as consumption* highlights how capitalist markets structure media use, in particular how interactions between people and texts are mediated by the purchase and use of artefacts in commodity form. Here, the two are combined in a cultural study of media use that investigates the interplay between culture and economy, thereby crossing the conceptual gap between consumption research and studies of media use. This puts a double perspective on media – as products for consumption and as means of symbolic communication. The chapter proceeds in four steps. (1) We start by discussing consumption as a process that begins with the phases of selection and purchase, whose real purpose is only realized at the phase of use, and ends when the product is disposed of, by being destroyed, given away, exchanged or sold. (2) In the next section, we investigate ways in which media have been defined and divided, by posing the obvious but surprisingly difficult question: 'What is a medium?' (3) The specific characteristics of media use are discussed in the third section of this chapter. It turns out that media use is a simultaneously situated and situating practice that places texts in contexts, and cannot be reduced to a linear transmission model built on a strict division of production and consumption. (4) This leads to an investigation of the multiple power dimensions of media use, which are crucial to a critical cultural studies perspective. We argue for a polydimensional conception of power, combining theoretical strands that are commonly kept apart. The interplay between communicative power and resistance, and more generally of structure and agency, is scrutinized, emphasizing their mutual dynamics and internal differentiation, against any effort to construct fixed dichotomies. This paves the way for the more specific investigation of practices of media consumption that follows in the subsequent chapters.

WHAT IS CONSUMPTION?

Research on consumption and on media use have developed with remarkably little mutual contact, based as they are in sharply contrasting concepts of consumption. In most recent research on shopping and consumption – whether marketing/economic or anthropological/cultural studies – consumption is understood mainly as the choice and acquisition of commodities or services, involving a transfer of money. However, in research on media use – whether in political economy or cultural studies kinds of reception research – consumption is understood instead as the use of these goods. In the first case, the focus would be on the act of buying or renting a video, whereas in the second, the act of consumption would be defined as watching the video. Consumption research has mainly focused on the phases of selection and purchase, but it has less often specifically studied media products and even less frequently their use. Most reception scholars on the other hand have dealt with the ensuing media use, but they have focused solely on reception, thereby isolating media from other articles used in daily life.

A striking example of this division is Daniel Miller's anthology *Acknowledging Consumption*, which presents studies in a wide range of disciplines, without ever noting the problematic conceptual slide between chapters. Consumption is generally understood as the acquisition of (non-media) commodities up until the last chapter, where David Morley's discussion of theories of consumption in media studies shifts the focus to reception and interpretation. By breaking down the process into separate research areas for shopping and media use, researchers have missed its interlocking chains with phases of shifting length and localization, intrinsic to the full process of consumption.

Until recently, consumption studies have mainly considered consumption as a financial transaction: a product changes hands, is transferred from a producer to a consumer for a sum of money. Today, consumption researchers have increasingly abandoned their exclusive focus on the financial aspect and started to regard consumption as a process that transforms the relation between a product and a person.[1] As it moves out of the sphere of production, the product is transformed by being associated with a particular individual or group. Consumption involves a complex encounter between textual products and individual subjects in distinct social settings or contexts leading to the creation of meaning, identity and shared life worlds. It also thus implies production – of experiences, meaning, identity, relations, communities, public spheres and new symbolic expressions. It includes both the financial act in which goods and services change hands, and the practices in which these products are then used in the creation of intersubjective experiences, individual and collective identities, knowledge, cultural constructions of meaning and social interaction and relations. Reception – meaning-producing interpretation – starts already in media production, since the product-makers' own interpretations of their raw materials and drafts contribute to the intended form. The moment of reception also permeates distribution; for example, the people in charge of buying products for a store and the sellers in the store must be familiar with the products in order to make profitable selections and presentations.

Consumption is here defined as 'the selection, purchase, use and disposal of all kinds of goods and services that have the form of commodities', i.e. are for sale in some kind of market. People gain access to objects and services in other ways too. Besides *commodities*, people regularly also encounter resources in the forms of *gifts* and of *public goods*. Specific artefacts may at any point transform from one form to another. Public libraries lend out their books for free, but buy them on the market, and birthday presents are also often first bought in shops. Still, these three methods of transferring control over objects and services each follow specific rules and principles. In this book, it is the world of media commodities that dominates, but we will also consider how it interacts with gifts as well as with public goods.

Consumption may actually be understood in either a broad or a narrow sense. In the wide or material sense, it encompasses all acts where living beings ingest anything, physically or mentally, thus disintegrating and integrating it with themselves. In this sense, a bird consumes a worm, an infant consumes her mother's milk and later a fairy tale, a birthday child consumes its gifts and a citizen consumes public goods. But what is at stake here is the narrower economic sense of the word outlined above, including a direct transfer of money in a market. Such consumption acts link people and objects with each other, while transforming them between a series of roles.

Each act of consumption can be said to pass through four phases: (1) selection, (2) purchase, (3) use and (4) disposal. These phases are interconnected. For example, there are no purchases without a minimal element of selection. Use presumes that something has been purchased (if the product is not stolen). The disposal of the product also presumes preceding instances of selection and purchase. Each phase can be studied separately, but also as parts of a whole since the shifting character of each phase together produces different consumption processes. This study deals mainly with individual acts of consumption where private consumers buy or use media products. But we also look at cases where selection, purchase, use and/or disposal of the product are carried out by a collective social institution such as a company (including the shopping centre itself or one of its shops), an organization or the state. Consumption is intrinsically a social process, founded on specifically organized relations between people, where some sell things that others buy from them. Different acts interlock, so that one act is added onto another when for instance a shop owner first buys goods from the distributor and then sells them to customers, restricting his own use of them to offering them for sale in his shop. The whole societal process of consumption is composed of innumerable such acts of shifting character, through which the members of a society are linked into commercial networks. In this narrow sense, a consumption act must always include the defining purchase phase. But there is also an intermediary sense of consumption, where all usage of objects that have once been commodities might also be included. For example, reading a book received as a gift can be said to be part of a larger consumption process, even though it was the giver who bought the book (and probably didn't read it). This means that although commodities, gifts and public goods involve separate logics for transferring objects between people, these three kinds of circuits frequently interlock, with commodities and thus consumption as a dominant form in capitalist societies. In this manner singular consumption acts are woven into complex chains of consumption, in which consuming acts in the narrow and primary sense are often combined with acts that are consumption in the intermediary sense, as gift acts and use of public goods that have once been commodities.

What happens when we think of media consumption in these four phases? The nature of the *selection* may vary, but normally it includes both a survey of the products being offered and a decision. When purchasing a durable product such as a television set, for example, a consumer may make a close examination of the market from his or her desk at home, comparing different tests and prices. After careful consideration a consumer may select a book from a book club catalogue that he or she has received in the mail, and place the order from home. On the other hand the selection may be based on a quick look around in the shop. When it comes to cable television, the selection might be made at the spur of the moment when flicking between channels, or well in advance by studying a television guide. Already in the selection, the first phase in the consumption process, two dimensions stand out as important – time and space. As is clear from the examples above, the time it takes to make a selection can be long or short. Home can be a prominent place in the selection, while in other cases it plays no part at all.

The *purchase* can also be carried out in several ways. It may be extended over a long period of time, for example by instalments through a bank account. The purchase can also be made in the shop, directly using cash, credit card or a cheque. Here too, time and space vary.

Use also varies according to the nature of the product, and includes the wear and tear as well as maintenance and care of the product. A television set is often used almost daily for many years and may require some repairs. A book is usually only read once during a few hours (it can also be read again and again), and though it still happens that people have their books bound and mended, such practices are unusual today. Television programs are ordinarily used when broadcast, but with the help of additional media machines (VCR or DVD) it is possible to record and save programs and perhaps watch them repeatedly. One uses one's own set at home, while a book can be enjoyed on the train, during a break at work or on a bench in a shopping centre.

The *disposal* of a product may have different purposes, take place in different locations and require different amounts of time. There are four main types of disposal: throwing away or discarding the product, giving it away, trading or exchanging it for another product, or reselling it. The character of these different acts of disposal varies widely, according to the type of product. (1) For example, both a television set and a book may be discarded, but whereas the destruction of the television might demand more time since it is a technical device with many parts that have to be taken care of in different ways, the paperback can be left in the paper collection for recycling. Television programmes on the other hand are normally 'consumed' as they are watched. (2) Both books and television sets, but more rarely television programmes (if stored on video cassettes), can be given away as gifts. (3) Books can also be exchanged, for example in a book circle, but this is rarer for television sets. (4) This last variant is very close to reselling the product. Then the consumer turns into a distributor/seller, for example, when selling a used book to a second-hand bookshop.

The consumption process, initiated by a selection, centred on the purchase and use, ending with some kind of disposal, also involves an extended encounter between a person/consumer and an object/product. Moving through the four phases, both consumer and product are at the same time transformed. During the selection and purchase, the person is primarily a customer and the artefact is a market commodity. Through the financial transaction the product changes hands, at the same time as the payment in the form of a sum of money (corresponding to the exchange value of the product) moves in the opposite direction from buyer to seller. When the product is being used the consumer turns into a more or less satisfied owner and user of the product, while the product changes into the article for everyday use that it was meant to be. This use value may be of extremely different kinds, from the very material to the highly symbolical or social.

It is common to misunderstand the concept of use value as covering only the most immediate and simple material uses of any product so that symbolic, relational or status values would be some different addition, specific to late capitalism. The idea is widespread in postmodernist versions of cultural studies, which announce a completely new era of simulacra, confining use value within an oversimplified vulgar materialism. A closer look at Marx's commodity analysis reveals that he also found it obvious that use values might well be of very indirect, social or symbolic kinds. Human needs always include social and aesthetic ones, and commodities – not least those of media and popular culture – have thus always had a wide range of such use values, including imaginary aspects of fantasy and social bonding. When looking at media commodities, this is even more striking, since media texts are always used for symbolic communication invoking aspects of imagination, rather than feeding the stomach or warming the body.[2]

The four variants of disposal provide a number of possibilities. When destroyed the product/article is turned into waste. When given away as a present it remains an article for everyday use, while the owner becomes a giver. When reselling it, the customer/user becomes a seller and the article of use becomes a commodity – though probably with a lower second-hand value than when it was new (apart from cases when it has become an antiquity or has a value for collectors). For the simplest case with an individual commodity and consumer, the complete process can be summarized in the following table:

TABLE 2.1: Phases of Consumption

Phase	Selection	Purchase	Use	Disposal: Destroy/give away/exchange/resell
Object	Commodity	Commodity	Utility goods	Waste/gift/barter object/commodity
Consumer	Selector	Customer	User & owner	Destroyer/giver/ barterer/seller

WHAT IS A MEDIUM?

Communication is a process that generates meaning; it is the production, exchange and sharing of meaning and cannot be reduced to the transference of messages or information. This perspective is the basis of the cultural or ritual perspective on media and communication.[3] Media can then be described as the apparatuses of human symbolic systems, a material base that makes it possible for these systems to mediate (transfer or share) meaning between and among people. If culture is based on communication, media as vehicles of meaning and tools for signifying practices are the material technologies and institutional apparatuses of culture.

Although most people would agree that one could write a message in sand with a twig, few would accept that a twig on a beach is a medium. Considerably more people would be prepared to accept that pen and paper are, and everyone would probably understand the press, radio and television as forms of media. What is counted as media varies, depending on whether material, technological or social aspects are emphasized. This enables a distinction among three main perspectives on media. (1) In a material sense, media are defined as sets of physical objects used for symbolic communication, including stone, wood, paper, copper, bodily organs, smoke, sound waves, light waves and electromagnetism. (2) From a technological perspective, media can be described as specific tools, appliances and machines that mediate symbolic forms and content, including oil paint, Morse code, typewriters, musical instruments, radio sets and computers.[4] (3) From a social or institutional perspective, finally, media are sets of genres, norms, regulations, professions and practices for symbolic communication, including the press, postal services, telecommunications, television broadcasting and the Internet. These three perspectives highlight different aspects of the concept of media and tend to let different but overlapping phenomena come to mind. Take radio for instance. It can be defined as a material medium of radio waves, as a technological medium of transmitting and receiving machines, and as a socially organized medium of central broadcast corporations, programme formats and dispersed listeners.

In practice, all three aspects are always interwoven. Communication technologies integrate material structures and are woven into institutionalized social practices. None of these perspectives alone suffices to form the basis of a clear-cut definition of media, or a univocal differentiation between media types. Moreover, none of them covers precisely the most common notions of media. For example, from all three perspectives money could be defined as a medium, but would hardly be regarded as such by most people. To start with, the use of money is clearly a form of symbolic communication, since like other symbols money has a meaning (to work as a means of barter with variable value) that is always tied to some form of materiality (gold, coins, bank notes, cheques, credit cards, etc.).[5] Money is a symbolic element in a monetary technology, where its value can be transferred between people with the help of different 'media' such as coins, credit cards, ATMs and computers that digitally register financial transactions, and finally as a social institution with fixed norms, laws, regulations, practices and institutions such as banks and markets. Still, most people do not regard money as media, but interpret it as belonging to the economic sphere (primarily co-ordinating the allocation of material resources), which is understood as differentiated from that of culture (primarily communicating meaning).

Asking, 'What is a medium?' can easily be perceived as mere academic hair-splitting, lacking any relevance for everyday reality and the social conditions of real people. For example, people hardly have an urgent need of a media definition in order to use their radio or television sets, CD players or computers. But today's rapid development of media technologies contributes to new ways of transferring symbolic forms and contents, breaking down conventionally accepted boundaries and distinctions between different kinds of media. As a consequence of this breakdown, common-sense views of media tend to dissolve. For example, is a newspaper that is published on the Internet still a newspaper? Is e-mail a form of mail? Is an e-book still a book in a conventional sense? Such questions are raised in the form of copyright problems, unclear boundaries between the private and public spheres, and as new conditions for forming public opinion. There is then a practical need to modify established and conventional uses of the concept of media. In the case of digital technologies, it is caused by material changes, but the relationship between technologies and institutions should be understood as dialectical in the sense that they are mutually dependent and affect one another. Sometimes technological innovations lead to institutional changes, but in other cases new institutional conditions can make room for new technological applications.[6]

In the Passages project, we asked people who visited the shopping centre how they defined media. We received highly diverse answers, ranging from those identifying media with people or with copper wire, to those who mentioned posters, books, telephones, home pages, CDs, or the more conventional press, radio and television. No absolute definitions can be given that once and for all establish what a medium might be. New technologies and new social institutions for symbolic communication continually arise, modifying its material base.[7]

Whatever concept of media is used, there is further an abundance of ways to divide the world of media into different media forms. Such boundaries are often legitimated by references to fixed physical, physiological or functional properties. For instance, media primarily intended to transmit meaningful messages across geographical space often have names starting with 'tele-', as in 'telephone' and 'television', while media for storing information across time have been given names ending in '-graph' and '-gram', as in 'lithograph', 'photograph' or 'phonograph'. This is not a rigid distinction, for as the word 'telegraph' shows, the two functions are typically combined. A book, photo or record stores words, images and sounds for future generations, but can also be used to transfer them from one place to another. There are similar problems with divisions based on which human senses are targeted, since many so-called visual media also have tactile components, while CDs are also material objects and, together with their covers, contain visual information. In fact, all media and symbolic forms of expression are actually multimodal, as there are inherent pictorial aspects of the alphabet and the printed page, visual gestures in music performances, and so on.[8] Another important distinction is between hardware (machines, appliances or tools of communication) and software (texts and programs of various kinds). We will discuss this further in Chapter 6, but it can already be noted that even though hardware and software as commodities tend to be produced and circulated in different ways, they are normally consumed in combination, which makes this division less suitable for a general mapping of types of media use. For instance, while cameras and photos are made and sold in distinct ways, in their actual use, the one presupposes the other.

Other divisions instead take their point of departure in the historically specific ways in which social institutions and technological systems organize communication. It is in this spirit that we here distinguish between *media circuits* as loose, flexible but tenacious groupings of media into rough categories that need not be very consistent or universal, but still have a presence and efficacy in the media world of a given society. The metaphor of a circuit may simultaneously suggest the spiral-formed processes of consumption and communication through which these media are used. The manner in which production, distribution, sales and consumption of media is organized results in a reasonably widespread consensus on what constitutes a media circuit in a given context, though there will always be border cases and contested fields.

In the process of media development, each new medium initially mimics the old, existing ones, in trying to improve them, thus promising brand-new tools for communication, while simultaneously being woven into the gradually evolving societal media networks, in a process of 'remediation' – a term coined by Jay D. Bolter and Richard Grusin.[9] They conceive of the historical development of new media as a process of remediation where limitations of previous ones are remedied by new forms that simultaneously always also copy and quote key traits of the old ones – both in form and content. This process is propelled by a dialectical interplay between 'immediacy' and 'hypermediacy'. On the one hand, there is a wish for transparent mediation that would enable media users to forget completely all the mediating apparatus and interact as if nothing stood between them and the media content. On the other hand, we find a reflexive attention to the peculiarities of mediating technology as such, making it an opaque object in the focus of activity. This dialectic works on several levels, including a transfer and adaptation of content to new media as well as the formal traits of how these new media are constructed and used. With Diane Gromala, Bolter has later developed other terms to discuss this oscillation between transparency and reflectiveness, arguing that 'every interface is a mirror as well as a window', and suggesting 'frames' as a third term between the two.[10] Each medium should then be seen as a constructed frame that can oscillate between being regarded as a transparent window (between people, or between users and texts) and a reflecting mirror (drawing attention to the media technology and design itself).

The digital age has intensified the remediation process, where new media constantly reproduce and replace other media, making intermediality and intertextuality key features of the media world. It should however be remembered that remediation is no new phenomenon. Film, for instance, has been used since its invention to remediate literature, and the content of each new medium tends to be related to older media. Bolter and Grusin refer to Canadian media scholar Marshall McLuhan's remark in *Understanding Media* that 'the "content" of any medium is always another medium', which implies that remediation is inherent in all media and is not specific to our epoch.[11] With the accelerating addition of an expanding number of media technologies into the growing network of media forms, it becomes more and more complex. The contemporary adaptation of older analogue media to digital format is a remediation process whereby computer networks mediate records, films, videos, newspapers or photos. Digital remediation also disconnects established relationships between media, form and content. As computers, fibre wires, mobile phones and DVD disks serve as media – in the sense of vehicles – for many kinds of form and content, it becomes more complicated to uphold stable distinctions between different media circuits.

But technology, commerce, consumption and use do not move at the same pace in this fusion process. The third generation of mobile phones makes possible an extremely interactive audio-visual media circuit that combines sounds, texts and pictures, whereas the formats of videos and DVDs still make up a distinct media circuit in terms of circulation, consumption and use. Media circuits are today (and have in a sense always been) in a transitional state of unsimultaneous simultaneity. 'Old' and 'new' media circuits coexist and are embedded in each other, at the same time as they balance between 'no longer' and 'not yet' in time and space. There are always new techniques that have 'not yet' been introduced in fully on the media market, while others (like vinyl records today) are at the point of 'no longer' being produced and are vanishing, but still continue to subsist on the fringes of the market.

The ongoing merging of communication technologies makes demarcations between media circuits arbitrary and raises a need for new media concepts. Instead of coining a brand-new and perfect definition, we use the term 'media' for technologies for communication, including those combinations of material artefacts, practices and social institutions primarily intended for producing and sharing meaning. Further, we choose not to divide media beforehand into strict types and kinds. Lots of differentiations may be made between media forms, depending on the perspective and purpose. Amateurs tend to manage with fewer categories than experts; producers, distributors and consumers group media differently; and categories shift between social settings. The ways in which media are defined and divided into media circuits (press, television, telephones etc.) are thus socially anchored and historically dynamic. There are institutionally supported stabilizing mechanisms whereby state authorities or large commercial actors strive to fix these categories in order to control and manage media use. But in a parallel movement, various actors always mobilize these boundaries around and within the media world. How these boundaries are drawn needs to be studied socially and historically.

This broad and multilayered view of media enables us to overcome the problematic external limitations and internal divisions of media studies, which have traditionally focused primarily on press and television. It is important to capture the interplay involving a much wider range of communication technologies, including records and photos, posters and postcards, books and journals, records, videos and films, telephones and other digital hardware from television and hi-fi to computers. All these are crucially interrelated in today's complex media world – in the cultural industries as well as in daily life.

MEDIA USE

Media studies have mainly investigated processes of reading, listening to and watching media. Those kinds of media reception are central among the uses people make of media, since it is these practices that define media as a particular set of phenomena, intended for communication. However, there are also other uses of the media that tend to be neglected. As will be discussed in later chapters, phenomena like gift-giving and collecting indicate that media use cannot be reduced to interpretation and reception.

By using media, people constitute various kinds of collectivities. As readers, spectators, or listeners, they form different kinds of audiences and publics, where the latter usually demand some kind of activity, performance and self-identification.[12] People's ways of selecting and structuring the media flow is both a precondition for and a constituting part of their media use. This structuring starts already in the selection and purchase of the media hardware and software, for instance by subscribing to cable channels or piling up CDs on the store counter. A record collection structures the media flow in a private home, framing the selection process that precedes every use of CDs, leading to a specific reception situation.

The key questions about media use can be summed up in the issues of when and where, why, how and to what purpose people use different media.[13] The questions of when and where have to do with the ways in which and to what extent media use depends on time and space coordination in contemporary society. For example, is everyday media use routinized – located at recurring times and identical places – or does it take place at shifting times and places? The ways in which people use media interact with the social relations in which this media use is embedded – the specific time, space and social context of media consumption. Drotner et al. distinguish between 'time-in' and 'time-out' culture, i.e. cultural practices that are integrated into everyday life versus those that stand out as separate events in time and space.[14] This distinction can also be made for media practices, though mediation tends to blur the distinction somewhat, since it might for instance be hard to know if watching television or listening to CDs is experienced as a background to home life at large or as sacred moments of reception. In any case, media use is framed by its social context, but it also actively co-constitutes this context. For example, watching television alone, together with the family or with colleagues may reflect one's lifestyle, but these media practices also contribute to the creation of a personal identity and social context for other activities. In this way social acts (for example, by having a ritual character) and social groups (for example, by being single gendered) contribute to determining the social context of media reception.

Statistics show that an average person in Sweden attends to mass media almost six hours each day. This figure excludes telephones and still images in the form of paintings, photos or posters, the 'use' time of which would be extremely hard to measure empirically. Sound media take 40 per cent of this time, followed by moving images (33.33 per cent) and print media (20 per cent). Television, radio and papers were part of almost everyone's average day, while books, CDs and the Internet were each used by roughly one-third of the population on an average day.[15] These figures vary considerably between countries, ages, classes, genders and ethnic groups. Since different media demand and invite differing use modes, it is always important to compare both number and length of uses, and to acknowledge that some media are used marginally each day while others may be used in a much more focused way on relatively rare occasions. Statistics thus demand careful qualitative interpretation in order to disclose any facets of when, where and how various media are actually used.

The answer to the question of to what purpose people use different media might seem obvious since almost all media that are produced as commodities have an intended or limited area of use. This area is, however, more distinct for some media than for others and can be extended as different media are combined. In addition, digital multimedia are open to a number of areas of use, such as e-mail, information searches, computer games, music making, image editing, and so on. The use of one and the same medium may vary significantly regarding what it is used for. For example, one person might use a television set for watching broadcast television programmes, while someone else is editing or watching videos he has made himself. The line between consumption and production is often problematic when it comes to media use. In Marx's terms, production is simultaneously also consumption, and consumption simultaneously also production.[16] Through the consuming use of media, people produce symbolic forms and contents in the form of photographs, videos, e-mail or audio recordings of their own musical performances. Conversely, the production of programmes by media companies requires consuming a wide range of media, including the communicative technologies of recorders, microphones, cameras, and so on.

The use of media is thus both material and symbolic production. Every instance of media use, whether it results in media texts or not, has productive phases, since the reception process always leads to a production of meaning. The meaning of a mediated message does not lie fixed and ready in the message itself, but is created when someone interprets it.[17]

Interpretation is accomplished according to taste, habit and competence in reading genres (media literacy). People develop tendencies to use media at specific times and places and to embed them in different types of social activities and relations, thereby contributing to the production of the context of which their media reception is an integral part. The production of context is not a sovereign process, but involves negotiating prevailing divisions of time and space in contemporary society, social power structures, and frames set by media technologies and institutions. Moreover, it is tied to conventions. In her study of women who read romantic novels, Janice Radway captured the situation of negotiation that the creation of such a context assumes when she described the act of romance reading as an ambivalent and conflicted occupation, but an act that the women themselves experience as a way of escaping the everyday chores and the rest of the family: 'This is my time, my space. Now leave me alone.'[18] In a similar way, by analysing 'the *how* of television watching', David Morley demonstrated how the 'domestic context' of television viewing is the result of a process of negotiation that depends on the power relations that prevail in a family.[19]

These two specific instances of media reception take place in a larger context. In Morley's words, the 'micro-contexts of consumption' are linked to 'macro-structural processes'.[20] For example, the family relations that determine the organization of television viewing depend on social contexts that include class, gender and ethnic relations. Because the contexts of media use are so enormously complex, there is always a risk that the richness of a concrete situation is reduced by researchers through a process Arjun Appadurai calls 'metonymic freezing', i.e. when a single aspect of people's lives is used to characterize or categorize them.[21] In addition, increasing globalization has gradually extended the contexts of media use to virtually global audiences, giving rise to glocal contexts, where global, national and local levels merge.[22]

Meaning is created in encounters between subjects, texts and contexts. This is a dynamic process, where all understanding presupposes and is grounded in some preconception, which at the same time is an obstacle to and resource for a fuller understanding. Because of the interplay between preconception and understanding, media texts are never completely decoded in a single act of reception. Media texts always carry 'an excess of meaning', making it impossible to exhaust them of their possible meanings.[23] This hermeneutic view of interpretation and reception breaks with all notions that the meaning of a text resides *in* the text itself. Meaning is produced in the contextualized encounter between the reader and the text. The meaning that a text conveys is produced in the reading of it, framed by the intratextual, intertextual and extratextual contexts of that relationship.

The intratextual context is the text as a whole, the interpretation of each specific part of that text. The intertextual context consists of other texts that are brought to the fore in the encounter between a recipient and a text, from the genre that a text is inscribed in to its references to other texts, and texts that deal with the same subject matters. These encounters between texts have no objective existence, but presuppose the interpretive acts whereby human subjects interrelate. The extratextual context can be divided into a text-related context (bound to the specific text) and a recipient context (linked to the user of the text).

The text-related extratextual context in its turn opens in two directions, which with Paul Ricoeur's metaphors can be described as 'in front of' and 'behind' the text.[24] When any subject encounters and interprets a text, an imaginary or virtual textual world opens up in front of that text, through the text's references to (and creation of) some kind of reality. Since texts are human artefacts, there is also a world opening up behind the text, including the intentions of the author and the historical context in which the text was produced, with the 'structure of feeling' in which it was originally embedded.[25] The recipient context has a series of subjective, social, cultural and historical dimensions, from a micro to a macro level, with everyday and lifeworld contexts in between. These fundamental dimensions may both converge and diverge, and can be further subdivided into a number of specific contexts in terms of family, gender, age, class or ethnicity.

This hermeneutic or cultural model of communication provides a critical perspective on the routine linear model of transmission. Harold Lasswell's famous 1948 formula was: 'Who / says What / to Whom / through what Channel / and with what Effect?' This kind of model was the basis for most media studies, which still tend to be rather strictly divided between studies of production, of texts and of reception.

The model was also central to information theory, with Shannon and Weaver as early examples.[26] While it can conveniently apply to certain aspects of modern mass media, it cannot fully conceptualize media use in general. Forms of communication other than press, radio and television problematize the frozen dualism of production and consumption, sender and receiver. In everyday dialogues face to face or on the phone, participants rapidly move in and out of the roles of speaker and listener. In interactive Internet or computer game uses, the programmers and the multiple users are all engaged in ways that are difficult to disentangle according to such a simple linear formula. Also, in poetic genres, it is more relevant to ask what people in a certain context make out of texts than what the author originally intended to express. The 'hypodermic needle' or 'injection theory' of media effects was soon questioned and modified in order to include contexts, feedback and interaction, but its basic divisions of sender, text and receiver remain in force, in theories of uses-and-gratifications as well as in Roman Jakobson's linguistic-literary model that inspired Roland Barthes, Umberto Eco and other semioticians.[27]

Serious attempts by British and American cultural studies scholars in the 1970s to distance themselves from the transmission view of communication nevertheless leaned heavily on semiotic ideas through which this view tended to sneak back in.[28] Stuart Hall's influential encoding/decoding model depicted media production as structured by specific cultural, economic and technical frameworks, leading to an 'encoding' of meaning structures into a programme or text as a 'meaningful' discourse. In reception, the audience then reconstructs a set of meanings through 'decoding' that same text, framed partly by other contextual frameworks.[29] This left room for a divergence between the two moments, but still retained a tendency to conceive of communication as a transmission of a meaningful message from fixed producers to receivers, and of media use as an unpackaging (decoding) of given contents. This may fit reasonably well for how, for instance, news journalism is supposed to function in its idealized form, but is unsuitable as a general model. Hall later developed a model of 'articulation', where locally specific historical configurations of texts and readers link meanings to texts. This is more consistent with the hermeneutic model of communication proposed here.

To take one example: who or what decides the meaning of any music video? Is it the artist, the music industry, or the totality of its time of origin – what Raymond Williams discussed as the 'structure of feeling' at the moment of textual production?[30] The answer must be, all and none of them! The meaning of any media text is never definitely fixed, as long as it remains circulating as a living cultural text. It therefore cannot be reduced to the original intentions behind it, whether they are analysed as residing in an individual artist, producing institutions, or the spirit of the times. Interpretation gives special attention to all of these but allows the text's meaning to evolve over history. For people who live decades or even centuries later, the meaning of an old text is never quite the same as it was for its original writers or readers. Though this may worry historians who want to find out a true first meaning, it is for many others who read the text no big issue, in particular not for fictional narratives or art works, where the experience and the interpretations that arise from each fresh encounter with a new reader are what count.

POWER DIMENSIONS

Consumption and media use are woven into a network of power relations, from the micro-power of everyday interactions to the macro-power of nation states and global corporations. Consuming practices raise questions about panoptic control and self-empowerment, ideology and resistance, where researchers alternate between regarding consumption culture either as the core of the run-of-the-mill everyday, or as an escape from it. Media practices, as processes of communication, include struggles for power over meaning and identity in space and time. Communication and power are always co-present, since power may be regarded as a (coercive) form of communication, and communication as a (communicative or symbolic) form of power. Power develops in all the kinds of spaces that have been discussed here: the spaces of media, of shopping, and of cities. Communication media are deeply involved in structuring time and regulating access to and use of space, and these are key dimensions for the construction of individual and collective identities.

We will here reconstruct the basic power dimensions of modern societies and locate media practices in these dimensions. We do this by combining theoretical sources that are rarely integrated. In particular, we make use both of Pierre Bourdieu and Jürgen Habermas, whose works in this respect productively supplement each other, offering a way out of the sweeping understanding of power that otherwise threatens to make cultural studies approaches vague or even self-contradictory.[31] By looking for differences and complexities, and situating communicative power in a force field of economic, political and cultural vectors, we hope to arrive at a richer and more useful model of media power.

A process of differentiation between power systems dates back to the formation of the modern nation state and capitalist industrialization in a long and globally differentiated process, gradually emerging from the seventeenth century onwards. The growth of media industries and institutions is a part of what Polanyi has called 'The Great Transformation' of European society, making all aspects of social life dependent on market exchange, but also separating economic power from other spheres of power.[32] The differentiation of power spheres was refined through the twentieth-century stratification of the bourgeoisie into economic, political and cultural strata. In modern and late-modern societies, power cannot be reduced to one single source. Three main types may be distinguished: economic, political and symbolic power. These are intertwined and interdependent, but also relatively uncoupled from each other, supported by distinct and sometimes conflicting institutional bodies.

(1) *Economic power* originates from work and the production of material resources, and is institutionalized in the form of markets, companies, capital and money. This power form structures material conditions for media use, from the decisions made in the boards of multi-national media enterprises to the everyday use of money in purchasing media commodities on the market. Economic power is

directly or indirectly present in all fields of activity and cannot be delimited to specific spheres of social action, but it is particularly concentrated in the market sphere of commodity production and circulation that links economic power to media consumption. Through the commodity form and the market institutions, economic power affects culture, arts, the media and the public sphere.[33]

(2) *Political power* originates from the need to govern, coordinate and regulate human activities, and is institutionalized in the form of state authorities, political parties, a juridical system and – as the ultimate coercive power – the military's armed forces. Its primary resource is the right to legislate and allocate authority to the holders of certain social positions to make political decisions, and supervise so that legislation and laws are obeyed (if necessary, with the use of physical violence). This administrative power determines the structured conditions for media use mainly through legislation, regulations and subsidies that restrict the influence of economic power on the media. The public service institutions in most European countries occupy a considerable space between the market and the state, taking form already in the early days of The Great Transformation, when the printing press contributed to the rise of state apparatuses, nation states and new cultural mass markets.[34] State-based and international politics still determine basic conditions for media use through censorship, regulations of free speech and subsidies to media that cannot survive on market conditions.

(3) Finally, *symbolic power* originates in a basic sense from the need to reduce the contingency in people's understanding of themselves, others and the world they live in, but could in a more specific sense be defined as the government and regulation of the meaning of symbolic forms and contents. In modern societies, symbolic power is dispersed through a range of social institutions such as churches, schools, universities, art academies, museums, theatres and the media. Modern symbolic power tends to be institutionalized into four main branches. A religious branch is concerned with the sacral, otherworldly and metaphysical aspects of human life. A scientific branch uses reason to interpret its profane and inner-worldly aspects. An aesthetic or artistic branch is concerned with human sensibility, expressiveness and matters of taste. Finally, a media branch is concerned with the transmission, diffusion and circulation of symbolic contents and forms. These branches of institutionalized symbolic power overlap, as they do with economic and political power.[35] Symbolic power is thus in late-modern societies differentiated into mutually competing spheres whose relative strengths shift historically. The so-called secularization process has for instance displaced symbolic power from religious to scientific, art and media institutions. Since the early twentieth century the media sector is a fast-expanding authority and centre of gravity of symbolic power.

Symbolic power has been differentiated into distinct subfields of cultural production, with varying degrees of autonomy, mechanisms of legitimization and consecration, and relations to economic and political power. The following model summarizes the dimensions of media power, combining terms and insights from Bourdieu and Habermas.[36]

TABLE 2.2: Forms of Media Power

Forms of Power	Primary Power Resource	Institutions
Economic power	Economic capital	Economic institutions (companies, markets, trade associations, private banks, etc.)
Political power Administrative power	Authority Legislation Physical violence/armed forces	Political institutions (state apparatus, political parties, parliament, local municipalities etc.)
Communicative power Symbolic power (religious, scientific, aesthetic, medial)	Means of communication Symbolic/cultural capital	Cultural institutions (churches, universities, schools, art academies, media enterprises, etc.)

This composite model allows a bridging of the gap between cultural studies and political economy perspectives in media studies, by acknowledging the political and economic force of societal institutions that frame and regulate mediated communications, as well as the communicative and symbolic force inherent in specific sociocultural interactions. The 'either/or' perspective on the sources of power is thus displaced by the recognition that power runs several ways. It is therefore necessary to investigate the intersection of many different forms of power in the world of consumption and media use.

Let us scrutinize the third, cultural level in further detail. What Habermas calls social and communicative power is based on the interactional resources of civil society, inherent in people's lifeworlds.[37] Social power manifests itself in any kind of enforcement or dominance in human relations, except in situations where people reach agreement through reasoning and thereby make use of the rationality of communicative power. These forms are blended in most human practice. For instance, social power manifests itself in the mobilization of social movements, and communicative power in the public arguments they use to support their interests or goals. Although dependent on other forms of power as well as some amount of expressive freedom, communicative power is a resource that both dominant and dominated social groups can mobilize, and is thus available for acts both of dominance and of resistance, indicating that there is no clear-cut distinction between resistance and power.[38] The state, the market and the civil society thus have different power resources at their disposal, and their interrelations may be characterized by consensus as well as by conflict. Around a particular topic, they may sometimes temporarily form alliances, giving rise to intersecting patterns of power and resistance between them. For instance, the official Swedish state policy for culture and the media has, since the 1920s, built on a strong ideological alliance with civil society in the form of social movements and associations, aiming to counteract what are described as 'the negative consequences of commercialism' and thus restricting the profit-seeking strategies of the media market. Pressure groups in civil society organize to counteract certain kinds of media content and convince state authorities to force media industries into self-regulation. The American Parent's Music Resource Centre (PMRC) did this in the 1990s, and similar alliances of parental, religious or feminist movements and associations working with state authorities have resulted in restrictions of violent, racist or sexist media content in many countries, including Sweden.

Such efforts depend on symbolic power, which works in both direct and indirect or mediated ways. It is incorporated into people's consciousness and corporeally embodied through processes of socialization and schooling, with effects later reflected in media habits, cultural consumption and taste patterns that differ according to class, gender, ethnic background and education. Bourdieu's concept of habitus, the embodiment of durable dispositions or generative schemes that determine people's orientation in the social world, is a powerful theoretical tool to grasp how such processes are related to symbolic power in the form of cultural capital.[39] Through habitus, symbolic power is built into actions and practices without direct external coercion. This habitus formation guides individuals towards adapting certain habits of consumption and media use, or taste preferences. Symbolic power thus works through people's self-regulatory practices, whereby they structure the conditions of their own media consumption.

But symbolic power is also at stake in the struggles for convertible forms of capital within the multiple and relatively autonomous fields of cultural production, including the educational, academic, journalism, arts and literary fields. The multiplicity of cultural fields contributes towards differentiating cultural capital into specific forms, like educational, scientific, informational and artistic capital. Complex struggles for symbolic power take place both between and within these fields of cultural production. They are hierarchically ordered, as are their relations to the overall fields of economic and political power, or what Bourdieu – parallel to Habermas' notion of political power – terms 'the field of power'.[40]

Media power is an institutionalized form of communicative power that hardly qualifies as an autonomous cultural field, since it is primarily controlled by economic or political forces. It is nevertheless perhaps the most important contemporary source of symbolic power. Based on the control of resources of communication and information, media power works through processes of selection, including the so-called agenda-setting function whereby dominant media set the agenda for public discussion by paying attention to some issues while systematically disregarding others. However, media power can be used either to reveal or to conceal other (economic, political or symbolic) power strategies. This makes it a central power source whose links to economic and political power are particularly controversial in public and political life.

Communicative power resides in acts of communication. As Habermas shows in *The Theory of Communicative Action*, building on speech act theory, all communication involves an exchange between subjects, balancing communicative and instrumental (goal-oriented, strategic) forms of interaction, and thus the exertion of social and communicative power.[41] Acts of communication always have effects – influencing something or somebody. This is true for expressive forms in images, music and all other symbolic modes. The force of language and linguistic argumentation has for instance been scrutinized by classical theories of logic, rhetoric and pragmatics. Further, a series of modern theories of communication, media effects, reception and semiotics have in various ways thematized the actual or potential impact of mediated symbolic forms in general. In the previous section on media use, we problematized the traditional production-consumption dualism that underpins a whole range of models of communication as a linear chain where meanings are transported from senders to receivers. Leaning on Paul Ricoeur's critical hermeneutics, we outlined a less dichotomous view of the processes of meaning-production as created in dynamic encounters between interacting subjects and plural texts in multidimensional contexts. All this has implications for how to understand the interplay of power and resistance, and, even more generally, of structure and agency. Here again, we question the common thinking in terms of essentialized polarities, and argue for opening up a more diverse and situated set of struggles.

Power breeds and needs resistance, as two sides of the same coin. There is always a play or struggle between these sides, and none of them can be understood as fixed essences. Front lines shift between situations, and those who at one time or in one respect are in a position of power may later or in another relationship be agents of resistance. Michel Foucault has underlined that 'power is exercised from innumerable points' and is 'immanent' in other relationships rather than exterior to them. 'Where there is power, there is resistance, and yet, or rather consequently, this resistance is never in a position of exteriority in relation to power', and power relations have a 'strictly relational character', depending on 'a multiplicity of points of resistance' that 'are present everywhere in the power network'.[42]

> These points of resistance are present everywhere in the power network … Just as the network of power relations ends by forming a dense web that passes through apparatuses and institutions, without being exactly localized in them, so too the swarm of points of resistance traverses social stratifications and individual unities.[43]

Power and resistance can thus not be separated from each other, Foucault argues. Nor is there any privileged source or type of power that explains all others.

> Similarly, rather than looking for the single form or the central point from which all forms of power derive, either by way of consequence or development, we must begin by letting them operate in their multiplicity, their differences, their specificity, and their reversibility; we must therefore study them as relations of force that intersect, refer to one another, converge, or, on the contrary, come into conflict and strive to negate one another.[44]

This book follows that advice, using the last chapter to study some specific relations of power and resistance that intersect in media consumption. However, we do not follow

Foucault when, in contradiction to these words, he then closes down his perspective to interpret all power relations 'in terms of the general form of war'. This might be useful to balance a tradition for studying power in terms of contracts and rights, but it seems more justifiable – and in line with Foucault's own apparent intentions – to admit that several levels and aspects of analysis may be needed, rather than again reducing power relations to one single privileged form. And since all forms of resistance make use of the power resources available to those who resist dominance, economic, political and symbolic resistance can be related to the corresponding forms of power.

Consumers might for instance manifest their resistance to economic power by their purchasing activities or by boycotts, and citizens might mobilize against political decisions or symbolically respond to dominant media texts with refusal, oppositional readings or alternative textual production. This also implies that different forms of power and resistance intersect, like when economic dominance is met with political or symbolic resistance. But in some instances the immanent relationship between power and resistance might go even further. For example, resistance might conceal power demands or even be combined with the exertion of power. As Paul Willis showed in *Learning to Labour*, resistance along one dimension may sometimes contribute to consolidating and reproducing existing structures of power in other dimensions, by the glorification of certain aspects of subordinated social positions and the reproduction of limitations that restricts the potential emancipation of the resisting act.[45] In Willis's case, the working-class lads' resistance to the school's middle-class values led to a triple reproduction of prevalent power orders, combining a misogynic fear of women, a xenophobic repudiation of immigrant ethnic groups and an anti-intellectual refusal of reflection.

Power and resistance flow through many kinds of social agencies, including institutions, communities and individual subjects. They are immanent in economic and political, as well as social and cultural fields. Each such power/resistance instance may be investigated in similar ways as media use, asking, who resists what, how, why and with which results, i.e. analysing different agents, targets, means, causes/intentions and effects of resistance.[46] To some extent, this is what we will do in our last chapter.

Communication and power are deeply imbued in one another, and there are several attempts in media and cultural studies to understand their intersection. Based on his model of encoding and decoding, Stuart Hall showed how power and resistance operate in media use. He distinguished three hypothetical decoding positions: a dominant-hegemonic, a negotiated and an oppositional one.[47] The sender has full power over the receiver – and resistance is thus absent – when for example a television viewer is operating inside the 'dominant code', faithfully reproducing the meaning structures intentionally encoded by the media industrial producer. Resistance manifests itself when audiences use either an openly 'oppositional' or a more compromising 'negotiated code' to decode the meanings of the received media messages. The interpretations of media messages may thus not coincide with the intentions of those who produce them. In many forms of communication, including the arts, this is the intended rule rather than a sign of failure or resistance. Still, Hall's reasoning is valid for many conventional forms of mass-media use.

It is more problematic to try to locate power and resistance in two opposite camps. Such a romantic, reifying and essentializing conception is widespread, not least in cultural studies, where for instance John Fiske – building on Stuart Hall's ideas – argued that the preferred meanings encoded by 'the power-bloc' in the products of the media and cultural industries tend to be decoded by 'the people' in unpredictable and oppositional ways. This move detaches interpretation from the strategies of economic power, and the 'semiotic power' 'to construct meanings, pleasures, and social identities' is transmitted from 'the power-bloc' to 'the people'.[48] These constructions of 'the power-bloc' and 'the people' conceal any internal differences and contradictions on both sides. Also, although meaning is produced rather than reproduced at the moment of media use, there are institutionalized and structural constraints in which this moment of interpretation takes place and which are not addressed in Fiske's analysis. It is important to recognize that texts are always interpreted in contexts where hegemonic ideological formations as well as material limitations constrain people's options. Resistant readings require efforts to break free of daily routines that tend to affirm existing structures, and each resistance on one level (for instance in class or generational terms) can easily in turn result in a reinforced pattern of dominance along another dimension (for example when it comes to gender, sexuality, or ethnicity).

The different forms of power are intertwined in everyday media consumption, giving rise to intersecting sets of resistance along the corresponding axes. Yet different schools of thought have continued to overemphasize either structural power or the agency of individual or popular resistance. Some forms of ideology critique, political economy and structuralist theories of social institutions or symbolic orders have exaggerated the power of structures to position, shape and steer individuals and masses. Others have instead constructed overly optimistic analyses of consumers' or subcultures' subversive uses of media contents.[49] In order to avoid such pendulum swings between extreme positions, it is necessary to distinguish between weak and strong forms of power and resistance. It was not wrong for cultural studies to break away from the old Frankfurt School view of the culture industry as moulding the consciousness and desires of the masses. The most totalizing and pessimistic analyses by Adorno, Horkheimer and the young Habermas failed to understand the complexities and inner contradictions of late-modern media culture. They are hard to sustain after Raymond Williams's critique of the whole concept of masses and mass culture: 'The masses are always the others, whom we don't know, and can't know. … To other people, we also are masses. Masses are other people. There are in fact no masses; there are only ways of seeing people as masses.'[50] But other and less totalizing lines of thought were also present already in the early and classical Frankfurt School, and Habermas's later work has productively integrated some of cultural studies' perspectives on the media to modify his own models in ways that deserve a more constructive treatment in cultural studies as well.

For instance, Adorno's critique of the culture industry can be reconstructed in light of his later philosophical and aesthetic writings to reveal highly sophisticated theoretical ideas on cultural power and resistance. He emphasized that people 'do not really believe' in 'the primitive wish fulfilments' of the culture industry and that it can never totally succeed in moulding their consciousness or needs. He also argued that modern subjectivity reflects the 'antagonistic' character of modern society in a way that makes individuals 'antagonistic in themselves', and 'both free and unfree'.[51] Hence, although the Frankfurt School emphasized the power of economic and bureaucratic forces in its analysis of the culture industry, it did not deny the possibility of resisting them.

In his later work, Habermas analysed the dialectics between the two large societal systems of state and market, and the lifeworld (the horizons of meaning and interpretation in which people act and communicate), whose interaction is steered by the tools of money and administrative power, structured by the institutionalized roles of employee, consumer and client, but which also depends on symbolic communication between citizens.[52] The lifeworld is rationalized and differentiated by the two modern systems, at the same time that it is threatened by their colonization. The outcome of these processes remains open, carrying both authoritarian and emancipatory possibilities. The modern differentiation processes have meant that society comprises a decentred network of plural but interconnected 'particularized forms of life and lifeworlds', whose mutual interlacing through communicative action binds society together, in spite of all its diversity. The lifeworld is in late modernity actually an increasingly open network structure of pluralized and particularized (though still collective) lifeworlds.[53] Habermas's notion of the uncoupling of the systems from the lifeworld is analogous to Bourdieu's idea of the differentiation of power and resistance in the modern evolution of relatively autonomous social fields.

Civil society and its public sphere are becoming increasingly mediatized. Media institutions do not entirely belong to the systems, or to the networked lifeworld. Although asymmetrically organized in terms of power, they mediate between the systemic level and that of the lifeworld(s). They function as sites for power struggles, both in terms of economic, political and symbolic power. Those struggles activate contradictions as well as alliances between economic, political and symbolic power, or between the advocates of the state, the market and civil society respectively. In this way complicated patterns of power and resistance criss-cross, as they frame everyday social and cultural practices, including media use. Some of these patterns of power/resistance stem from systemic demands, others from lifeworld contexts, which can never simply be seen as sites of resistance to systemic power, since the latter is also always anchored in and dependent on the lifeworld practices that reproduce it. Personal, social and cultural dominance are built into lifeworld relations and maintained either with the support of systemic power or in contradiction to it. Hence, civil society's demands for liberation from the administrative power of the state or the economic power of the market cannot by definition be regarded as progressive or democratic, as clearly revealed by the histories of fascism, racism and sexism.

Economic, political and symbolic power are thus each linked to corresponding forms of resistance. Certain sets of oppositional acts turn against the dominant market forces. Such economic resistance may be local and/or global, and it may also be either limited or radical. Smaller enterprises may for instance counteract the hegemony of large corporations, while cooperatives or open source networks pose more general alternatives, and radical anticapitalist movements openly confront the capitalist market system as a whole. On the political frontier, minority parties oppose ruling governments, while alternative social movements work for more radical forms of democracy. There are finally also symbolic or cultural forms of resistance, subdivided along dimensions partly linked to the identity orders to which people tend to relate: class, gender, sexuality, age, generation, ethnicity, nationality and so forth. In the last chapter, we analyse these various forms and dimensions in greater detail, based on ethnographical examples.

With such an understanding of power-resistance dimensions, it is possible to deconstruct the romantic idea of resistance as a pure and homogenous counter-bloc to an equally essentialized power-bloc. It is often thought that in revolutionary situations, various streams of power and resistance may converge and clash against each other, but on closer inspection, things are never so simple. There is never any perfect fit, but only idealized imaginations of such utopian moments. In reality the fragile alliances that coalesce to tip over balances of power in one historical moment always contain internal tensions and contradictions that make history continue. In ordinary daily life, resistances shift and intersect in highly contradictory ways, and there is little point in idealizing resistance as such. It is never possible to praise all forms of resistance, since resistances often counteract each other, and the success of one leads to the opposition of another. This implies no total relativism, since each case of power/resistance front line must be evaluated in relation to the long-term articulated structures in which it is integrated. But these structures are never completely rigid and cannot be outlined once and for all. For instance, when new topics develop on the social and political agenda, old front lines may be reduced in relative importance. Any interpretation of power and resistance thus has to be contextually situated and contains within it the potential to overturn any ahistorical and universal model.

THE CROSSROADS OF MEDIA CONSUMPTION

This chapter has argued for more complex tools of understanding of media consumption. In a series of areas, we have problematized closed dualisms and dichotomies, arguing for more multidimensional and dynamic perspectives, from the basic definitions of media and consumption to the analysis of power and resistance in practices of communication. We have argued that the processes of media consumption and of communication overlap, and run in several phases. Both involve encounters between products and individuals within social frameworks – contextually situated interactions between texts and subjectivities, resulting in the production of meaning, identity and power. These processes are framed by institutions and structures that have evolved in modern societies, placing media use in a multidimensional force field of economic, political and symbolic power.

A shopping centre is one such place, central for the economic, spatial, institutional and social processes that are typical of late modernity. It is a prismatic space of consumption and communication, where the intersecting passages of people and media goods result in a number of encounters: social encounters between people, intertextual encounters between genres, and interactive encounters between consumers and media. The next four chapters will move into such a centre, to discover how consumption and communication are organized and intertwined in a set of media circuits. Chapter 3 starts with the old circuits of print media, Chapter 4 continues with images of various kinds, Chapter 5 discusses temporally mobile media of sounds and visuals in motion, and Chapter 6 approaches the hardware machines that link other media circuits and create new, hybrid media forms. After this journey through the late-modern mediascape, the subsequent three chapters will again bridge the gaps and scrutinize intermedial connections, time and space. The final chapter then returns to the dialectics of power and resistance and proposes a new agenda for media and cultural studies.

3. PRINT MEDIA

There are several shops in the shopping centre that sell newspapers, magazines and books, i.e. media in which the written and printed word has the centre stage, but which may also contain pictures. Print media are among the oldest and most widely used mass media, historically fundamental for the growth of the modern society and culture, and still an important part of daily life. In an ordinary day, 81 per cent of the Swedish population read a daily paper, 39 per cent read some kind of magazine and 37 per cent read a book. Only television and radio can compete with these figures.[1] In this respect, the Nordic countries tend to present comparatively high figures, but the reading of printed texts is a key cultural practice all over the world.

In the shopping centre, newspapers, magazines and other periodicals are sold primarily at the confectioners and tobacconists, but also in some grocery stores, where paperbacks can be found as well.[2] Otherwise, books are primarily sold in the two bookshops, representing Sweden's two largest chains of bookshops. But books, newspapers and magazines are also available in a non-commercial space: the large, modern and well-attended municipal public library, located in the shopping centre. The library is one of few buildings that the city did not sell to private interests when it sold land to make room for a new shopping centre at the beginning of the 1960s. Today, the library has a large reading room where people can sit and read newspapers, magazines and other periodicals, though they cannot be taken home. But, as is normal in libraries, one can take out books and 'non-print' material such as audio books. Many people think of the library as a place where people mainly borrow and read books. Certainly, lots of books are borrowed from Solna public library, but almost half the visitors (44 per cent) do not borrow or return books.[3] Instead they read newspapers and magazines (18 per cent), borrow/return CDs or videos, study, or use the Internet-linked computers. Though books dominate, many other media are today represented in the library.

Nor do bookshops only sell books. In Sweden, bookshops have always depended economically on selling stationery, and today it could even be said that the bookshop is the line of business with the widest selection of different media. Bookshops sell postcards, classical music CDs, children's videos, audio books on cassette and CD, and CD-ROMs with games and encyclopaedias, just to give a few examples. This multiplicity of products have made the conditions for selling books more like those for newspapers and magazines, which have long been sold in stores in which they are not the main attraction; newspapers and magazines in kiosks and grocery stores have shared the space with tobacco, sweets, games, soft drinks and stockings. The difference, compared to books, is that in such an environment newspapers and magazines have had no connection with the other products on sale. Their function – especially the newspapers – is as a kind of loss leader, luring customers into the store where they will hopefully buy something more profitable. Books, on the other hand, have links to their new company. Among other things, the growing media supply has to do with the fact that more and more media are connected to one and the same phenomenon or story. For example, a story first published as a novel may become an audio book or a computer game, but also an animated cartoon or a feature film, which in turn might provide images for the cover of binders, pen cases and letterheads. The bookshop is in fact an excellent example of a commercial place where intermedial relations and intersections between different media circuits can be studied.

In the shopping centre there are thus two kinds of book spaces, both traditionally viewed as temples of bourgeois culture, as opposed to the traditionally more popular aspects of the places where newspapers are sold. But today bookshops can be said to have become more democratic, partly through their location in shopping centres and malls, but also because of their broader offer and sales strategies, which are no longer exclusively aimed at the educated classes.[4] A similar development can also be observed in public libraries. The traditional image of libraries is as strongholds of highbrow culture, where learned men (and a few women) sit silently leafing through half-bound volumes among dark, wainscoted bookcases. This image does not correspond well to today's public libraries, which in the last few decades have been 'popularized' in the same way as bookshops, and they are nowadays both depending on a large group of female readers. Libraries, like bookshops, have also even come to be located in shopping centres, side by side with tobacconists.[5]

Traditionally, studies of media reception have been confined to media use understood in terms of reception: the reading, watching or listening to media. This runs the risk of forgetting other media uses that are important in everyday life, such as giving away media as presents. Media consumption, when treated as synonymous with studies of media reception, runs the risk of neglecting the function of media as commodities that is crucial to understanding the place of media in everyday life. This requires a reformulation of consumption as the purchase of products into a definition of consumption as the stretched-out process discussed in the last chapter. Here, we analyse the selection, purchase, use and disposal of books, newspapers and magazines in commercial and non-commercial spaces. This approach also indicates the importance of the places where media are used, illustrated by the contrasting roles of the bookshop and the library.

BOOKS, NEWSPAPERS, MAGAZINES

Several criteria have traditionally been employed to divide media into main types. Some of the divisions seize upon the form of expression that dominates each medium. In this respect one can say that text and picture are central in the circuit print media. Other divisions focus on the ability of different media to store information over time or to distribute information in space. Newspapers, magazines and books can be stored over time, but the duration of the storage is limited by the durability of the paper. On the other hand, the perishability of paper can be compensated for through storage on microfiche. The extent of the distribution in space is highly varied: from a national perspective one can distinguish between, on the one hand, print media that are available in principle for everyone in the country – for example the largest morning and evening papers and some magazines and books – and on the other hand, less available print media such as local newspapers, more exclusive magazines and books that lack nation-wide distribution. Yet another possible categorization is by genre. In this way, one can place newspapers and some magazines and books in the macro genre information/ analysis/debate, though many of these media, both in terms of content and form, are increasingly mixed with entertainment. Correspondingly, many periodicals and books can be classified as entertainment. None of these criteria offer an unambiguous distinction between newspapers, magazines and books, as all criteria flow into one another.

So what are the characteristics of print media as commodities, compared to other media circuits? One thing that books, newspapers and magazines have in common is that they contain visible text and images already at the time of purchase, something that distinguishes them from, for example, videos and CDs, whose use requires some kind of hardware. It is thus possible to claim that print media are autonomous or *single media*, circulated and used without any necessary additional technological support. Another characteristic of print media is their specific materiality: the paper and the ink. Through their materiality, paper books, dailies and magazines – unlike web 'papers', e-zines and broadcast media – are products that demand a much more concrete physical transportation across space.

For readers, the materiality might have specific dimensions. For example, when Celal, a 28-year-old Kurdish man born in Turkey, talks about reading newspapers from his native country, he attributes a special significance to the smell of the printer's ink: 'When I buy *Hürriet* I smell the ink and my fingers become black, which is not the case with Swedish papers ... I have to smell that smell, perhaps to some extent I feel like, okay, I have not cut my contact with home.' Print media products have both tactile and visual aspects. In both the newsagents and the bookshop, customers touch the products all the time. Through their availability on display, media products can be held and examined: is it four-colour print on glossy paper? How small or large is the print? Is the book bound in leather, in paperboards or is it a paperback? What does the blurb say and what are the headings in the table of contents? What articles and pictures are found in the magazine? In the bookshop, unlike on the Internet, customers can touch and leaf through the books. The tactile and visual dimension of moving around among the products, among the material objects, is a competitive advantage of bookshops in face of e-trade.

However, in spite of all the similarities between media constituting this circuit, there is one criterion that distinguishes newspapers and magazines from books, and that is periodicity. There are daily newspapers, periodicals published weekly, monthly or less often, but still clearly regularly, whereas books, with some exceptions, are not submitted to demands of periodicity.[6]

Newspapers and magazines are perishables that are often only read once and then disposed of. In this they differ from records, films and books, which have a longer normal lifespan and are often kept by their consumers who may sometimes return to them long after the purchase. These different aspects of time – the 'speed' of their lifespan – also affect the tempo in the shops selling print media.

SELECTION AND PURCHASE

The shops where newspapers and magazines are sold are characterized by a fast pace and great visual accessibility. Most such shops have glass walls from floor to ceiling, making it possible for prospective customers to get an overview of the products from the street. The shops lack doors in a strict sense, which also facilitate accessibility and allow customers to come and go easily. Nor do customers stay long in the stores – most seem to know what they are looking for when they come in; they walk straight to the product, pick it up and then immediately go to the counter, pay and leave. This behaviour is also encouraged by the shops themselves. A tobacconist says that representatives from the two major distribution companies, whom he meets a few times per year, advise on how the magazines should be arranged on the shelves. According to them all magazines on the same subject, for example, mobile phones, should be placed side by side: 'The customers must be able to find the right title quickly; otherwise they leave.' Only the latest issues are left on the shelves, and all back issues are tucked away in stores. Children's magazines should be placed on the bottom shelves and porno magazines on the top shelves, where they cannot be seen. Each magazine should be placed so as to get maximum exposure, for example by not being placed on top of each other, and the lighting must be good. These directions emphasize the perishability of the magazines and are meant to optimize exposure. The placing of the magazines according to theme or genre has the obvious purpose of making it easier for customers to find what they are looking for, but might also tempt them to buy more than they had planned. Distributors and shop owners address their customers as subjects who are always on the go and have the power to leave suddenly without making a purchase.

The bookshop entrance is likewise designed to draw people into the store. The spacious, open entrance, barely marking the border between inside and outside, attracts presumptive customers. When customers enter, they immediately encounter platforms displaying the season's articles and special offers. At the start of the new school year, stationery dominates: glossy wrapping paper for textbooks, strawberry flavoured pencils and beautiful, collectable erasers, displayed en masse in racks on top of a rounded platform. Close by is a pallet full of notepads, sold in such quantities that they are not stacked on platforms or shelves, and the customers pick them up as they are delivered.

The sales figures and the marketing in the bookshop, like in the rest of the retail trade, are rooted in annually recurring events. This can be understood as a way of creating the periodicity that is built into the products of the newsagent. The events may be tied to the calendar, such as Christmas, Father's Day, Saint Valentine's or

Easter, or to events not named in the calendar, for example, the Nobel Prize for literature, beginning of term, end of term and the annual sale. In connection with these events there are established campaigns. Around Christmas, which is the season with the largest turnover, large gift books with eye-catching covers are arranged in piles on a platform: novels in hard covers, cookbooks, gardening books and books about interior design share the space with gaudy illustrated books. For the traditional book sale in February the shelves are removed and the space is arranged so as to accommodate the best-selling discount titles. For the summer, pocketbooks and paperback crime novels are displayed with a sign: 'Take four, pay for three'.

The pace in the bookshop is much slower than at the newsagent's. The platforms and gondolas make it possible to display a large number of titles, arranged according to genre like the magazines, marked with clear signs on the shelves. But like tobacconists, booksellers choose to focus on the latest items, presented here in the form of top tens, special stands and displays. Similarly, the chain of bookstores chooses to display many copies of fewer titles, so that presumed best-sellers are displayed in stacks or on the shelves that cover the pillars in the store. The platforms in particular help to attract attention to the products and bring them literally close at hand. It is easy for visitors to look at, touch and read the books; many visitors stay in the store for a long time and examine titles, hold books, leaf through them, read blurbs and tables of contents. A bookshop regards the customer as a flâneur, for whom the process of selection is important. This fact illustrates the place of the bookshop in a field of tension between different values. On the one hand, there are the economic values, where turnover, sales and profit are central. On the other hand are the cultural values that are associated with reading and books in our society. Books are bearers of a cultural heritage, having for centuries been associated with education of the middle classes. This accounts for the bookshop's serene and peaceful atmosphere without pushy or obtrusive salespeople, in contrast, for example, to the shops where media hardware is sold.

But in spite of this relative serenity, neither booksellers nor newsagents encourage any more extensive in-store reading. In shops that sell magazines and newspapers one can find signs saying, 'Buy before you read', but in the bookshop there are no such signs and some reading is tolerated, but not too much. This is underlined by the absence of chairs and armchairs, unlike some other bookshops that have developed to more or less literary salons. But the bookshops in the shopping centre seem untouched by this trend, probably because of their profile as popular bookshops for 'common' people. The antipathy to reading about media products can not only be explained by the fact that the articles must not look used when they are eventually sold, but also because the stores want to push consumers forward at different paces in the selection process toward the final goal – the purchase. The different paces depend on the way the different shops construct their customers, leading to different sales strategies. At the tobacconist's the various products are made available through a process of continuous weeding among the newspapers and magazines so that the latest issues are brought to the fore and can easily be seen and picked up in mid stride by hurried customers who did not actually plan to buy a magazine or newspaper, but cigarettes or sweets. The bookseller, on the other hand, counts on people entering the shop because they are interested in books, and that the customers possess a certain amount of cultural capital. Such customers do not want to think of themselves as consumers. They cannot be pushed into making a purchase, but have to be coaxed, and this is why browsing is tolerated. The slower pace in bookshops is thus a sales strategy, just as the speed at the newsagent's. In this, the bookseller's sales strategy coincides with the interests of the customers – creating a space that is experienced as being free from raw commercialism, something that both the employees at the bookshop and the customers pointed out in our interviews.

The significance of place is even more central for people in relation to the non-commercial alternative – the public library. Both book and newspaper readers say that the library satisfies the need for reading, at the same time as it saves them the cost, but they talk just as much about the peace they experience when they sit and read there. The library is a place without stress, a place for reflection. To some extent the library shares this relaxed atmosphere with the bookshop, but in part it has different causes. In a library people can sit in peace and quiet, reading for pleasure or study, but such reading is absent in the shopping centre's bookstore or at the tobacconist's, where the focus is on the purchase. A common ground for the contemplative atmosphere seems to be the unique aura of the book, passed on by heredity for centuries, which gives some of the association of education, quiet concentration and calm to this medium. This characteristic affects the library as well as the bookshop. In the former, the aura of the book creates a place that works as an oasis in the middle of commercialism, in the latter a place that can be seen as a commercial oasis.

The library functions as a macro consumer. When selecting what products to purchase, and at the moment of purchase of newspapers, magazines and other periodicals, the library can be regarded as an individual, institutional player represented by staff who (though in consultation with their colleagues and, in this case, acting on the suggestions of their visitors) choose, order, pay and receive the products. In strict economic terms, libraries are consumers who through a financial transaction become the new owner of the media products, using them by lending them to individual citizens.

When the media products are purchased, their use is multiplied as the library in principle makes the media products available to a limitless number of users. Since the library is financed with tax revenue, the use is not strictly speaking 'free', but it is free of charge. This dynamic, whereby taxpayers invest in a service, delegate the administration to the municipalities or the state, and then enjoy the services free of charge or at a discount, are central mechanisms in the modern welfare state.

PERIODICALS, PLACE AND IDENTITY

People born in Sweden and whose families have lived in Sweden for generations, and people who have experienced migration just a few years or a generation before, meet in the shopping centre. Those who have experiences of migration are placed in and occupy specific social positions in the new country and develop heterogeneous communities, identities and attitudes to both the host country and to their country of origin. In anthropology and cultural theory, for example, there is a growing literature about different kinds of communities, subjectivities and identities, which the current global migration creates. This literature examines the histories, experiences, discourses and communities of exiles, immigrants and guest workers in the diaspora.[7] However, there is not only migration between countries, but also internal migration, between parishes and cities within a nation state.[8]

The relationship of migrants to their places of birth is complex. For diasporic communities, newspapers and magazines published in the old countries can play an important role in maintaining a connection to 'home'. Correspondingly, provincial newspapers are important for internal migrants. Some of the media products that are sold in the shopping centre are foreign and provincial newspapers and magazines. They are purchased by both external and internal migrants and they are also available at the library as a service for city residents. Here we focus on migrants' use of newspapers and periodicals; a use that links two places: the library's reading room and the visitors' birthplace.[9]

Celal, one library visitor, sees his country of birth as the place where he was formed as a person: 'I did not come to earth from the sky, but grew up in a specific place, in an environment, in a district … that's why localization is important for me … but if one cannot strike a balance between localization and globalization it is easy to become a nationalist or localist racist.'[10] Celal and Pablo, who are both refugees, associate the distance that separates them from 'home' with a lack of control of, or influence over, the events there. The fact that Celal cannot return (for fear of imprisonment) makes him see that country as 'a utopian country, far away … waiting over there'.

For Pochi and Carlota, who both came to Sweden only a few months before the interviews to live with their boyfriends, the 'home country' is the place where they have their roots, a constant reminder that it is important to continue talking about.

The prospect of returning is not the all-pervading vision for all those we interviewed. Pablo has decided to stay and regards Sweden as his new home, where he has been given opportunities that he did not have in his native country. Carlota and her Swedish boyfriend have not yet decided what to do, while Ingemar regards the very north of Sweden as 'home', even after forty years in Stockholm. Although he is about to retire, he does not want to return to live there because that region is 'dying'.

The reasons why the newspapers and magazines from 'home' are important vary, but many answers recur in the interviews. Most often people say, 'I want to know what is going on there.' The will to know is expressed both by those like Pochi and Celal who express a strong sense of longing, and by those like Pedro who emphasize that they do not feel any nostalgia. To be well informed about what is going on in Colombia helps Pedro to imagine how his family is. Another reason mentioned is a wish to maintain contact with one's native culture and language. Celal thinks that newspapers from Turkey express a view of the world that is different from the one in

Sweden, and when he lives here he wants to have access to both. The young woman who described herself as 'half Swedish, half Pakistani' thought that since the image that one gets of one's own culture here is tainted by the Swedish perspective it is important to get an image of one's culture in which one recognizes oneself.

Pochi expresses a feeling of great ambivalence about her new life in Sweden. She experiences the move from the 'tropics to the Arctic' as a great adventure and a great shock. The new, foreign language and culture lead to an experience of alienation and loss of one's earlier life: 'I feel "dead" but live on.' Although she is an academic, she has to return to the 'nursery … to re-learn to read, write, speak and think'. The Colombian newspapers she reads on the net in the library make her feel 'less dead'. Through her reading she returns to her old, mature, competent self. The information that she gets from the Colombian newspapers is also used as a resource in her self-assumed mission as ambassador for her own culture, for example by informing people about Colombian artists.

Recognition is also an important reason for reading newspapers from 'home'. Anders and Carl, who moved comparatively recently, think that it is especially fun to read about people they know. For Ingemar, it is not a question of people (after forty years, few of those he knew are still there), but instead a question of practical everyday information. If there is a winter market or an auction somewhere, it is good to know when and where. If a bus has run into a ditch he wants to know where, so he can see the place when he drives that road. For those like Ingemar who visit their old district, the local newspaper is an instrument for finding a way into its current concerns and maintaining a place within it.

The ambition to stay informed about what is happening 'back home' was also found among most of the transnational migrants we interviewed, though the degree of the commitment and engagement in 'home' was expressed with varying degrees of fervour. On the other hand, the old country is not the only place outside Sweden that is the object of migrants' interest. It is striking that so many of them also read the international press such as *Time*, *Le Monde*, *Die Zeit* and the *International Herald Tribune*.

However, most of the migrants who were interviewed are not only oriented to the transnational. They show a strong commitment, though in different ways, to their lives here and now. They have learned, or are on the way to learning the new language; they continue their education or plan to; they work and worry about qualifying for the profession they had before they came here; they dig the soil on their allotments; they are consumers of both commodities and public services; and they use the Swedish media. For those who are learning the language, Swedish newspapers have a double role as sources of information and educational material. Pochi and Carlota have daily access to Swedish morning and evening papers in school and at home, and their boyfriends help them when an article is too difficult. Celal subscribes to Sweden's largest morning paper and Pablo reads it in his workplace. Both also read *Metro*, the free daily paper distributed in Stockholm's underground stations. Pablo, who only occasionally reads news from his old country, says that for many years he has read news mainly about Sweden. Celal makes a stronger connection between reading newspapers, gathering information and actively participating in Swedish daily life. Because of this attitude, he thinks that Swedish papers are more important than Turkish ones at present; whereas Turkey is far away and beyond any possibility of influence, Swedish newspapers give him resources to 'control what is important in life, or closest in life', the life he lives here and now. Cédric reads Swedish newspapers in addition to *Le Figaro* in the library. News in Swedish newspapers about the outsourcing of production, for example, makes him reflect on the consequences of globalization for Sweden. He is particularly concerned by the threatening dismantling of the welfare state. These examples show how Swedish newspapers are resources these migrants use for constructing their local lives and for reflecting on what is happening in Sweden as transnational relations intensify.

The library also provides the opportunity to read newspapers, magazines and journals online. So-called 'public computers' are available for the general public. Some can be reserved in advance and others may be used on a drop-in basis. Pochi and Carlota are frequent users of this service. They visit the library several times a week to read and write e-mail, and read Colombian and Spanish newspapers, respectively. Their reading habits clearly show how the context of reading contributes to the form and characteristics of reading: at these computers there is always a time limit – one hour when one has made a reservation and fifteen minutes for the 'drop-in computers'. Because of this, reading newspapers online must always be done quickly. When she wants to have more time or wants to scrutinize a text, Carlota uses the paper copies. In this way the rules that the library imposes on the visitors' computer use foster different user regimes.

Through its foreign, provincial and national newspapers, the library is an important centre for forging place-bound relations and identities for both external and internal migrants. The newspapers, magazines and other periodicals contribute to the creation and maintenance of transnational and translocal relations, at the same time as they produce and reproduce the local and national sense of community. A phrase that was often used by our informants – 'I want to know what is going on there' – is consistent with press research that shows newspapers and magazines as information sources that are basic to the ability of citizens to exercise their democratic obligations and rights. But migrants' uses of newspapers and magazines have more sides than this. The reading of transnational and translocal newspapers and magazines is a kind of place-related memory work, connected to life stories and identities, which in this way are kept alive with the help of specific media for want of the real place.

WAYS OF USING BOOKS

Now it is time to leave the city library, where migrants' use of newspapers and magazines was the focus of attention, and walk over to the commercial book space, asking why people want to *own* books. What distinguishes the library loan from the bookshop purchase is the desire to own books and also to give them away as gifts. This shopping centre has both a library and two bookshops. Such a combination of commercially and municipally managed 'book spaces' is rare in a shopping centre. The residents of Solna are therefore well situated, with a rich availability of books – a basic prerequisite for books to be sold, borrowed and read in the first place.

Being part of Sweden's largest chain of booksellers, The Academy Bookstore (Akademibokhandeln), the largest bookstore in Solna Centre is connected to a wide range of products that it cannot influence. The range of products is not exclusive: the shop is ordinary in that it sells most things that are typically supplied by bookshops in Sweden, from stationery to best-selling novels. Early in our fieldwork, our attention was caught by the fact that so many books were purchased as gifts. This was especially evident during the Christmas rush, when gift sales dominated, but books are commonly given away during the whole year. There is no Swedish statistic for what portion of the total sales consists of gifts, but the large percentage that is made up of Christmas shopping (circa 20 per cent) suggests that books are very often bought as gifts, and that in Sweden perhaps a quarter of all bought books might be intended as gifts.[11] Compared to other lines of business, the book trade distinguishes itself in this respect (together with the recording industry).

Through the staff in the bookshop we got in contact with a book discussion group on the Internet. In this way we got access to a new field, a 'book space' in cyberspace and the fieldwork took a cyberethnographic turn.[12] At the time the group had between 220 and 230 members, and twenty-seven of them (twenty-four women and three men) were willing to answer questions about owning and giving books.

Selection processes take place in and outside the bookshop and eventually lead to the purchase of books. After the purchase the book transforms into a piece of property and is used by its owner. So, how does one use a book? For many people the obvious answer is 'by reading it'. This use is of course primary, both for borrowed and bought books. But owning a book in itself provides opportunities for specific uses that library books do not give, which is evident from the discussion in the reading group and from the answers from the twenty-seven 'bookworms'.

The bookworms all agreed that the most important advantage of owning books is that one can reread them whenever one wants. And the current trend in Sweden of publishing more and more titles as paperbacks makes it even easier to buy, and hence to own books. 'Long live the paperback!' a member of the discussion group writes. 'I gladly pay the small amount to own my reading experiences.' Some specify which books are essential to own – one's favourites. To borrow books from the library is also all right, 'but I want to own my favourites!' Others underline that it is important to own non-fiction and encyclopedias so that one can look up things quickly.

One can thus say that the ready availability is a partial explanation of why people want to own books. Although they acknowledge the economic reasons and also the space they save by borrowing from a library (several people complained of crammed shelves), our informants say that the opening hours and queues for new literature are restrictive. Libraries are called 'test arenas', a place where one can borrow and read books by unknown writers, to test whether one likes a certain author or title. But if one does, one has to buy the book to own it and be able to reread it whenever one wants.

Some say that one of the advantages of owning books is that one can lend them to friends: 'Books should be read and not collect dust!'[13] One of our book lovers had even made a system for her own book lending: her 'library', as she calls it, is visited by a small band of good friends. In return for the borrowed books they buy new ones for her. But others say that they do not want others to borrow their books since it is so hard to get them back:

> I am also completely manic about buying books. I want to own all the books I read, so that I can write my name and the date in them when I have finished them. But I am a bit stingy about lending my books. I am reluctant to lend them since I find it so tedious to have to beg to get my own books back and then have them back in a worse state. But of course some of my friends can borrow, and it is fun to lend and give tips about good books to those I know take good care of them and return them when they have read them. (Female, 32, student teacher)

Many explain that filling one's bookshelves has to do with *identity*. To write one's name and the date in books like the woman above is a way of inscribing the book in one's own life story. Several others discuss the subject of identity by saying that books are mementoes. Children's books bring memories of childhood back to the nostalgic reader, and other books are time machines that take the reader back to a special time and place:

> In addition, some books can work as souvenirs, for example, from a trip. I see one of my worn paperbacks and remember that I brought this same book with me on a trip to Stockholm a couple of years ago, and I read this once on the ferryboat to Umeå. Things like that are nice, and that's why I seldom throw away or give away books. Moreover, it is always nice to look at other people's books when one visits them, and I don't want to deny my friends that pastime. (Female, 20, student)

Like the woman quoted above, many informants emphasize that books reveal a lot about people, not least about themselves. Someone's books reflect his or her personal development and identity. It is also striking that so many of the informants talk so warmly about their books, calling them 'friends', even 'family', and say that one cannot throw away books one likes. But books are not just friends; they are also identical with their owner. A 55-year-old man expressed the connection between him and his books succinctly: 'For me books forge identity; one can partly see who I am by studying what books I have.' Walter Benjamin regards ownership as the most intimate relation one can have with an object: the bookworm lives in his or her books.[14] Books certainly seem to offer this to our book lovers. They are a part of their lives, woven into their identity to such a degree that losing their books would be a loss of their personal histories and identities. This is why books have to be owned, since one's life history and identity cannot be returned to the library, or as one of them writes: "I would rather read books that I own than books I borrow, perhaps because I am afraid of returning them later, when they are read?"

Books may also improve one's status, some of them thought, which is related to the ways in which identity is constructed and communicated to the outside world. Book lovers expand their book collections through various status-raising practices. It might be a question of hiding or cleaning out. One man admits that he organizes his books in such a way that he keeps 'questionable' literature out of sight; a woman says that she gets rid of 'crappy books' that she does not want to show on her shelves. It might also be a question of holding up literature that is counted as 'high-brow', as for example this 27-year-old woman librarian:

> It could also be status! I blushingly admit that I have a few books visible on the shelves just because they represent bookish culture itself. Do I have to say more than 'In Remembrance of Things Past' by Marcel Proust? If it is not status, why then is there greater demand for leather-bound 24-volume encyclopedias than the same facts collected on a shiny CD-ROM for the computer?

Judging from the answers, beside the reading experience itself, it is the rereading, lending and identity forging aspects that provide the most important utility values in ownership. But other uses also appear in the answers, though less frequently. Many of our informants emphasized that books are aesthetically pleasing. 'Books are beautiful,' one of them writes. 'I think that bookcases crammed with books are such a beautiful sight,' someone else says. It is thus not only the content that is important, but also the aesthetic form. If books are pleasing the owner can also use them when he or she is not reading them, taking pleasure in the sight of shelves filled with attractive books.

From the above account of the discussion group's answers and discussion, the following factors emerge as to why it is important to own books and what specific uses come with ownership: (1) the reading experience, (2) the opportunity to reread books, (3) lending them to friends, (4) the construction and communication of identity, and (5) the aesthetic satisfaction. Consequently, books that are owned have uses that borrowed books do not have. The remainder of this chapter will dwell on a further (sixth) utility value for bought books that paradoxically involves a deliberate disposal of them.

BOOKS AS GIFTS

All commodities are charged with meaning and are thus communicative.[15] When commodities are transformed into gifts, they also mark special occasions and specific relations between a giver and a receiver. Gifts are not given to just anyone; the donor has to have some kind of relationship with the receiver – he or she is not a complete stranger. Nor are gifts given at any time, rather they mark specific, festive occasions such as Christmas, birthdays or weddings. Gifts can also be given at less special events, as a present to a dinner party's host, or just as a surprise in everyday life. In this context the gift works as the marker of something special – the everyday is turned into a party through the gift.

The anthropologist Nicholas Thomas criticizes 'gift theoreticians' such as Marcel Mauss for not being sufficiently attentive to the objects, the things given.[16] Whether it is a ritual tool, food or sex, these scholars incorporate the objects into a general gift pattern, although different objects have different importance and symbolic meaning.[17] The following discussion about books as gifts should therefore not be seen as automatically applicable as a whole to other material objects.

A few factors that determine what books will be chosen as gifts can be discerned in the book lovers' discussion. A fundamental factor was the type of relationship between the donor and the recipient, whether the relation is close (intimate and emotional) or distant (formal, yet friendly). One has close relationships with family and a few friends, and distant with everyone else.

The giving of gifts in Western culture is based on the ideal of unselfishness and generosity. Unselfishness dictates that the donor does not think of himself but only the needs and interests of the recipient. The idea that the recipient's interests and personality should decide the nature of the gift is reflected in our informants' first statement that it is the recipient who chooses what book to give, or as one of them said, 'It is not much use giving Hermann Hesse's *The Glass Bead Game* to an illiterate golfer.'

However, this kind of answer is almost always followed by 'but if both of us like the book, so much the better'. This ambiguity is also reflected in the fact that although many people emphasize the importance of the recipient of the gift, it is remarkable that it is negated by another statement. For example, a woman who first says that the book must 'of course' suit the recipient, immediately thereafter says that she only gives away books that she likes herself. In theory, it seems, the interests and personality of the recipient should decide, but in reality the donor is more central than many people would want to admit. The anthropologist Daniel Miller points out that the relationship to the other is constructed through the objects that a subject is thought to desire.[18] In other words, gifts involve a construction of the other based on the donor's ideas about who the other is. The gift of a book reveals more about the donor, or rather the donor's idea of the recipient, than the donor intends to disclose. It is this instinctive insight that makes the answers of our informants in the discussion group ambivalent in this respect.

However, the donor's ideas about the recipient might coincide more or less with what the recipient would like and in a close relationship the chances of getting it right are greater. If one knows the other well the choice of present becomes simpler; our informants said that they just buy something that suits the personality and interests of the other. But for them the ultimate book gift should both 'suit' the recipient and the donor should already have read and liked it. The recipient is then constructed as similar to the donor, as a twin in terms of taste.

In a close relationship, the donor is 'allowed' to be visible in his or her gift, contrary to the norm that the gift should reflect the wishes of the recipient. In Mauss's terms one can say that the gift is 'charged' with the giver.[19] Although all gifts are the responsibility of the donor, it seems to be the case to a higher degree and more consciously in close relationships. This is only 'permitted' or desirable in a close relationship because it is felt to be too personal, intimate and revealing to be shared with anyone else, or in the words of one of our informants, 'It depends on how well I know the person and how well I would like the other person to know me.' In this way, to give a book can be experienced as giving away a part of oneself. Such an act reinforces a close relationship, which is based on mutual, intimate knowledge about the other. In this way, the gift of a book becomes an acknowledgement of the close relationship: 'You know who I am and I know who you are.'

That some gifts of books are felt to be less intimate and personal than others is illustrated by our informants' discussion of the type and contents of books. In general, people buy paperbacks for themselves and hardbacks for others. But in close relationships the material side of the book is not as important as in distant relationships. The most important thing in the former is not the type of book (paperback or hardback) and the price, but rather the substance, the content of the book.

> To begin with, with people who are really close, the form is totally unimportant; it is the reading experience that counts. That is why I often go to second-hand bookshops where I hunt for books that mean much to me (it is of course out of the question that I would give away my *own* copy!). I hope to bring the same sensations (not necessarily joy, because some books are supposed to disturb) that I had when I read a particular book. Here one must adapt to the recipient, since, for example, both politics and religion are virtual minefields that have destroyed many a good relationship. But of course people in close relationships should be above such worldly reasons for discord (a definition as good as any!).
>
> When it comes to more distant relationships and 'dutiful gifts', of course the form is more important, and for Christmas I raid a large bookstore (*everyone* gets a book, and someone may even get a title that they really want) so that those who think that the cover of the book is more important than the text itself will not think that I'm being stingy. (Male, 39, electrical engineer)

The giving of a book is regarded as less important in a close relationship. The main thing is the book's ability to symbolize the shared, intimate relationship. However, it should be emphasized that the material dimension is not entirely unimportant – indeed, for birthday and Christmas presents the significance of the book's contents increases, as in close relationships, when the ideal giving of gifts includes generosity as well. The norm of generosity is also reflected in the fact that magazines are considered 'skimpy' gifts, if they are not an expensive specialist journal, or a subscription to a magazine.

A close relationship between two people is reinforced and becomes deeper when the donor of a book provides the other with a key to his or her identity, to him or herself. But this key requires mutuality: for the close relationship to survive, the recipient must return the gift with something similar. So it is now possible to refer to reciprocity, though not wholly in Mauss's sense. He describes the norms of giving gifts as an obligation to give, receive and reciprocate.[20] This of course is the case with gifts between tribes or between states, as in Mauss's analysis, whereas in close, intimate relationships people do not give primarily out of a sense of obligation, but because of closeness and ultimately love.[21] The norms of giving books in a close relationship could thus be described as: (1) it is an act of love to give; (2) it is an act of love to receive gifts; (3) it is an act of love to reciprocate gifts. This is not to say the personal gift is entirely free of obligation.

As opposed to the personal gift of a book, our informants talked about 'impersonal', 'general' and 'universal' gifts, such as books about gardening, cooking, landscapes and buildings, suitable for giving to acquaintances and distant relatives. Such books reveal little about the giver or the receiver, but much about their relationship, since it symbolizes their formal and impersonal relationship. As we have said, the giving of books in a close relationship, on the other hand, says a lot about the donor, the recipient and their relationship. In the distant relationship the giving of books emphasizes differences: 'I don't know you and you don't know me.' This is not a mutual exchange of keys to one's identity, but an obligatory exchange of gifts in order to maintain, but not necessarily to develop a relationship. One could thus say that Mauss's gift norms – emphasizing obligation – apply to the giving of books in distant relationships.

In the distant relationship, substance becomes significant in the gift process: it is more important to fulfill ideal notions of generous giving to people one does not know well. This is so because an acquaintance cannot estimate the gift from a mutual, intimate knowledge of the other, but is obliged to resort to evaluating it from general cultural norms about ideal giving. For example, one of the informant book lovers said that she buys 'new' books for people she is less familiar with, 'which also means that they will be more expensive'. The male electrical engineer (see above) emphasized that quality is important in 'dutiful gifts' to distant relatives so that they 'will not think that I am stingy'.

The discussion among our book lovers works as a commentary on Mauss's gift theory. It shows that gifts are not always a question of duty but about love as well. It also shows that the gift process transforms commodities to something that certainly has points in common with everyday objects but at the same time is still clearly different from them. According to Miller the processes of everyday shopping can be analysed to contain three stages, which can also be applied to the giving of books.[22] The first stage – the utopian vision of plenty and pleasure – is also found in the idea of the generous gift. There are shades to this generosity, however, depending on the distance between the donor and the recipient: either one is generous with one's money, or one is generous with oneself. The second stage, frugality, however, is not as applicable to the gift process. Stage three – the return to social relationships, strengthening of social bonds – is central to the giving of books, not to say *the* most important aspect, in both close and distant relationships. The latter determination of two kinds of relationships is important for understanding the gift of a book. Love is central in close relationships whereas duty is more crucial in more distant relationships. But love is not limited to the close family that stands at the centre of Miller's analysis of everyday shopping, because the gift of a book transcends the limits of this particular social constellation and shows that loving relationships are not limited to the narrow circle of the close family or the opposite sex.

The comments in the discussion group can be read as a memento for media studies, in that uses of books as property and as gifts show that focusing on the act of reading does not suffice to understand everyday media use. Also, our informants' answers implicitly problematized certain aspects of consumer research, in that their selection, purche, use and disposal of books is far from the ways of 'economic man', guided by rational and egoistical motives. Instead the gift of a book seems to a certain extent to be about love, unselfishness and generosity, both with oneself and one's financial situation.

4. MEDIA IMAGES

One is surrounded by images in a shopping centre. What is more, the shopper moves through a visual environment that consistently reinforces a sense of being looked at, by cameras, by shopkeepers and service personnel, by other shoppers, and where one repeatedly meets one's own image in the many mirrors on the walls and ceilings of this space. Sociologist Erving Goffman wrote in the 1970s of the effects of advertising on the visual performances we enact in social space.[1] The sense of being under surveillance has certainly not diminished since then. The awareness that one can at any moment 'be taken' by a camera or by another's glance is a growing aspect of the everyday experience in the contemporary media environment. We live in the midst of an unending stream of images, and whether or not one agrees with Debord that this creates 'an excess of display', concealing the truth of the society that produces it, it is hard to argue against the postulate that consumption and vision are mutually constructing practices in the ongoing legacy of late modernity.[2] A key question for this study has been how this expanded visual field is reflected in the ways people use images in their own lives. This, in turn raises questions regarding the forms of reflexivity that arise in these visual practices. Pictures never operate in isolation, but are interwoven in complex networks of meaning with other media and sensory experience.

The consumption of media images is a many layered activity. There are, first, the images 'in' the media, on television, in advertising, in film, in magazines. This is the usual way of thinking of media imagery. Pictures in the media are the most commonly discussed and analysed media images. These are also the images that are frequently at the centre of debates about the effects of media on consumers: advertising's effects on young children, the effects of media violence on youth behaviour, the effect of fashion advertising on young women's self-image, or the availability of pornography on the Internet. There is widespread concern over the meanings and messages conveyed by the visual content of (mass) media. While not denying the importance of such questions, the focus here is rather on images 'of' the media and their uses.

Contemporary society is permeated by images of media. The media's visual presence is as much a part of contemporary culture as the air we breathe. Existing media statistics do not include any counting of the number of images seen on an average day, or the length of daily time spent on seeing images in the form of photos, posters or painted images in the streets or at home, and it would indeed be methodologically virtually impossible to measure the presence of images in society and everyday life, or assess the relative importance of images compared to sounds or words. The visibility of media and their significance as cultural artefacts means that people consume media through the images of media. This form of media consumption includes media as symbolic representations, or pictures of media, and also media in use; that is, the media practices that we see around us. Because of media's visibility and the centrality of media in our lives, we use the images in and of media to make judgements about media products and technologies themselves, what they look like and how they are used. For example, Ericsson is said to have lost an important segment of its cellular phone market when its new models had less visual appeal than Nokia's. Images of media use can also give rise to cultural stereotypes; for example, when Europeans observe the ways tourists from Asian countries use their cameras on their city tours.

Mediated images of media exemplify what might be called '*media reflexivity*', where media mirror themselves (or other media). Just like other forms of reflexivity, media reflexivity seems to increase in late modernity. In fact, the various forms of reflexivity are closely interrelated. For instance, individual self-reflexivity uses reflexive media as a tool for personal self-thematization, scientific reflexivity in academic research interacts with reflexive forms of mediated communication, and mediatization is a key factor in the whole institutional reflexivity of society at large through which societal structures increasingly deal with problems they have them-selves created.[3] Media reflexivity is also closely related to the notion of 'hyperme-diacy', the intense attention to the tools of mediation that counteracts the transparency of mediation and makes people highly aware of the mediating apparatus as such.[4]

The distinctions drawn in Chapter 2 among three levels of symbolic communica-tion can be applied also to image consumption. Here, the material base is the image itself, with its symbolic form and content. The technological level of these media includes the apparatuses that are used to create and distribute these symbolic forms as visual artefacts. At the third level of social institutions, institutionally anchored sets of norms and rules guide and regulate the visual performance of media and their use, governing both images in and images of media. Images proliferated throughout the shopping centre, in all sizes, shapes and formats. Media were also highly visible, both as pictures and being used by shoppers. And finally, through the research group's investigations of media consumption, we learned a great deal about the cultural, social and institutional rules that shape how media are used, including the visual performance of media in the shopping centre.

Material from two case studies in the centre illustrates the cultural, social and insti-tutional rules and the individual choices that shape image use.[5] The case studies take as their point of departure the two photographic shops, and a card and poster shop located in the shopping centre. All three of these businesses are franchises, belonging to national and international chains, and use media in all forms of their advertising. The content of the images available in these shops draws heavily from the mass media, pointing at intermediality as a key feature.

The chapter begins with a discussion of the mall as an environment of visual display, itself a medium if you will. The concept of display can be helpful in investigating how visual forms are used to communicate ideas about aesthetic value and hierarchy, about history and power within the context of specific cultural environments. We consider, first, the commercial pictures of products, how they represent, their intermediality and how they are used to inscribe hierarchies of value. From this more general consideration of images, we then shift the focus to specific visual media and the chain of consumption that takes its point of departure in the shops selling these products. Here the focus is on photographs, cards and posters, and the technology used in their production and use.

PICTURES IN THE MALL

In Chapter 1, we described the visual environment as an expression of the histories and conflicts over Solna Centre as a place. Here, the focus is on the specific characteristics of the images displayed in the shopping centre environment, where they are found and the values they construct. This is not an exhaustive analysis of all the images on display in the shopping centre, but is based on a selection, with the aim of understanding how images work in this environment in relation to hierarchies of power and value.

We begin with the most obvious – the pictures that advertise goods that are for sale in the shopping centre. In shop windows photographs are used repetitively, often citing another item in the window, or even repeating themselves. They frequently engage a visual play with scale, showing for example an oversized copy or details of an object. Poster formats are the most common, suspended in the window or mounted onto the display in a wide range of sizes. Pictorial illustrations, including photographs, have been common in advertising since the rise of mass consumer publications in the 1890s, but what is noteworthy here is their use behind glass. The show window was a display form originally developed to protect attractive goods from weather, dust and the consumer's touch; now we find instead the expendable mass-produced image dominating the shop window, sometimes even replacing the object it represents.[6] Why has the photograph replaced the goods in this display form? Let us look at some examples.

In the cellphone shop, three-foot-tall photographic enlargements of the latest cellphone model provide a practical solution to presenting objects that are too small or too valuable to stand so exposed in the expanse of a show window. More significant, however, is the visual impression of power and value established through the repetition and large scale of the images. In other windows photographs represent products being used, a common strategy in shops selling sports equipment or children's clothing. In these cases, the image is often less distinct or even blurred, conveying a sense of movement or a mood, while the product itself is unclear. The object being advertised is on display, too – the sports shoe, the child's winter parka – a concrete sign next to the photograph that represents the product as a swash of colour. We are presented simultaneously with the product and its image, a photographic image that projects the desired qualities associated with the product – power, luxury, style, fun, etc. – but that are not evident in the product alone. The real object and the hyper-real are woven together in the display. In the contemporary store window, the photograph serves the purpose of enlarging and transforming the object, and represents using it as an expression of visual, aesthetic pleasure.

Many of the pictures on display in the shopping centre refer to other pictures, in other media. Disney film characters show up on clothing and accessories, as well as in cards, posters and videos in various shops throughout the shopping centre.[7] Harry Potter's familiar face on the cover of the bestseller stacked high at the bookstore entrance also beams out at us from the video store and on posters for sale in the card shop. James Bond aims his gun at passers-by from a poster advertising a wristwatch that does everything. In a wall painting next to an elevator, Greta Garbo poses in front of an old movie camera, a reference to the Swedish film industry that once had its studios nearby. The list of examples could go on, constant visual reminders that the shopping centre is an intermedial space.

Another characteristic of the images in the shopping centre is that many of them represent the private sphere, depicting a domestic scene or a personal relationship. These representations are evidence of the growing intimization of the public sphere, a characteristic commented upon by many media scholars.[8] In the shop windows of the children's clothing store hang large posters showing children at play. Children are also a common theme in the photographic shop, offering visual lessons of what the ideal family looks like. In the windows of the travel agency hang oversized posters showing a man and woman enjoying a romantic meal – the heterosexual vacation ideal. These photographs project an image of intimacy and also a model of media practice in the sense that consumers should be able to recognize themselves and project their own desires onto the display. They should, in the words of Solna Centre's slogan, 'feel at home' in the images that surround them in the shopping centre. We assumed that it was no accident that the central image in the management's marketing campaign showed a Caucasian man and woman and their daughter, seated together on a couch in the middle of the shopping centre. The image of this 'family' appeared on information brochures, in ads in local papers, and on the posters and flags hanging over the entrances and passages in the shopping centre. This was certainly a representation of the primary target group as seen by the Solna Centre management.

This photograph remained on the information brochures, but was gradually replaced by a series of other photographs in the 'feel at home' displays on flags and posters throughout the centre. The first of these showed a young bi-racial couple, a black man and a blond woman, smiling into the camera. Several months later, this was replaced by a different social grouping, a photograph of a middle-aged woman standing behind a boy of about eight, a clear representation of a single mother with her son. This in turn was replaced by a photograph of a young professional-looking man and woman, both with dark skin and hair (suggesting they are first-generation Swedes), looking over some papers spread out in front of them. In this case we recognized the woman as someone who worked in the information desk in the middle of the shopping centre. Who, we asked, is being invited to 'feel at home' in Solna Centre?

These photographs looked like they were designed to appeal to a broader segment of consumers, a more diverse population. The campaign, employing visual signs of cultural diversity, does represent the demographics of the city of Solna more accurately than the initial image of the family. According to the manager, however, the campaign was not designed to appeal to Solna Centre's diverse population of consumers but rather to 'create involvement' among employees. All the people in the photographs, with the exception of the little boy, work in the Solna Centre, and the manager could identify most of them: the man in the image of the 'bi-racial couple' is actually a Norwegian who works in a men's clothing store, and the 'single mother' is co-owner of one of the cafés. The idea, the manager said, was to have a little fun and at the same time encourage employees to feel connected to the workplace. This claimed lack of intended diversity meaning does not make the first reading false, since the producer's expressed intention does not confine the signifying effects of any picture, but it certainly adds another dimension to it. Do consumers 'feel [more] at home' if they happen to recognize the people from these posters as they do their shopping?

These photographs of people obviously have a different purpose than those we see displayed in store windows. They are part of Solna Centre's own promotional campaign and occupy the arenas of common commercial space. The people in the pictures are locals, 'real' people if you will, who work in this place. However, it is important to recognize that they do not portray themselves. They appear in poses and contexts that are visual representations of specific social relationships, which may have nothing to do with who they 'really' are. Despite their local origins, these photographs draw their meanings from visual stereotypes that are national and even global. We don't see the café owner herself, but a single mother. We don't see a young store clerk who speaks with a Norwegian accent, but a representation of a tolerant, multiracial society. In the context of this display, they have lost their subjectivity and been mediatized. Whether the manager wants – or understands – it or not, the images in their contemporary cultural context do invite interpretations in terms of positions in the dominant orders of identity and difference.

SELLING PICTURES

We turn now to the shops that sell pictures in various forms. What is on display in the environment of the photographic and card shops, and how do customers select and use what they buy in their daily lives? Two of the largest transnational photographic companies, Kodak and Fuji, have shops in Solna Centre. Both the Kodak Image Centre and Fuji's Photo Gang (Foto-gänget) sell and develop film, and offer a broad selection of both digital and film-based cameras and equipment.[9] Both sell albums, picture frames and other means for displaying and storing photographs. Each shop has a scanner and customers can order digital copies of photographs. Both shops also have a simple set-up for taking identification portraits while the customer waits. The Gallerix shop belongs to a Swedish chain of more than eighty stores, all similar in appearance and what they offer: 'pictures, cards and frames'. The pictures include posters and prints in a range of sizes and formats, both framed and unframed.

There is also a framing service in the shop. The Gallerix assortment of greetings cards is the largest and most varied of any Swedish company.

There is no accepted descriptive term that encompasses both photography and the purchase and exchange of cards and posters. Photography in the primarily private sphere is usually referred to as family or amateur photography. Elsewhere we have argued for the term 'vernacular' as more appropriate to cover the range of activities and meanings these images have in daily life.[10] Photographs taken by amateurs are appearing with greater frequency in the public sphere, including news photographs, and the iconography of these images is often imitated in advertising and film. The vernacular develops as a kind of visual dialect that borrows elements from popular culture in its construction. In this sense, the term can easily be used to include the ways cards and posters are used by the people who buy them.

Despite the importance that people attach to the images they take, make and collect for their private use, these practices are a neglected aspect of media research. The everyday uses of photographs, cards and posters confound traditional divisions between media production and consumption. Examining how media consumers select, purchase, use and eventually dispose of these images can, in line with the theoretical framework of the research project as a whole, extend the boundaries of media research.

The two photographic shops have very different profiles, already evident in their respective names. The Kodak Image Centre, like its counterparts the world over, is dominated by the company's yellow colour and familiar logo. The floor plan and design are standardized according to the company concept. The birch counters are complemented by shelves and countertops in a light slate grey, a colour repeated in the employee's shirts. In the centre of the shop a large basket is piled high with film, the current special offer at Kodak Images Centres across Sweden. Fuji's Photo Gang, on the other hand, is part of a locally owned chain of five shops in the Stockholm area. In the shop Fuji green mixes with hand-painted signs and labels in a range of bright colours. Boxes covered with silver paper and containing an assortment of photo albums are arranged on the floor. A TV monitor behind the counter is always on, showing either the Eurosport channel or, more often, a Disney video. The staff do not wear name tags or uniforms.

The pictures on display underscore the shops' different profiles. In the Kodak Image Centre, four identical illuminated photographs are mounted on the back wall, clearly visible from the shop entrance. These are changed several times a year. During the summer, two little girls giggle from under their straw hats, and in the winter we see a father with his children on a ski slope against a deep-blue sky. These photographs are not like images from a family album; they represent instead the dream of the ideal family vacation. The pattern is repeated in other images throughout the store. The same picture, often of a smiling blond child, appears again and again on signs, posters and other labels in the current advertising campaign.

In the Fuji shop there are even more photographs on display, yet here all of them are different. Some are large colour prints of people dressed up in fancy party clothes and humorous costumes smiling and making faces into the camera. Other photographs show tourist attractions, including exotic people from far-off places. A mural of these photographs, all taken by people working at Fuji's Photo Gang, covers three of the walls in the shop. An employee explained the display: 'Our customers aren't pros, and they want to see pictures they can relate to … Not to mention any names,' he said in an obvious reference to the Kodak store, 'but snow-covered mountain tops aren't what the typical Smith family is interested in.' The photographs also reinforce the message that in this shop there is a 'team' or 'gang' ('Foto-gänget'), a group of friends who work together – important to the employee's identity – whose camaraderie is an important ingredient in customer service. The two shops, with their different displays of photographs, also present the consumer with different models of photographic practice. On the one hand, in the Kodak Image Centre we find a standardized uniformity that also suggests uniform standards of products and service, tied to the image and reputation of a transnational company and its trademark. At Fuji's Photo Gang, on the other hand, a transnational trademark is mixed with signs of the local and a more personal, varied, even homespun interpretation of how to address the consumer's photographic needs.

In the Gallerix shop, these distinctions are evident within the same space. The name 'Gallerix' is a clear signal of what the consumer will find. In a 'gallery' one expects to find art on sale, but here the term is given a twist toward popular culture's visual aesthetic. The name links art and mass media, the visual forms found in advertising, comics and film ('pix', 'Asterix', 'comix', etc.), communicating that Gallerix offers art for everyone. This mass art is nevertheless arranged according to a clear hierarchy of economic and aesthetic worth. Outside the shop, piles of greeting cards are arranged on two collapsible tables. These follow the conventions for 'bargain' goods, accessible for passers-by who pick up and sort through the cards. This, together with the fact that the tables are set up on the outside, the wrong side, as it were, of the show window, signals that these are the least exclusive of the shop's cards, probably last year's stock. The consumer will find better and newer stuff by stepping inside.

Inside the shop, one finds greeting cards on the many rotating display racks and on permanent racks along the walls. The cards are arranged not according to price but according to function and theme. Nearest the door, accessible to the occasional tourist, is the shop's rather meagre selection of postcards. Further in are groups of birthday cards and other special occasion cards. Cards for children, and cards that play music and joke cards are displayed thematically. There is little distinction here between high and popular cultures; regardless of price, the greeting card display suggests that this is merely a consumption item.

Among the prints and posters, however, there is a clear hierarchy of display; at the same time the shop strives for a mass effect in its visual presentation of goods. Pictures cover virtually every surface, often in multiple versions, if not of the same image, then by the same artist or of a similar theme. Smaller pictures are displayed on the lower shelves, and larger formats further up on the walls. Artists and pictures that are known to sell well are prominently displayed. One example is the popular artist Lasse Åberg, referred to in the Gallerix catalogue as the 'in-house artist', whose popular images of Mickey Mouse appear in every possible format throughout the shop, including a single large framed print on the top shelf. The wall space directly behind the counter, referred to by the shop manager as the 'gold wall', is reserved for the most expensive framed and matted prints. Consistent with their presentation as exclusive works, these are single images that are not displayed in other formats elsewhere in the shop. The juxtaposition of this display with the shop's framing service underscores the singular quality of these pictures. At the other end of the scale of quality are the mass-produced posters, sorted under thematic categories such as 'Kids & Animals', 'Music & Movies', which can be seen only by leafing through them in the large flip files mounted along the back wall of the shop.

On the one hand, quality is associated with exclusivity, prints available in smaller editions (although they still number in the thousands), displayed as single framed and matted paintings. On the other hand, quality in this context resides in the techniques of reproduction, and not in any assumed artistic or aesthetic value. The work of the unknown company name Joadoor hangs on the 'gold wall' side by side with a print of a familiar van Gogh painting. Most Gallerix prints are representational, often in popular and easily identifiable art historical styles (Impressionist, Surrealism, and so on). Non-figurative art, considered difficult and inaccessible to a broad public, is nevertheless present as what could be called 'abstract – light', colourful, nearly abstract pictures by Gallerix's own 'trend-artists'. The shop manager half jokingly referred to the accessibility of the shop's art as 'prints for the people'. Benjamin foresaw how mass reproduction brought the work of art closer to a broader public, at the same time that it broke loose from the fabric of tradition, with its dependence on the original as unique.[11] As a work of art becomes widely available, it loses its authenticity, its 'aura'. With this move into the domain of mass culture, the work is divorced from its function and value as a ritual object, and is transformed into an object for display. The work of art has become an object of consumption. In Gallerix, not only individual works of art, but also pictures that paraphrase other known works or styles superimpose Benjamin's thesis onto the visual landscape of late modernity.

The pictures in Gallerix continually refer to other pictures within the shop as we have just described, but also to pictures found throughout the shopping centre and in the media at large. This intertextual phenomenon, the meeting and mixing of visual images, is at the same time intermedial. The pictures that can be purchased here, to send to a friend or to hang on a wall, often refer to other media. Pictures of the young magician Harry Potter, first seen on the covers of the best-selling books and then in film, soon showed up on posters and cards available in Gallerix. The television cartoon figures from the Simpsons and South Street, popular among schoolchildren, can be purchased as cards and posters. The same is true of popular singers such as Britney Spears, and film stars such as Keanu Reeves from the *Matrix* films, which in turn can be rented on video. Although these intermedial references are most evident among Gallerix's posters, certain media figures have also ascended into the higher echelons of cultural display. Old advertisements and classic Disney figures, including the above-mentioned Lasse Åberg renditions of Mickey Mouse, are presented as framed works, worthy of display on the wall of a living room or office.

ADDRESSING THE CONSUMER

There is a commonly held conception that the photographs people take and exchange, and the images they hang on their walls, are highly personal and intimate expressions of personal identity. A closer examination reveals that these practices nevertheless take place within a framework that is highly constrained by the range of media goods available on the market. A vast majority of consumers use compact automatic cameras, and the film one can buy over the counter in camera shops follows this format. Colour print film is preferred. Only 10 per cent of consumers take colour slides; certain types are no longer developed in Sweden but must be sent to a lab in Switzerland. Black and white film is a negligible part of today's amateur market. The two-hour developing service, which many customers take advantage of, is available only for the most common film and prints, in a standard size of 10×15 cm. The so-called 'specialized' services include a reduced price for double or even triple copies of prints – intended for families with young children who want to give pictures to both sets of grandparents. Yet even this is standardized. Cropping to improve a picture's composition, or compensating for faulty exposures, are not services offered by the local shop. The choices available are within a limited range of formats; standard or panoramic images which some cameras are capable of, or having film developed in the 'classic' mode, in the 'exclusive' format which includes a print with an overview of the entire roll as small images, or on a disk. Other innovations are introduced at regular intervals; for example, having a white frame around the prints, which gives the contemporary consumer's pictures a retro-look, reminiscent of an older snapshot aesthetic.[12]

Turning to the card and poster shop, we find similar constraints. The vast majority of greetings cards have pre-printed messages, and a broader range of stationary is not available at Gallerix. Greetings in the cards follow the standard holidays and celebrations observed by the Swedish majority culture. Christmas, Easter and school graduation cards are displayed according to the season, and congratulations for weddings, christenings, retirement and birthdays are available all year round, but pre-printed cards commemorating other religious holidays are absent from the display racks. There is little here that would appeal to the customer looking for a souvenir from a visit to Solna – the few available postcards are outdated views of the city, and anyone wanting a souvenir or greeting from a football match at the nearby stadium would be advised to go instead to the local team's shop elsewhere in the centre. The themes and styles in the prints follow the same pattern found in Gallerix stores across Sweden: standardized offerings reflecting current trends in other media, popular culture and interior design.

The framing service presents an exception. In this special section of the shop, a customer receives personalized service and is offered a wide range of passepartout mats and frames to choose from. Framing is represented as a craft, requiring skill and experience, and the shop employees who perform this service have gone through special training. The greater degree of choice and reliance on specialized skill raises the quality of this product – the individually framed print – and distinguishes it from the standardized mass production of Gallerix's other offerings. Elsewhere in the shop, employees were reluctant to offer customers advice on their selections, but they felt free to make suggestions on the choice of a frame or the colour and width of matt. Whereas selecting a card or print was seen as a question of personal taste, and was therefore outside the employee's remit, framing a print required expertise, and in this area the trained employee was seen as more knowledgeable than the customer.

Still, there were obvious limitations to the degree of individual service offered. Frames in prefabricated formats and styles dominated, and even if it was possible to order customized variants, the stock of profiles was considerably smaller than in the largest specialized art-framing shops elsewhere in the city.

The individualized services available in the photographic shops had a somewhat different character. Many communications and public relations companies are located in Solna, and according to the manager of the local Kodak shop, these provide a substantial part of their business. When a 'pro' (the term reserved for these key customers) entered the shop, the manager stopped whatever else he was doing to talk to him. The individualized service this customer received could include ordering of special products not available in the standard assortment, or advice about the latest products on the market. The 'pro' might also show or describe some new product or development to the shop manager. It was significant that all the customers identified as 'pros' were men. These conversations had the character of an exchange of information between equals, mutually confirming each other's status and shared enthusiasm for new techniques with joking references to 'toys for boys'. Other individualized customer services, such as advice about buying a new camera, or handling complaints about print quality, could be carried out by other shop employees; only the 'pros' were on a first-name basis with the manager.

The clearly identified group of photographic 'pros' was, nevertheless, an exception to the shops' descriptions of their circle of customers. All identified their customers as a broad, even all-encompassing group – 'everyone from a relative of the royal family to a homeless guy', according to the Fuji Photo Gang shop manager. Gallerix's target group is defined as both women and men, from teenagers up through middle age. On closer inspection, however, the majority of customers in all of these shops were women. Women accounted for the largest number of purchases, if not for the largest volume of sales. The 'typical' photographic shop customer was the mother who dropped off her film and ordered triple prints, one for each grandmother and one to keep for the family album. Gallerix's display of 'trend artists' to the exclusion of classic prints is intended to appeal to the younger middle-aged target group, and we assume, primarily to women who often carry the main responsibility for home decoration. Retired customers' purchases are almost exclusively confined to greetings cards for special occasions.

Within the framework of the shops selling pictures we found a fixed repertoire of available images and products available, seemingly allowing little room for variation and individual choice. Individualized service was the exception, confined to a limited range of products and, in the case of the centrally located photographic shop, was reserved for the professional male customer. Despite a broad definition of their customer population circle, we found that the majority of consumers in these shops were women. Let us turn now to a closer examination of the patterns that characterize these vernacular forms of image consumption, of photography, cards and prints.

MOBILE PICTURES

Challenging the relative constraints on image consumption imposed by the shops, people developed ways to personalize their image use. In their pictures, we found few of the strict conventions seen in images displayed in the photographic shops. The ways people displayed and used the pictures they had made or purchased did not always follow the marketing framework. We found people who combined purchased prints, children's drawings and their own photographs on the walls of their homes, others who had mounted all the greetings cards they had received in albums, people who refused to purchase pre-printed cards, preferring instead to pen a greeting on one of their own photographs to send to a friend. We found networks of image exchange that were highly personal and individual, often interwoven with other media in innovative communication forms. Image consumption was inextricably intertwined with production of individual and social meanings and identities, as pictures moved from their point of purchase, out into communication flows among family and friends.

The themes and occasions documented by the amateur or vernacular photographer are well known: family and friends, particularly on special occasions such as birthdays, Christmas celebrations and holiday trips. These photographs often have a social, communicative use, which we will return to shortly. What is less understood is the ways these images are used in individual narratives and histories, and as means of reworking or negotiating personal identities. One particularly active photographer, in addition to the customary photographic occasions, took pictures of her own paintings and handicrafts, and how she displayed them in her home as a way of charting changes in her personal life and work. She also took pictures of public places that she knew would be changing over the years. These private and public subjects together became a means of reflecting upon her personal life in relation to the history unfolding around her.

Making, taking and collecting images is described by some people as giving pleasure in itself, regardless of what they plan to do with the images. The pleasure associated with acquiring pictures of specific subjects was mentioned by many of our subjects. A particular desire to photograph flowers, or being drawn to images that show sharp contrasts, were two examples. Another was the woman who had started collecting small reproductions by Marjolein Bastin, a Netherlands artist included in the Gallerix collection. She often ended her obligatory shopping with a stop at Gallerix where, after selecting the greetings cards she needed, would look for a new Marjolein Bastin print that she could buy as a small present or 'reward' to herself. Another couple we met had a group of pictures with a sailing theme they planned to display on one wall at home. They described themselves as 'boat people'; sailing was a family hobby, and they were shopping for frames that would tie this small collection together. One can imagine that this private picture display reminds family members of holidays at sea, and affirms their common interest and identity. However, the images people display at home are not only private; they also serve a social function. At the same time that they express and affirm the identity/identities of a person or people who live there, they communicate that identity to others.

A more obvious example of the social functions of vernacular images is the practice of showing photographs to other family members or to friends. Passing around holiday snaps during a coffee break at work, for example, is a way to share the holiday experience with others. The social and communicative functions of pictures are the primary reasons most people take, purchase and display photographs. One of our informants described simply carrying a camera and taking pictures as communicative acts, something she does in order to demonstrate the importance of personal documentation to others she knows. The common practice of ordering double or even triple prints when taking in film for developing underscores the double function of photography, as personal memory and gift or medium of exchange. It also points to the value these personal photographs have. By ordering double prints people avoid the dilemma of parting with their only copy. They have one to keep and add to their collection, and one to give away.

Giving or sending personal photographs is particularly important to families and friends who are separated by long distances. Even in the contemporary media landscape of the Internet, e-mailing copies of photographs to family members remains an important way of keeping in touch. Children are often central to a family's history because, as one informant expressed it, they change so fast. Multiple copies, enlargements and framed pictures of children make handy and much appreciated gifts for grandparents, particular those who don't get to see the children very often. When distance prevents someone from attending an important family occasion, such as a funeral, wedding, christening or birthday, people take account of this in the pictures they take, by taking more pictures 'to show what it was like'. Photographs provide a means of bridging the gap, providing a kind of presence by proxy. One woman showed us a picture she had taken of her husband lighting a candle in their local church, in memory of his father. He could not afford the long journey to attend his father's funeral and had asked his wife to take the picture. They kept a copy for themselves and sent one to his mother.

Private pictures become integrated into other personal communication networks in different ways. Family members separated by long distances often have agreed times when they telephone each other, and we were told of a woman in Chile who always has a recent photograph of her son by the phone when she is waiting for him to call her from Sweden. In this simple and moving example of intermedial use, she can look at his picture as she hears his voice.

The social functions of greetings cards have many similarities to personal photographs. One of the more surprising findings of our study of vernacular images was the time and care people devoted to selecting these seemingly simple mass-produced images. And, similar to the use of photographs, it was not unusual for people, particularly women, to purchase duplicates of cards they especially liked so that they could keep one and send one to a friend. Sometimes these cards followed particular themes that they both collected. One woman reported that she was looking for a card with a picture of a pig on it to send to a friend. She laughed and explained that they often exchange pig cards 'when we're feeling fat'. This is a form of exchange where the only reason is contact between friends, a form of female bonding. Men may also spend a great deal of time finding just the right card to send, but always on an occasion when congratulations or holiday greetings are in order.

Many people in our study reported that they *never* throw away the cards they receive. One woman told us she had saved every card she had received since she was five or six years old. Her collection of greetings, congratulations and postcards, carefully mounted into albums, was clearly a way for her to create and maintain a life history. The greetings card's materiality further adds to its value. The fact that it is initially a mass-produced product does not prevent it from carrying meaning as a metonym of personal history. Postcards on the contrary are an example of how public images can move into the private sphere as gifts, when the card is received from a significant other.[13] Even people who reported using electronic mail for most of their correspondence said that e-mail messages could not replace the significance of personal greetings cards. When gathered into an album or series of albums, pictures and cards become a compendium of personal history, similar to a book in form, but with the critical distinction it cannot be mass-produced. Each album is unique.

This multifaceted pattern of personal image consumption suggests that the flow comes to a near standstill as pictures increasingly pile up in albums, boxes, cupboards, and now in computers. How do people deal with this ever-expanding collection of personal pictures? Whereas few people maintain a personal attachment to a particular television set or video player, and have no problem disposing of an older model when they have the means to purchase a newer media machine, their relationship to their pictures is different. A girl may replace the posters on her bedroom wall, but usually keeps the old ones, and how does she then as an adult throw away the pictures that meant so much to her when she was a teenager? The box of family photographs that is accidentally thrown away during a move continues to be mourned by the child who feels she has lost a record of her childhood.

Strong emotional ties are not exclusive to picture collections. There are other media goods that many people regard as valuable and important to the construction and maintenance of personal history and identity. Books, records and films are also objects that, alongside photographs and other pictures, are often seen as building a personal collection, and that present particular problems when we consider how people dispose of media items. We will therefore return to the phenomenon of collecting at the end of the next chapter.

5. SOUND AND MOTION

The previous two chapters indicated that the media for printed words and images are in a state of transition, where new generic and technological forms tend to dissolve the borders between and around these circuits. Still, they have a long tradition of relatively stabile institutions of production, distribution and consumption that safeguard their identity. The media for storing and transmitting sounds and pictures in motion are relatively more recent, with key innovations starting in the late nineteenth century. They are therefore somewhat less fixated and more porous, but as these temporally organized media circulate in specific forms through the shopping environment, they deserve a separate treatment as a distinct media circuit here, in turn subdivided into partly overlapping flows for music, films, radio and television.

In quantitative terms, media for sound and moving pictures are clearly dominant in our times – in Sweden they together make up for roughly 75 per cent of the average daily mass-media use, though it should be noted that these statistics exclude phone talking and watching various kinds of images.[1] In any case, 'audio-visual' media have been so strongly present in modern everyday life over the last century that they are often seen to define a whole phase of media history, after the oral and print eras. Today records, films and videos tend to merge into one media circuit by the DVD (Digital Versatile Disk) format combined with networked digital computers capable of storing and transferring film and music files. This is part of a general development where different media circuits intersect and no single medium can any longer operate in isolation from other media. The phenomenon of remediation introduced in Chapter 2 is evident in the diffuse media circuit for sound and moving pictures. There is no universally valid terminology here. The term 'audio-visual media' seems for instance too wide since books and photos are also visual, and 'electronic media' is likewise problematic in a time where electronics is not even confined to digital cameras but is integrated in virtually all media technologies. One might argue for reusing the old term 'telegraphy' as shorthand for all ways to telecommunicate, even so-called interactive ones, and thereby to regard telephoning, televising, telephotographing, telegramming and SMS-ing as one media circuit. That would then imply a wide and general semiotic concept of text as any kind of inscription in any kind of material substrate ('-graphy'), and thus applicable to all kinds of symbolic communication. However, conventional definitions of media circuits linger on and according to them 'telegraphy' still refers to an old and nowadays outmoded form of tele-communication. Also, such an extended interpretation of 'telegraphy' would not make the boundary to photography and books any clearer. It is possible to discern a wide circuit of media involving watching and listening to images, words and sounds that are presented in a temporal sequence, defined not least through the specific practices of marketing and consumption found in a shopping centre.

In Solna Centre as in most other similar places, videos/DVDs as well as records are sold in retail shops that offer few other commodities, except for complementary goods such as fizzy drinks, sweets and snacks to be consumed while watching or listening to a record, tape or disk. Conversely, these audio-visual software media for music and films can themselves turn into supplementary goods in other retail shops. Sports and grocery shops may for instance sell the most popular DVDs and chart music in addition to their main commodities. Bookshops often offer a small range of classical music and jazz to strengthen their image of 'high culture', though on closer inspection this reveals itself as a 'light', middlebrow version of the fine arts, since most of their records are from the low-price series of record companies such as Naxos, EMI and Decca.

The sales of music and films in Solna Centre adhere to the traditional borders between high and low culture. It is the library that has the most extensive and diversified supply of so-called quality films and serious music, while the shops are dominated by the more popular genres. This reproduces a basic structural opposition between low culture as being commercial (for sale) and high culture as non-commercial (not for sale). It is true that the demarcation line does not solely depend on this criterion, or is ever perfectly clear, since it often interplays with other oppositions that tend to blur and disguise its effects. One such opposition is confirmed by the head librarian: the opposition between giving people what they want and what they ought to like, which has accompanied any cultural policy built on classical *Bildung*-efforts during the last two centuries. The mixture of high (that which passes 'qualitative judgement', in the words of the librarian) and low culture ('pulp fiction') in the library is a concession to a recent more service-minded and liberal cultural policy.

'Mainstream' seems to be the most fitting genre and taste category for what is available in Solna Centre's two main shops for records, videos and DVDs: Mix Records and Video 48 Hours.[2] Both of them offer high cultural as well as subcultural items, including 'quality films', classical music and rather obscure film and music genres, which nevertheless seem to confirm that middlebrow is the high standard of taste and mainstream the dominant taste category in this shopping centre. The most conspicuous feature of both shops is the Top Charts, comprising the hundred most rented videos and DVDs in Video 48 Hours and the twenty most sold records in Mix Records.

This is, however, just part of the music and film consumption found in the centre. The soundscape, a pleasant atmosphere for shopping, is created with the help of recorded and/or broadcast background or foreground music. Audio-visuals are also used in marketing, ads and sales promotion, not least in event marketing where live music is often included. The promotional circuits of audio-visual media do not end at the centre's physical borders, since visitors to its website are given the opportunity to play interactive computer games. Such computer games also testify to the arbitrary character of any definition of media circuits today. It seems as reasonable to include as to exclude them from the circuit of software audio-visual media, since they operate through mobile vision and sound while their interactive character places them close to the hardware thematics discussed in the next chapter.

Audio-visual media are not restricted to sites of ordinary shopping. Web-based transmission of music and film by file sharing has been described as the worst 'threat' ever to the music and film industry, and is targeted by fierce anti-piracy activity. The intensity of this struggle results from piracy's tendency to transgress the borders regulating consumption, leaving out its most significant moment where a commodity is bought and sold. File-sharing movements potentially step out of commodity exchange and replace it with either a gift economy or a public resource. Active measures against illegal copying and distribution were taken in Sweden in 2001 when the so-called Anti-Pirate Agency (Antipiratbyrån) was formed by the film business with the aim of tracking down and prosecuting so-called pirate copiers. Hacker groups responded with an ideologically based critique of the business, claiming that all information as well as any other web-distributed material should be free. The heated debate raging around these issues indicates that cyberspace media consumption has not yet found its proper form. This is one of those 'not yet' cases that characterize the contemporary stage of remediation.

The outcome of this struggle is still unresolved, but it has already affected the established trade with audio-visual software. The record and film industries have for several years reported decreasing sales figures, and retail shopkeepers testify to a decrease of customers. If no retail innovations arise, we might witness the end of retail trade and traditional face-to-face consumption between seller and buyer within this media circuit. The only safe conclusion at the present is that digital copying and web distribution of these media have become a giant commercial and legislative problem. Illegal copying plays an increasingly significant role within a wider software audio-visual circuit of media consumption, of which money-based commodity exchange is only a part. It indicates an uneven pace of development of technology, commerce and legislation, where technology lies ahead of consumption and legislation that have not yet found proper forms for integrating copying into the legal sphere of consumption.

SOUNDTRACKS OF SHOPPING

There are a lot of entrances to software audio-visual media in a shopping centre like Solna. One passes through one of them as soon as one steps into the centre and is exposed to the music that flows from shops, restaurants and coffee shops. Music can draw attention to itself by its high volume and recognizability, or disguise itself by low volume and anonymity. The latter is a characteristic feature of the prefabricated background music commonly called muzak that is often used in commercial spaces. This kind of music is also present in Solna and flows from time to time from a central source through the whole shopping centre, but mostly with a softness and anonymity that makes it almost unheard. The volume increases at Christmas, Easter and other holidays when consumption booms. It then shifts from background to foreground music, when well-known carols contribute to a festive mood. However, there is no strict distinction between music experienced as foreground or as background, as this depends on a situation-bound combination of cultural, subjective and situational factors. In the commercial space of the shopping centre they are as plastic and transformable as Goffman's sociological distinction between front and back regions.[3]

At such times, the almost unheard background music also competes with the foreground music that flows from some shops, with the dual purpose of attracting the attention of by-passers and creating a sound-image that supports the overall image of the respective shops. Hence, music is used in many ways in the shopping centre, but above all to catch the attention of potential customers and to create a cosy sound atmosphere for shopping. In both these functions, music interplays with interior decoration, the display of commodities and the style of the staff who might for instance intend to give an impression of youthfulness, efficiency or exclusiveness.

As is customary in record shops, Mix Records is more or less constantly filled with music, which turns into an advertisement for itself. The music played is mostly current hits or 'golden', but not too old, 'oldies', underlining the mainstream orientation of the shop. Music is used as a marketing device, directed towards the initial selection moment of consumption, by generally making potential customers feel at ease, or by more directly influencing them to make up their mind to buy certain commodities. It is, however, doubtful if and to what extent this really works. (This is actually surprisingly true for much marketing and advertising in general.) The taste for music varies and it is easy to arouse dislike even by the choice of relatively soft and harmless background music.

Individual taste is revealed in customers' choice of commodities, and tends therefore to be a controversial subject in media shops. In Video 48 Hours, taste is openly discussed when couples or groups of people browse through videos to decide what film to rent or buy.[4] On average, the selection process lasts longer for groups than single customers, which probably reflects that a common activity, like watching a film in the company of friends, demands a joint resolution based on negotiation. But although taste is thus displayed in the shop, the staff considers it a delicate issue and refrains from making definite recommendations when customers ask for a 'good', 'funny' or 'thrilling' film. In contrast to Mix Records' way of constantly displaying music, Video 48 Hours makes no great efforts to influence its customers' precise choice of films. Excerpts from films are displayed on a small monitor behind the desk, but the medium on offer is not itself much used to influence customers' choices. This difference between the two shops may be derived from the fact that it is easier to remember a piece of music than excerpts from films, at least in terms of taste. A catchy tune is something one can grasp immediately, while a film trailer may certainly catch someone's attention, but can scarcely be used to give a fair judgement of the whole film. This also corresponds with the common use of music as a marketing device. In Solna Centre, advertising on TV screens is quite a rare phenomenon, clearly overshadowed by the use of adverts and still images. This centre thus reveals a quite low degree of (audio-visual) mediatization, compared to certain other, flashier shopping environments.

CONSUMING MUSIC AND FILM

While most print media tend to be mainly used individually, tapes and records can more easily be used by many people simultaneously. A distinction between the social and private use of music and films is emphasized by their differentiated types of hardware, from fixed collective hi-fi sets and projectors to portable disk and MP3 players designed solely for individual use. Reception studies have emphasized that the use of a medium like video is strongly embedded in social and cultural contexts.[5] In a process since the mid 1970s, video has become domesticated and is today frequently used as a core technology within the family circle. The domestic character of video is a prolongation of the way television – the medium it is usually used in combination with – became a form of family entertainment in the 1950s and 1960s. The domestic integration of both these media forms has at times been met with critique and resistance, and is in some respects still a controversial subject. Parents, for instance, are aware of the discourse on the impropriety of using video or television as babysitter, but also of the difficulties avoiding it. The same goes for teenage peer groups, where the use of DVDs is deeply embedded in a wider normative discourse on proper education and upbringing.

Moral as well as taste standards are therefore activated by the use of videos. This is reflected in the decision of Video 48 Hours not to offer its customers pornography, although, according to the shop staff, this decision was based on commercial as well as moral considerations. The mainstream orientation of Video 48 Hours might explain why few challenges to legitimate taste and moral standards could be detected among its customers. Film swappers and other social groups involved in such challenges tend to build their own networks for the procurement and exchange of more or less controversial films.[6] This is an example of how commercial media circuits may be transformed into social circuits, like fan or collector circuits, by people who organize their own networks of cooperation, information and exchange. As a step in what Kopytoff calls 'the biography of things', videos, DVDs and records are used in a diversity of ways, depending on in what social and cultural context they are embedded, after they have been sold and bought for the first time.[7]

One such re-embedding context is made up of people's own music making. During our fieldwork in Solna Centre, we encountered a girl rock group called Miss Gandalf, whose four members were 16–17 years old.[8] They rejected the mainstream orientation of Mix Records: 'They have nothing to offer, no good records and if they have a good record it's too expensive. And on top of it, the shop is filled with boy groups and other scary things.'[9] They also preferred old vinyl gramophones as vehicles for sound transmission rather than 'light' equipment such as portable CD players or mini-disks.[10] In the same vein, the only record shop in Solna that passed their critical judgement – apart from the quarterly arranged record fair – was a small second-hand shop. Otherwise they preferred shopping for records in Stockholm. By using records primarily as an inspiration for their own music making, the band members blurred the borderline between production and consumption. Also, the contemporary diversity of music transmission technologies promoted a reflexive and critical attitude towards those media, which were systematically integrated into their judgement of different kinds of music and thereby had lost any sense of transparent immediacy.[11] A similar drift towards hypermediacy is found in the use of videos and DVDs, where the introduction of the latter medium, and its commonly acknowledged superior visual and auditory qualities, has drawn attention to these media in themselves. This tendency is counterbalanced by the representational character of audio-visual media, in that the DVD medium claims to give a more 'realistic' and 'total' film experience than the video. This is further reinforced by home movie equipment, which has adapted domestic film experience to cinema standards. These interacting tensions between hypermediacy and immediacy in video use are also found in the use of music media, but were not prominent in Miss Gandalf's discourse on music. Maybe these tensions are hidden by music's supposedly non-representational character, which makes it hard to discern a relation between an auditory medium and what it represents. Still, while a studio recording may be heard as an autonomous artefact, judgements of live recordings often thematize the degree to which they capture the atmosphere of a 'real' public performance.

The use of audiovisual media is part of the routinization of domestic life. All media use follows routines and customs, but the watching of television, videos or DVDs, and the listening to radio and music are among the media activities that get most time in domestic settings.[12] Video has become an important time management tool for co-ordinating TV watching with domestic duties and other activities. Recording programmes on video and saving them for more suitable occasions has become a daily routine among some of our informants, who often recorded new programmes, deleting the old ones before they had time to watch them, while saving others as cherished gems for repeated enjoyment. In this way, videos as well as CDs can become objects of more or less systematic collecting.

DILEMMAS OF COLLECTING

The collector is a paradoxical consumer: on the one hand, a true hero of consumption, always looking for something thrilling to acquire, but on the other hand repudiating any hedonistic consumption mentality. The motive for acquiring cherished possessions does not seem wholly selfish, since it is permeated by care for the objects in themselves. Such paradoxes make it interesting to take a closer look at the practice of collecting in general. Who becomes a collector and why? When do media items form a collection? There are media-specific distinctions between collecting pictures and collecting records, but also cases where these distinctions are blurred. Through history many media have turned into collector items. Benjamin identified a relationship between changing patterns of media consumption and collecting, describing collecting as a practice that adapts and transforms itself according to the historical development of commodity production and media innovations. This transformable capacity is reflected in the elusive character of the phenomenon of collecting.

Among our informants, video recording was not only a way to control viewing time. Video recordings of favourite films or televised programmes were also saved and watched several times. In this way, video recording from television can result in substantial collections that also include purchased films as well as self-produced amateur videos. The introduction of video in the 1970s has thus also made it possible for anyone to collect films, transforming film collecting from an exclusive hobby for a select few to a widespread popular practice. By that time, records had been collectibles for decades and gone through several cycles of material and technological remediation, in that shellac records had been replaced by vinyl records and supplemented by tapes, and the introduction of CD records was in its infancy. However, the invention of the phonograph around 1900 transformed rather than initiated the practice of music collecting. In the eighteenth century, devoted collectors could already fit rolls or disks in automatic pianos and street organs, and collecting music scores for piano playing was a popular practice among women in bourgeois families long before records became collectibles for the listening public at large in the twentieth century, with the 1920s as the main breakthrough decade.

Most people who have a video or DVD player also possess at least a rudimentary collection of favourite films, without considering themselves devoted film collectors. Differences among collectors are gradual rather than substantial, making it hard to draw a clear line between collectors and those who do not collect. In contrast to the vernacular practice of collecting photos, record and film collectors are not primarily occupied with saving memories of special occasions or events that reflect their own life course. Like books but contrary to photography, records and films do not serve as a primary biographical material for those who collect them. Book, record and film collectors can easily be described as book, music and movie lovers, while there does not seem to be a necessary relationship between collecting one's own amateur photos and a deep devotion to or even interest in photography as such. Record and film collectors seem to collect in a more determined, systematic and purposeful way, while collections of photos often have a more occasional, unintentional and unsystematic character.

Our interviews confirmed that the collector is a vague, but nevertheless real, social figure in people's minds. The same goes for efforts to define what a collection is, which to a great extent could be explained by the intersecting meanings of words such as 'saving', 'accumulating', 'hoarding' and 'collecting'. People's views on collectors and collections seem to rest on family resemblances of the sort Wittgenstein had in mind when he wrote that 'phenomena have no one thing in common which makes us use the same word for all – but they are *related* to one another in many different ways.'[13] Some collect for taxonomic, others for aesthetic or economic reasons, and some even out of necessity, like the ragman. Although there is no single property or motive that all collectors share, they are conceptually united by the fact that they resemble one another in various ways.[14]

Hence, it comes as no surprise that people hesitate when asked whether they consider themselves collectors. Even the most prolific photographer among our informants did not consider herself a collector, but rather a 'big-time consumer'.

People who 'collect' photographs seem to fall in the same category as collectors of art, as distinct from people who may have a collection consisting of thousands of personal photographs in albums or (equally common) shoeboxes. The couple looking for frames for their collection of sea images were not 'collectors', since they were dealing with a small, finite selection of pictures. On the other hand, the woman who buys every print she can find by a particular artist and keeps them for herself may be seen as a 'collector'. But what about the woman who has saved all the postcards she has ever received – is she a 'collector'?

Surprisingly enough, even Erik, a 26-year-old music journalist with a collection of more than a thousand records, had doubts about classifying himself as a record collector in the light of what he designated as 'more devoted' collectors. In comparison, Victor gave the impression of a more secure identity as a collector by giving a straight 'yes, definitely' answer to the question as to whether he regarded himself as a collector; a response that seemed grounded in his participation in an extensive network of special media, second-hand markets, clubs, web pages and other channels of information exchange for record collectors. Elisabeth, a 51-year-old journalist, who together with her husband had a record collection of 'a hundred old vinyl records and about fifty or seventy-five CD records', on the other hand had no doubts whatsoever that she was still not a record collector, since she was not devoted to collecting records and did not buy more than three or four a year.

Classifying oneself or others as collectors has a phenomenological as well as a social side. This was revealed by both Victor and Erik when it came to collecting records, but also by Elisabeth when she described herself as a collector of miniature houses. Each of them had a distinct experience and memory of what aroused their motive or instinct to collect. Victor described it in a comic way as 'love at first ear-sight', while both Erik and Elisabeth, in a corresponding but a more destiny laden way, designated it as 'something one had waited for ... the whole life, actually' and 'predestined', respectively. In short, their experiences could be characterized as peak or extraordinary experiences of consumption, triggered by an encounter with what was retrospectively conceived by them as the right kind of collectibles. In Victor's and Erik's cases the experience could also be characterized as aesthetic, since it was a certain kind of music that turned records into collectibles for them. Elisabeth's experience seems to have more of a self-biographical character. But common to all three of them was that a certain class of object mediated an extraordinary personal experience that also assigned them a subject position as a collector. In the last instance taking on a collector identity seems to be the result of an extraordinary encounter between a human being and a thing where they mutually construe one another as a collector subject and a collectible object. Hence, a kind of double construction, where the subject is transformed by the object and vice versa: the subject becomes a collector and the object a collectible. Collectors' affective bonds to certain things are of a special kind since they are both particular and general; tied to a special *type* of object as well as a particular object in itself. Bibliophiles are devoted to books, discophiles to records, and cineastes to films.

The multifaceted value structure of collectibles opens for clashes, tensions and contradictions between different values. This is for instance reflected in the view, common among record collectors, that people whose primary motives are economic or social (status, prestige, companionship, etc.) do not count as true collectors. Such motives are scorned as 'selling out' and regarded as a concession to 'commercialization' in the rhetoric of record collectors. As explained by Victor, a devoted record collector in his forties, who regularly participates as a seller in the quarterly arranged record-swapping fair in Solna, 'the day you estimate what you can get paid for a record, then you're sold … then collecting is finished, then you become a hawker.' The determination of who is and who is not a genuine collector primarily belongs to a discourse on motives, and among collectors themselves. Such discourse does not result in a clear demarcation between collectors and non-collectors, since collectors are rarely conscious of their own motives.

Benjamin notes that collecting is strongly related to memory: 'Collecting is a form of practical memory, and of all the profane manifestations of "nearness" it is the most binding.'[15] Collecting things preserves memories as well as history in materialized form. And nearly everyone could be characterized as a collector in this sense, since most people save things that remind them of something, such as photos, souvenirs or letters. These objects have strong affective value for their owners. Yet different kinds of objects carry different kinds of affection. Susan Stewart draws a distinction between the souvenir and the collection, and argues that personal photographs, albums and scrapbooks should not be seen as collections but as souvenirs.[16] The souvenir is a metonym of personal experience and thus retains its tie to the past; it always 'speaks to a context of origin'.[17] Because it has the capacity of tracing the owner's authentic experience, the souvenir carries value both as an individual item of personal history and for its place alongside other items/souvenirs. The souvenir can always serve as a point of departure for a narrative of one's life. According to Stewart, each item in the collection, on the other hand, is valued in relation to other objects in the collection; classification replaces origin as its raison d'être. The value of a single item can never be as great as when it is inserted into the complete entity of the collection. It is the collection as a whole, rather than its individual parts, that distinguish its value. Another difference is that the souvenir maintains a trace of its original use value in its instrumentality. Old letters can still be reread, photographs can be looked at again and again, and in these acts the souvenirs retain aspects of their original meanings, even as these meanings change. For the item in the collection, however, use value has faded, to be replaced by aesthetic value. As Stewart states: 'The collection represents the total aestheticization of use value.'[18] This interpretation points at an important tendency of collections to be a culturalizing factor, but there is actually no strict dualism between souvenir and collection. Most collections do not at all erase the souvenir character of the items they include, but manage to combine the two sides. It may be true that some souvenirs never get organized into structured collections, while the items of some institutionalized or neglected collections may seriously weaken their links to past lived experience. But most cases lie between these extremes, so that the souvenir and the collection should rather be seen as two overlapping aspects or perspectives.

Affective value is primary for all these forms of saving and collecting. Affective values are personal, even when attached to mass-produced things such as records, books or clothes.[19] An item's affectionate value cannot be communicated or shared in the same way as other kinds of use and exchange values. Benjamin touches on this aspect when he remarks that 'the phenomenon of collecting loses its meaning as it loses its personal owner.'[20] A collection may be transferred from one person to another, but not its affective value. This is as true for the souvenir as for the collection. Because the affective value is personal, these objects or goods can be withdrawn from economic as well as symbolic and practical exchange. The tangible things themselves may of course be exchanged, books may be given as gifts or photographs exchanged, but not the affections they hold in terms of memories, associations or familiarity. The new recipient/consumer may also have affections for the object, but these too are personal and individual. A person who acquires a collection may have as strong an emotional attachment to it as the prior owner, but this only means that one affective value is replaced by another.

Contrary to an exchange value or a use value, an affective value cannot be transferred from one person to another; hence, it can be neither bought nor sold.[21] In this respect, collecting in many instances bears the mark of what Bourdieu designates as an inverted economy, which allows for symbolic profit but is based on a denial of or a disinterest in the economic in the narrow sense, and a refusal of commercial interests.[22] The inverted economy of collectors prioritizes the affective value of things rather than their potential to accumulate symbolic profit. The affective value of things is personal and in this sense withdrawn from economic as well as symbolic and practical exchange. The tangible things themselves may of course be exchanged, but not the affections they hold for certain people in terms of memories, associations or familiarity.

As a practice, collecting affects every stage in the process of consumption, from the acquisition to the disposal of an object, although not in a uniform way for all kinds of collectors. Benjamin speaks of a 'shudder of being acquired' that runs through an item when it is enclosed within a 'magic circle' by a collector.[23] This shudder points to the affective side of collecting, which manifests itself not only in a collector's acquisitions, but also in the possession and care of the items that make up the set of things demarcated as his or her collection. Often, but far from always, collectors also remove the items comprising a collection from their normal use. Contrary to Benjamin's view on 'the bibliophile as the only type of collector who has not completely withdrawn his treasures from their functional context', put forward in the 1930s, most contemporary collectors of records and films do use their beloved items in a functional way, that is, they play and listen to their records and view their films.[24] This again indicates that Stewart's dichotomy of souvenir and collection is untenable. However, there are many collectors of stamps, comic books or pictures of celebrities who completely withdraw their items from their intended or conventional functional uses that might degrade them, by always keeping them concealed and never removing them from their special plastic protection.

By such practices, collectors redefine use values, rather than obliterate them. Collecting practices express and assign different kinds of use values to things. Affective and symbolic values are also use values, only of a different subtype to the kinds of communication for which media commodities are normally intended. Status value is another use value that may be added to the mediating and affective values. A vast, unique or beautiful collection may give its owner prestige or even honour, and consequently may also be used with that in mind by him or her. Nevertheless, the status value of items in a collection probably contributes to the quite common outlook on collecting practices as being non-utilitarian or even pointless. The redefinition of a tangible thing into a collectible one, normally also affects its exchange value. With stamps as an historical example, some things may accumulate considerably higher economic value when they become collectibles than they did when they were merely considered as mundane but useful, even beautiful objects.

In the same way as collecting gives a special character to the selection, acquisition and use of an object, the disposal of collected items is treated with care and is often experienced as loaded with strong feelings or anguish by collectors. This is often revealed when record or video collections are put up for sale on the Internet, as in the following case:

Personal Record Collection Clearance
(and a few music videos)

Genuine reason for sale not commercial.

Due to a change of lifestyle and an extreme shortage of storage space,
the time has come to part with my beloved 'Record Collection'.

Collecting records has been a hobby of mine for many years and the
thought of taking these along to a car boot sale just didn't seem right!
So I am offering them here on the Internet in the hope
that they can find a trusted home.[25]

Collecting or saving objects, in whatever form it takes, thus disturbs the ordinary chain of consumption. As Benjamin points out, a collector's care of things seems 'archaic' nowadays and in many ways stands in opposition to the easy come easy go mentality that is often attributed to contemporary consumerism.[26] As our examples reveal, collectors unwillingly part with their collections and mere economic profit is seldom the reason to do so. In the case of the personal photographs or postcards collection, it is questionable whether it would carry any economic value on the open market, unless the collector is a famous person. As a specific type of consuming, collecting thus also transgresses the borders of what is ordinarily considered as consumption.[27] In some cases collecting even serves as a way to withdraw certain objects from the consumption market by, for example, transforming them into museum specimens. But second-hand markets show that collecting also plays an important part in reintroducing objects into the market economy and once again transforming them into commodities after they have passed through the initial stages of consumption, thereby saving them from being disposed of.

6. HARDWARE MACHINES

It should by now be clear that media circuits notoriously impinge on one another. The previous three chapters started with different kinds of media texts, studying where, when and how they are sold, bought and used. There is a kind of historic progression between these chapters, in that print media are the oldest form of mass media, followed by visual media and somewhat later sound and moving images media. This is not a matter of linear succession where one media form chronologically follows and replaces the other. They work in a dynamic sequence as new media interact with older ones, imitating and modifying them in processes of remediation, combining with them in multimedia cooperation, hybrids or other kinds of intermedial relationships. Print media were the dominant form of the classic public sphere, and papers and books remain key elements in forming opinions, with a comparatively high social status. Visual, auditive and audio-visual media have gradually extended the scope of public spaces, offering more and richer channels of exchange, across larger distances in time and space. During recent decades, the digital revolution of computers and global networks has accelerated these processes, leaving no traditional media circuit and no inherited boundary untouched.

In order to approach this complex media compound systematically, this chapter does not deal with one particular media circuit. Instead, it focuses on the machines that are used in several of them. The historic development of media technologies has gradually increased the number and complexity of such machines, with digitally networked computers as a recent example. Media machines are usually called *hardware*, in contrast to the *software* of those multiform texts that mediate meanings. Mediated communication lets people interact with symbolic forms of multiple kinds, material artefacts designed to invite the construction of meaning that is called interpretation. These software 'texts' (in the widest sense of the word) are materially embodied in, for example, stone, wood, paper, sound waves and photon streams. In modern societies, the making, spread and use of textual artefacts increasingly often rely on hardware, so that communication presupposes a combination of two consumption acts, in what might be called a '*two-step flow of media consumption*'.[1]

Media hardware can be required in various parts of communication processes. Some are needed to produce media texts, with the printing press, the (still, film or video) camera and the sound-recording microphone-and-tape device as classic examples. Such media-producing machines belong to the complicated socio-technological apparatuses that constitute modern media. The products of such machines can sometimes be used directly by consumers and audiences. If you don't happen to need glasses, you can take a book, paper, placard or postcard and read it as it is. However, in many cases, machines are also needed to use and interpret media texts. Some kind of apparatus is definitely needed if you want to hear the music or see the film that is loaded on a digital disk. It is those machines necessary for (certain) media consumption that are the main focus of this chapter. Print media usually do not need any hardware, whereas hardware is central to audio-visual media, and the previous chapter has already gone into them in detail. Here, we treat hardware separately from software because it is often bought and sold in separate shops and thus engages phenomenologically different 'tracks' of selection and use. Hi-fi equipment, mobile phones and computers therefore deserve special treatment in this overview of media consumption starting from a shopping centre. This chapter will also be an opportunity to develop the hardware side of those media circuits discussed before, highlighting connections between various media circuits. We also include telephones and computers, media that are less obviously sold and consumed as commercial texts and thus tend to be neglected when studying mass-consumed media texts.

The borders between different kinds of media hardware are blurred. Many machines can be used both for production and for reproduction in consumption: a tape recorder can be used for listening to music but also for recording and making music. Some hardware also includes functions of distribution, mediating between production and consumption. This is particularly true for the hybrid Internet-computer-cellphone combination where each machine enables multiple, interrelated and overlapping functions. It is, however, in most cases still possible to discern different kinds of media hardware use, and to distinguish the roles and effects of hardware from other elements of the media world.

DOUBLE MEDIA

The definition of media and of 'a medium' is a contestable social compromise rather than a fixed and universal concept. Sometimes it is textual types like books, CDs or television programmes that are classified as media, at other times media definitions refer to types of (production- or reception-oriented) media hardware such as printing presses, record players or television sets. These texts and machines are connected in social and institutional *media circuits* including media producers, genres and users as well as all technologies entering into the circulating process. Both hardware and software do mediate and may thus be seen as media, but it is the socially constituted media circuits that define the main media categories. When we talk of 'book media', for instance, we usually refer to the whole institutional circuit binding together publishers, printing technologies, printed volumes, text genres and readers. The term 'book' is then used metaphorically (or rather as a synecdoche – a part of a phenomenon used to signify the whole phenomenon in question) to refer to the whole media circuit in which the book as such is a prime element. Those encompassing circuits are socially defined and in historical flux, since their definitions and mutual boundaries are open to change, depending on developments in cultural industries and markets, technologies, genres and forms of daily life.

Let us call those media that for their use require specific combinations of textual units with decoding machines, *double media* – in contrast to those single media that may be used without the help of any particular technical apparatus. Double media insert a separation of hardware and software into the mediating process of communication. This divides the consumption process into two main parts, each with its own organizational form, spatial localization and temporal rhythm in the interplay between purchase and use. This is the two-step flow of media consumption.

Double media thus complicate the analysis of their consumption, since they involve a combination of two distinct but overlapping acts of consumption. A record without a record player is as silent as the reverse. A television set is useless without antenna or cable. The VCR makes things even more complicated since it won't function without tapes but also has to be connected to the television set, which is an example of intermediality, a phenomenon that will be discussed in the next chapter. In the case of CDs, people usually acquire the machine in a different way to the record, in other kinds of shops, as a larger investment and with different considerations. Though they have to be used together in order to function as intended, each can still communicate meanings separately. The CD cover can be looked at and admired, as can the brand-new CD player on its shelf at home. Some of their ('secondary') use values can be fully appreciated separately, but in order for them to work as that kind of medium or media circuit for which they are primarily made, they must be used together. The two consumption chains thus have to converge at a single time and space in order to make possible the use specific for communication media, namely reception.

Hardware and software need not be bought in the same way, place or time. The software of different media has varying use periods. Without a VCR/DVD machine, a televised programme needs to be seen at the moment of broadcast, paid via cable rents (for commercial television) or a combination of taxes and fees (for public service). In this case the normal viewer owns the same television set for several years and lets a flow of program units pass through that machine during its total lifetime. For CDs the situation might be highly different, in that a CD itself may be a relatively durable possession. A music lover might cherish her record collection dearly and save records for ages, while perhaps updating her player regularly in order to improve technical listening quality and visual design according to her changing taste. In that case, the consumer will experience the same software goods via a series of different machines. The hardware/software concepts are thus not always synonymous with long-term/short-term use, though they do sometimes coincide.[2]

Many media circuits have borderline cases and can therefore appear in both single and double form. Photographic prints work like single media without hardware for watching them, whereas slides normally require a projector or other viewing device to be consumed as intended. Computer media could be called *triple media* since they use at least three main components: machine hardware, programs and documents ('texts'), and both these latter software components can in their turn be stored in many different disk forms. This is one of many reasons to talk of *multimedia* – besides the perhaps more obvious ones that they combine different sensory modes (writing, image, speech and music) and elements from older media types (books, photos, records etc.).

Some (single, double or multi) media are independent in that they may in principle function by themselves in the normal act of consumption. Others are dependent in that their use requires the simultaneous use of another medium. The VCR is an obvious example of the latter, since its normal use presupposes a link-up to a television set – at the very least a monitor. It is a matter of convention among producers, retailers and consumers if such combinations are considered as a cooperation of two media (one of them dependent on the other) or as a case of one double (or multi) medium. For example, we normally think of the VCR as a separate medium to television, whereas we would probably regard antennas or digital decoders as accessories to TV sets rather than as separate media of their own.

Media machines are often included in what are sometimes called capital goods or durables since they command larger sums of money and are intended for long-term rather than momentary use. They function as tools for producing and consuming software texts, and have as means of production and/or consumption a particularly central role in media use, since access to such machines makes possible the production and reception of a wide range of texts. Media machines have thus become an important power resource for human interaction and thereby also for control over communication processes.

It is media hardware rather than software that may be seen as extensions of the human body, in the way first developed by Marshall McLuhan in the 1960s. This has been further developed by theorists of human prosthetic uses of technologies, where machines supplement the finite body, extending its control over the environment even as it is increasingly dependent on technical aids. It is machines rather than texts that function as tools that expand human capabilities, creating the cyborg – the 'cybernetic organism' fusing human and machine.[3] In the direction of perception, machines interact with our senses, while in the direction of production they reinforce and widen the expressive power of our voices and bodies to make traces in the material world. With a radio we can register signals otherwise unnoticeable by our bodies; with a camera we can produce and save images for the future; with telephones and PCs we live our daily lives in close symbiosis with communication technologies that collaborate with our eyes and ears, voice and hands. Machines multiply our capacities to check vast archives of symbolic forms, create complex texts and communicate instantly with others across the globe. This extension of the self is particularly effective with micro technologies that can be attached to the mobile human body.

HARDWARE LOCATIONS

Communicating through media of inscription and transmission compresses time and space, letting people access meanings across distances by reading texts, watching pictures and hearing voices that have been stored for ages or disseminated from the other side of the globe.[4] Still, all actual media use is located in time and space. Media are always used by someone somewhere, and at some specific time. There is an intricate dialectic here, in that media use gives time and space meanings and even creates its own virtual times and virtual spaces, while also remaining bound and framed by particular places and moments. Investigating media hardware in the context of a shopping centre thus invites reflection on how this particular location of such machines relates to issues of power.

Mobile machines are found in most places where people move. Modern micro-technologies make many media machines mobile. However, much hardware still tends to be relatively fixed in space, due to large size or a need to be connected to a fixed network of antennas, cables or electric power. In some places, even mobile apparatuses may be hard to use, due to physical conditions (for instance under water) or rules of conduct (when silence or utter concentration is demanded). The question of where hardware machines are located – and their accessibility – is therefore an issue subject to conflict and contestation, since they establish a kind of communicative power over space.

The consumption processes of media machines follow the same basic phases as with other commodities, but are modified by the specificities of these machines and the fact that they are tools for media use and always connected to some kind of software. Within the space of Solna Centre, this process can be summed up in three main steps: (1) shopping for media hardware in the centre, (2) using media hardware in the centre, and (3) using media hardware that has been bought in the centre, outside the centre. Here, only brief comments will be made about each point, with a focus on their spatial aspects.

(1) First, media machines are selected and *purchased in the centre's shops*. In Solna Centre, the most general such shop was Expert, a chain store for all kinds of hi-fi equipment and media hardware: stereos, TV sets, radios, VCR and DVD players, photo cameras and computer technology.[5] The Technics Store (Teknikmagasinet) had a similarly wide range of goods, but geared more towards smaller and cheaper electronics, tools, gadgets and games.[6] There were also a couple of short-lived small shops specializing in computer goods and game tools, including both programs and hardware. In addition, some shops for mobile phones were sometimes connected to a particular company for telephone subscriptions.[7] Finally, there were two competing photographic shops, Kodak Image Centre and Fuji's Photo Gang, described in Chapter 4. Some media hardware could also be marginally sold in other places as well, in conjunction with other media, or with children's toys.

(2) Second, regardless of where they are bought, media machines are *used in the centre*. Some machines are owned and used by companies and their staff and management, others by customers. The TV monitors and sound systems discussed above belong to the first sub-category. Also, telephones and computers were used by Solna Centre and its shops, both for internal communication (as with faxes and e-mails between managements and shops) and as sales tools to stimulate or assist customers' choice and purchase of other goods (as with TV monitors showing commercials).

Similar kinds of hardware were also used in the centre by its visitors. Phones could for instance function as tools for selecting or purchasing other media commodities, like when customers call their partners from the video rental shop in order to decide which film to hire for the night.

A mixed case was machines owned by commercial establishments but used by customers and visitors. Phone booths were sparsely placed at strategic places in the centre. The library had computer terminals too, both for staff and for visitors. They could be used as a means of registering loans or library cards, or for information access in archives or on the Web, or for other kinds of communication. This is an example of one medium (computers) in the service of others (books, journals, and so on). The library also had equipment for listening to CDs and looking at microfilm etc., comfortably located for public access but ultimately controlled by the staff according to laws and rules of conduct. Visitors trying to access or create porno-graphic or Nazi websites on the library terminals could count on being thrown out, if they were discovered.

ATMs and computer terminals of various kinds were found in post offices, banks and at cash desks, used for carrying out money transfers and accessing related finan-cial information. Here, particular kinds of money-transfer media produced symbolic communication acts (transfer of numeric signs) that were truly performative, having direct real and material effects in the form of economic values shifting place or owners. To our knowledge, no media studies seem to acknowledge ATM machines as media, as their use is so clearly restricted to one specific purpose. Still, they do mediate symbolic messages, and their existence underlines the principal difficulty of defining what is a medium and how do delimit media circuits, as discussed in Chapter 2.

One interesting case was the use of strategically located monitors and loudspeakers to provide information, modify the atmosphere of the place or advertise specific products. In the centre, nearly a hundred monitors were displayed that were not for sale. One third of these stood turned on in hi-fi shops, as part of the interior design.[8] The rest were placed in the windows of other shops, by entrances and inside shops, with the purpose of supervising or steering visitors' movements, decorate the visual space, supply information or entertainment for children and adults, and/or advertise commodities for sale by showing fiction, sports, music, documentary images, textual material and pure commercials. Many were found in food and hardware stores, but some were also placed in media shops that did not sell television sets and thus exem-plified intermedial cooperation.

There was a small cinema in the centre, called Sagittarius (Skytten). Its film projector was an example of a tehnological fixture around which was built a whole room for cultural experiences. This was one of two dozen similar suburban and shop-ping centre cinemas around Sweden, managed by the Eurostar company. This little cinema, squeezed into an awkward intermediate space near one of the bookshops, was not well integrated into the centre and led an obscure life. The centre would have liked to establish a large multiplex cinema within its confines, in line with the concept of integrating shopping and the production of experience that has proved highly successful. But this was difficult due to competition from a new but separate multiplex complex adjacent to the centre, in the area of the old studios where Greta Garbo and others once had produced the classics of the golden age of the Swedish film industry. The unsuccessful efforts in this direction by the management were part of a more general wish to make the centre a 'centre of events', as it was formulated in one advertising slogan. In line with current management trends towards a cultural-ized economy, visitors should be offered exciting experiences, and a cinema would of course be an eminent site of experience production. One needs only to recall the number of references to current films in the intermedial products on sale throughout the centre to understand the vacuum Solna Centre's lack of a cinema represents.

But there were apparent limitations to that trend towards experience management. The centre had once organized a sales event including the Bananas in Pyjamas show for kids.[9] The centre managers repeatedly referred to this particular event – as a warning. The reason was that Bananas in Pyjamas attracted large and noisy crowds that obstructed other customers' shopping activities. If strong and focused aesthetic experiences for their own sake are defined as a key aspect of cultural events, one could say that Bananas in Pyjamas was not too little but rather too much (experience) culture for this shopping centre.

A related problem was the lack of appropriate space for a cinema, its location a potential disruption to the smooth sales machinery of surrounding shops. Cinemas are often placed in shopping centres and were actually also included in some old-time department stores. One of the very first public places showing films in Paris was the Dufayel department store in 1896, where it was supposed to attract customers.[10] But with longer narrative films the competition between commerce and film reception made such cohabitation difficult to sustain. Today multiplex cinemas are returning to shopping centres, but they usually occupy a separate floor or wing. They clearly require careful strategies of containment and planning, in order for the powerful media machine of the cine-projector not to interfere with the surrounding commercial sales apparatus.

(3) The final main type and phase of consumption was *the use outside the centre of machines bought in that centre*. Visitors interviewed by Martina Ladendorf easily remembered which TV sets, cameras, record players or phones they had bought in the centre, and this historic root often gave that machine a specific meaning for them. In such use, the links back to the place of acquisition were often maintained, for example by guarantee conditions and service access, by the continuing delivery of software to the hardware, but also in the aura around the machine that was some-times kept alive in memory. It felt different to have bought a machine in a more exclusive shop than in a mass chain store, or having paid a reduced sales price, for instance. This could give the machine an aura of either nobility or simplicity, of high or low cultural value, as a waste of money or a bargain. Media machines helped to structure time and space, shaping memories and spaces of interaction by creating and

delimiting opportunities for media use, thus enabling and restricting various kinds of social action.

One example is when mobile phone users create a space for talk – a virtual parlour – around themselves. Such a communication space creates a bridge connecting the two speakers across physical distance, while erecting a wall that separates them from people in their immediate vicinity. Someone chatting on his cellphone makes him- or herself incommunicable to those who happen to be physically close, but can share only half of the electronically mediated dialogue. Together with the ways in which patterns of media use distinguish different kinds of people according to class, gender, age, ethnicity and taste orientation, this spatial dialectic shows how media not only transgress borders and distances, but also create them. Another example is the use of video by families to control the temporal rhythms of everyday life, using time shifting in order to reconcile conflicting interests of adults and children into a functional structure of media use.[11]

POWER OF ACCESS

Communication is a form of power, demanding that people listen, see and make sense of symbolic forms of various shapes. By arguing in words, sounds and images we can strive to affect other's ideas and actions, and by spreading sensuous and affective expressions the moods and behaviour of audiences can also be more or less deliberately manipulated. Communicative power interacts in both directions with other forms of power – in particular with the strategic power of money (the market) and political administration (the state). Economic and political forces frame and steer the execution of communicating force, which in turn – through debates and discourses in the public sphere – simultaneously binds and delimits the range of pure commercial profit or state authority. The position of media machines in this configuration is thus also a position of power. This is particularly clear in the case of media machines that are more or less openly subject to intense negotiation and regulation by societal institutions.

The sounds and images streaming from TV screens and loudspeakers in the shopping centre influenced visitors' movements, more or less consciously. Even a turned-off monitor can make people move around it or watch the screen (in vain). Media machines can thus be tools that the centre and shop managers use to control the flow of people through their premises.

A basic condition for communicative power is access to the means of media production and/or consumption. Through regulation by censorship, legislation, taxation and subsidies, the state tries to regulate media access – positively by guaranteeing public resources, freedoms and rights, and negatively by restricting abuse. Through marketing strategies and other forms of competition, businesses likewise do their best to manipulate conditions in favour of their own market shares. For single media, and for media texts in general, censorship and public service are central issues of debate and struggle between the conflicting interests of civil society, the state and the market. Here, freedom of expression immediately becomes an issue of content and thus of ethics and aesthetics.

For media machines, the situation is somewhat different, since they do not automatically favour one particular kind of text: they are to some extent content-neutral. The existence of telephones or radios does not in itself (at least not in an equally obvious manner) determine which kinds of messages people get access to. On the other hand, they are absolutely necessary for producing and/or consuming media texts. In this case, freedom of expression becomes an issue of access to the technological means of production and consumption, and thus primarily of economic and political considerations.

Access to the means of media consumption (reception) plays a slightly different role than access to means of media production. Cheap record players are different from cheap portable music studios. Cultural policies of distribution focus on issues related to reception, making efforts to let all citizens enjoy the widest range of media texts, through libraries, distribution support and public service broadcasting. Cultural policies of production are instead concerned with control over tools for producing texts. In certain media circuits, the border between the two is blurred, in particular for digital media like telephones, computers and the Internet, where production and reception are densely intertwined through interactive technology.

Media machines are communicative tools with implications for democracy. In a tradition of political information as well as in media research, culture (both art and entertainment) is not seen as politically or materially significant, and the public sphere is effectively reduced to its political branch. This underestimates the role of fun, form and fiction in shaping world-views, identities and social relations. This is the result of a widespread logo- or rather verbocentrism that traditionally prioritizes speech and writing and does not really know how to deal with images and sounds. But there are also important efforts in cultural theory to acknowledge and understand the cultural public sphere, for instance in relation to issues of citizenship.[12]

The Passages project made a close study of how the state and the market were involved in regulating media resources, and of the struggles of power and resistance taking place within and between these systems, as well as vis-à-vis individuals and groups in civil society.[13] We found a complex set of tensions and open struggles between commercial actors, state authorities and individuals and groups in civil society.

There are many kinds of *citizens' rights* in modern society: civil rights (of expression and private ownership), political rights (of democracy), social rights (of economic life resources) and cultural rights (of access to media and cultural forms). In Sweden, almost every citizen has access to television, telephone and radio, around four out of five to video, CD and mobile phones, closely followed by personal computers. The cost of purchasing these machines is also constantly declining. When they become widespread, they also become regarded as a natural or minimal resource of everyday life, both by citizens themselves and by various state authorities. It becomes a right but also a duty to have such machines and to be able to use them.

This can be studied by examining how minimal standards of living are established. In Sweden, colour TV has been seen by the National Board for Consumer Policies as belonging to a minimum life standard for citizens since 1978, to be joined by CD records in 1993. In 1996, video was added but just for families with children, and it is probable that cell-phones and computers will soon be added to the list. These products have been transformed from luxury goods to necessities. This is not only a statistical fact but also a normative demand. It is difficult to practice one's rights as a citizen if one does not have access to television or radio (for public information) and de facto also to the Internet. Citizens can thus not only expect to have access to these media, but they are also expected by state authorities to have such access.

In Sweden, there is a public enforcement service that follows certain rules for what can be expropriated and what may be kept when people are declared bankrupt. Media hardware and software each constitute about 15 per cent each of sales in auctions where confiscated goods are sold. When asking the enforcement staff in Solna about their rules and practices, it turned out that they always let families keep one TV set and (if they had children) one video. There is thus an official right to keep oneself informed through such media machines. This citizen media right is in a way also an obligation, in that state authorities regard such channels as sufficient to reach the whole population in the event of a national emergency.

The commercial market delivers tools for communication, but this delivery is uneven and constricted by inherent limitations in that market system. There is historically a steady trend that large distributors swallow up smaller ones, and today's media hardware market is extremely centralized in this respect. In home electronics, for instance, in 2000, the Expert chain in hi-fi stores had 14 per cent of the Swedish market, 92 per cent was controlled by large chains and only 8 per cent by smaller independent shops. This has effects on how customers can acquire media hardware, what choices they are offered and which social and cultural contexts frame their acquisition, as chain stores are for instance generally less locally specific.

Were there traces in Solna Centre of civil society based resistance against such commercial interests? One example was the maltreatment claims against home electronic companies made to the National Board for Consumer Policies. Between 1995 and 2000 there were 2,700 such cases, more than 70 per cent from private individuals, and three-quarters of these came from male customers. A predominant cause for complaint was misleading marketing, and some discontented consumers have become real activists by publishing lists of bad firms on the Internet and by opening websites for debate and mutual support.[14] Another form of resistance through disobedience is pirating, which is widespread in the case of media software among young people (games, records, films, and so on), but less so in hardware, except for accessories to media machines (phone shells and the like).

In the eighteenth and nineteenth centuries, the early modern public sphere was largely based on communication through print media: papers and books. These remain important media of the political and cultural public spheres of today. Most of the later media additions depend on hardware machines for their use by consumers. Double and triple media add new dimensions to issues of access and of freedom of expression and reception. Media hardware is therefore increasingly important for the development of democratic freedoms and rights. It remains crucial to discuss issues of software content, but media studies need also to analyse these hardware issues. This implies studies of cultural industries, media technology, distribution of hardware machines and their acquisition and use by institutions and individual consumers in everyday life.

CONSUMING MEDIA TECHNOLOGIES

The modern public sphere, including its political and cultural branches, as well as the various alternative public spheres on its margins, nowadays has the character of a networked set of media publics, where people talk and communicate through and with technological machines of many kinds. To access and/or produce different forms of media content (texts), people need access to hardware. This costs money and demands time as well as skills. Though most households have access to many kinds of media, this is not true for all, and many actually cannot afford to buy TV sets and DVD players – instead they rent them from Thorn or other rental firms. This makes their access to these forms of communication vulnerable to fluctuations in the economy. What does it mean to be without these and other media technologies in a late-modern society where all are supposed to be able to relate to new TV programmes, records and websites? People lacking access are excluded from important societal networks of information, discussion, empowerment, enjoyment, imagination and recreation.

This book started with a critique of the one-dimensional view of the consumer as 'economic man'. In this chapter, however, it has become clear that economic aspects also have key importance for cultural, social and political media issues. 'It is not the economic origins of culture that will be presented, but the expression of the economy in its culture,' Walter Benjamin once wrote about his Arcades project.[15] A study of communication hardware offers strong evidence of such expression of the economy in media culture. Studying media as commodities and mediated communication as a consumption process highlights economic aspects that need to be acknowledged in cultural studies. There is no contradiction in combining elements of political economy and critical theory, including ideas from Benjamin and Habermas, with models from hermeneutics and cultural studies. Instead, such combinations help us understand how economy and culture is increasingly intertwined in late-modern societies.

To conclude, this chapter has dealt with two main themes. The complex intertwining of consumption and communication processes in double and triple media is one of them; the issues of access and power is the other. Together, these themes indicate how recent developments of advanced media technologies have demanded a renewed reflection on basic issues of mediated communication – in media research as well as in public debate.

7. INTERMEDIAL CROSSINGS

The previous four chapters have travelled through a wide range of media circuits and looked upon specific issues that each of them raise. The media world can now be put together again. How are acts of communication and of consumption intertwined in media use? Which general patterns and forms of interaction between people and media can be discerned? This chapter connects back to the general themes of media use and consumption introduced in Chapter 2, but goes further to elaborate on distinctions and extensions of previous media studies. It will summarize implications of the previous chapters for the understanding of how media circuits are formed and intertwined in communicative processes of consumption, and thus prepare for the subsequent discussion of temporal and spatial dimensions of these processes.

PASSAGES AND ENCOUNTERS

Media use consists of temporal processes, giving the encounters between media and people a processual character, which can be pursued through consumption chains including linked acts of selection, purchase, use and disposal of media texts and hardware technology. Walter Benjamin inspired a model of passages and flows, which is helpful when trying to understand the mix of communication and consumption in shopping spaces. Instead of freezing media use into still moments of reception, one may investigate the shifting passages through which media and people encounter each other. As was explained in Chapter 2, this means restoring the full arc of consumption acts that has been bifurcated by the division between consumption research and media studies. Acts of media consumption add up to form a multitude of dispersed and mutually interlocking chains of encounters between people and media, each comprising several consecutive phases of shifting length, character and location, and which might be broken off at any stage, as commodities may be transformed into either gifts or public goods, thereby stepping out of commodity consumption and entering one of these alternative spheres of relations between people and media.

Late-modern shopping centres are spaces for *passages* (see Figure 8.1). The inner passages over experiential thresholds have a social and material basis in specific passages of media and people through spaces of consumption, which give rise to a series of encounters where boundaries are transgressed or drawn. The shopping centre is an arena for two interlaced passages: flows of people through spaces and media, and flows of media through spaces and people. Together they give rise to several principal kinds of *encounters* or meetings.[1]

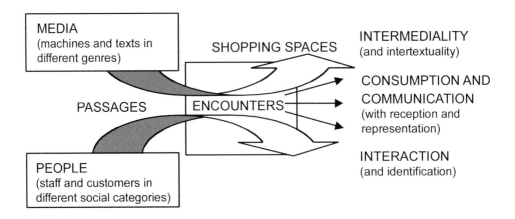

FIG. 7.1. Passages of media and people through consumption spaces.

First of all, people encounter media in processes of *consumption and communication.* Such encounters may sometimes lead to some kind of interpenetration. In processes of reception, media flow through people who make meanings by interpretations of the media texts they use, so that media are incorporated into people's lives, minds and bodies. Conversely, people flow through media as representations, where media texts are populated by symbolic representations of human subjects.

A second general kind of encounter occurs between people in forms of social *interaction.* People meet each other in front of media (talking in front of a newspaper placard) or through them (by using mobile phones). These interactions may lead to mutual interpenetration in the shape of identification, through which individuals influence each other's understandings of themselves and of others.

A third main kind of encounter is the *intermediality* between different technologies and texts in encounters on bookshelves or in the streets. Here again, texts may not only stand beside but also penetrate each other, in processes of intertextuality, where mediated texts are criss-crossed by other texts, through open or candid references.

All these passages and encounters may lead either to transgressing contacts and hybrid fusions or to confrontations and separations. It is due to these encounters that the passages of consumption are communicative practices, since they entail a meaning-making interplay between subjects and texts in contexts, when consumption develops into reception and representation. The spatial framing of these processes in a shopping centre may at first seem self-evident, but quickly turns out to be an extraordinarily ambiguous space, replete with liminal zones and a lack of consensus among people as to where its borders are. Sometimes, it is perceived as a relatively clearly delimited building unit, while at others it may not even be noted as such but only transgressed as if it was a completely transparent and neutral passage rather than a specific space of its own.

It is almost the same with media use: sometimes people using media are acutely aware of these communicative tools, at other moments their use is so routinized that they become almost invisible. This brings to mind the dialectics of hypermediacy and immediacy mentioned in Chapter 2: the phenomenon that media technologies can either become the reflexive focus of their users' attention or function as transparent channels for users who are completely focused on the communication content.[2] A related distinction is that some media use is highly conscious and focused in time and space, while on other occasions media are almost omni-present but scattered across the background of a wide range of social activities. The typical use of a book by reading it is, for instance, much more focused than when reading the message of an advertising poster in the street. There is always a certain degree of fuzziness around all categories, including those of media use and shopping space. Still, people continuously use such categories, and so do we in our research. By not taking them as given, but exploring how they are constructed in everyday practices, the false illusion of their naturalness may be broken.

Communication and consumption are parallel and interrelated processes, each comprising several phases. Consumption studies have tended to focus on purchase rather than use, while media reception studies tend to focus on a particular facet of use: that of reading, watching or listening. Such reception may be seen as the core and 'preferred' activity of media use, but there are also other ways to make use of media commodities where the user does not step into the symbolic universe of media content. By acknowledging the existence of use forms other than reception, and of other consumption phases than that of use, one may get a larger picture and understand the wider contexts that are relevant to understanding how reception in the narrow sense works.[3]

TYPES OF MEDIA CONSUMPTION

The media world is internally structured, but the division lines vary between different contexts and perspectives. Users, salespeople and producers have varying ideas on what constitutes one particular kind of media. Instead of at the outset fixating a definite and limited set of media, we have included all possible kinds of media and media use that could be found within the shopping centre. The conventional limitation of media studies to the press and television misses their interplay with a wider range of communication technologies in the cultural industries as well as in daily life. This brings up questions about what constitutes a communication medium. Again and again, we were reminded of how vague and difficult the very concept of 'a medium' is, and how divergent are people's conceptions of media.

A close reading of classical and contemporary texts in media studies actually offers surprisingly little clarification when it comes to a media definition. There is simply no straightforward consensus on the extent of the concept of media. Much research is still tied to the journalistic practices of producing information and news, while systematically neglecting mass-produced genres like entertainment, fiction and games, as well as interpersonal communication through phone, post or computer networks, or interactive/productive media uses such as photography or web pages. There is generally no real theoretical justification for this limitation, which is rather based on historical and conventional links, and the interests of certain media industries and media researchers. This fact makes more general studies of mediated communication to a large extent absent in media and communication studies, relegated to other disciplines and fields like sociology, ethnology, anthropology, literary 'media history' or separate departments for digital media.[4] A more inclusive concept of media offers a better chance to see how specific media – including those favoured by conventional media studies – function in a wider context in a society like our own, where all media forms in practice are closely interrelated.

It is thus only possible to make a heuristic and provisional division of communication technologies into a set of media circuits. Even though differentiations between main types of media and key phases of communication and consumption are constructed, context-bound and changing, such distinctions are routinely made at all levels. Media industries and research have conventional ways to define and differentiate media types. We have shown in previous chapters how these boundaries – both the external ones around what may function as media and the internal ones between different media – are challenged by technical, social and cultural transformations, in particular by the intermedial flows and hybrids that have been intensified by the development of digital and telecom technology. Still, such divisions are regularly (and often unconsciously) made by all the actors involved, relating to shifting forms of production, distribution and consumption. The divisions made by market actors at the point of purchase form a particularly influential prism in the process of communication – a hub where the various actors meet and negotiate their shifting differentiations, and where the interests of producers and consumers are balanced through ongoing processes of negotiation. In these processes, there are certain *stabilizing* mechanisms, tending to fix boundaries and keep media circuits apart. The distribution of media commodities on different specialized stores and their competitive division of the market between them is one such stabilizing mechanism. But there are also *mobilizing* mechanisms that tend to mix and hybridize media circuits. These will be discussed in the next section.

Our overview started with the oldest mass media: printed books and journals, with written words in focus, but also including graphic designs, photos and other pictorial forms. It continued with another classical circuit that is partly integrated in the press but also has an existence of its own, that of photos, posters, postcards and other printed or digital images. It is at once obvious that there is a grey zone between them, where the balance between images and words is more even. The inclusion of images in books and magazines, and of words in various kinds of pictures, is a mobilizing force that blurs these borders. The separate organization of networks for selling books and photos on the other hand tends to stabilize their distinction. The third circuit added was a further extension to other kinds of audio-visual media, including sounds and/or moving pictures. Again, there are many overlaps with the previous circuits, balanced by separating forces in the sales departments of the shopping centre. Finally, the focus on media hardware cut across the previous circuits while also pointing out a wider set of media types such as telephones or computers that are not primarily used for consuming mass-produced contents but rather are intended for producing one's own texts and interacting with others.

All media may be used for very different purposes. First, there is the standard mass communication pattern of making messages, reproducing them on (more or less) a mass scale and sending them to their consumers, who then receive them and use them according to their own circumstances. Both individual and collective actors are involved in all phases of such transmission chains of dissemination and reception. Individual artists as well as large media corporations produce and distribute such messages, and they are used by single persons and families as well as by large social institutions, including shops and whole shopping centres. John Durham Peters has outlined the complex history of communication as a tension between dialogue and dissemination, and different media have historically been developed with one or the other focus, even though all of them may be used in both ways.[5] *Transmission* (the transfer of messages from sender to receiver) is the main function involved in dissemination processes of the mass media, but there are also elements of individual *consultation* (where people look for specific information, for instance in libraries or on the Internet). Other uses of media technologies are for *surveillance* and *registration*, whereby individuals willingly or unwillingly supply information to central archives of various kinds. A third set of uses includes *dialogues* between individuals and groups. Such dialogues may be truly mutual and open forms of communicative action, but they are more typically framed by unequal power relations and include aspects of coercion and strategic action.[6] Each media circuit allows for many variants and combinations of these communicative forms, and specifically in new digital multimedia, these forms are notoriously mixed. With a wired pc, one can switch continuously between fetching and reading prefabricated texts, writing one's own texts, editing images, filling in forms and interacting with others.

Thus, the dynamic sets of media circuits are intersected by equally complex types of communication. When processes of communication and media use are seen as processes of consumption, a further set of main types can be discerned. As was shown in previous chapters, each phase of consumption runs at a different place and pace for different sets of media and people. Some phases are fast, others slow; some are located in public places, others at home. Also, the forms of consumption differ. Media (texts as well as machines) can be bought, hired, borrowed, stolen, self-made or received as gifts. Some media are sold as *commodities*, owned as private property for the intended direct communicative use or transformed into items for collecting. Others are supplied as common *public goods*, for instance as library loan or as free public service broadcast. Yet others are transferred as interpersonal *gifts*. Media and mediated texts move in and out between such consumption forms, and again many combined forms are found, such as 'free offers' in shops or libraries' annual sales of unwanted books.

Those media commodities that are sold and used in discrete units may be called '*simple*': books, journals and printed pictures. Other media are '*double*' in that their use requires a combination of software (texts) and hardware (decoding machines):

radio, television, records, videos, telephones and computers. Sales may be organized by the piece (books) or through some kind of subscription (journals, television). Among double media, the software units may be packaged as things (materially separable units, like tapes or records) or as flows (as with broadcast media). Some such differentiations between single/double, piecemeal/subscription and thing/flow media are relatively fixed across time and space, but there is rarely a purely physical and thus universal determination here. The consumption forms of different media are always the result of historical processes where technical, economic, social and cultural factors combine. They may also be variable between countries and between instances. Intricate social conventions regulate how media circulate as various kinds of commodities, common goods, loans, private gifts and self-produced use values. All these variants can be further explored and systematized only with careful attention to the temporal processes of intersecting acts of consumption. Their significance is lost or misrepresented when consumption research is reduced to studies of shopping, and when media reception research focuses exclusively on how media texts are interpreted.

Media use is a process that involves multiple triads of people relating to other people and confronting interconnected symbolic artefacts in multifarious spatial and social settings. Mediated culture is composed of such signifying composites of subjects, texts and contexts that produce identities, meanings and power structures. The complexity of such processes is multiplied by the fact that they are never confined to one single individual, artefact and context, but instead take place in an ongoing temporal flow of intersecting triangles, where intersubjectivity, intertextuality and intercontextuality are always present within the signifying act.

It is common to identify communication as a linear chain sender → text ← receiver, based on a straightforward dichotomy of production and reception. To some extent, this fits commercial commodity production, but cultural practices in general are better analysed as plural hermeneutical triads of subjects–texts–contexts. It is the commodity form that institutionally and experientially separates production from reception. However, such chains of transmission are always integrated into more complex interactions between consuming users, mediators and producers. All these actors move in and out of each of various positions that are often but not always institutionally separated into different times and spaces. From a subject-centred perspective, people move through spaces (contexts) and encounter and use media (texts). Interpretations start by differentiating texts out of contexts – perceiving them as texts in the first place, out of the more or less chaotic flow of things and signs – and then relating them again to each other in acts of interpretation. From a context-centred perspective, it is subjects and texts that move as floating objects inside spaces. And from a text-centred perspective, texts move between subjects in contexts in chains of transmission.

INTERLACED MEDIA CIRCUITS

An expanded media concept makes visible how media circuits are both kept apart and interconnected in intertextual, intersubjective and intercontextual practices.

There are several key forms of intermediality. The Harry Potter phenomenon may be used as an example here. At the time of our research, these popular books for children had a marked presence in the whole shopping centre, and it was not only the books themselves that were marketed and displayed in the bookstores. The films were first shown in the cinema and then sold in the video store, and CDs were sold with the film music. An informant had heard the Stockholm Philharmonics play this music in their concerts, thus contributing to the ongoing blurring of the high/low divide in the hierarchy of cultural commodities. Postcards and posters relating to Harry Potter were found in the Gallerix store, and the bookstore also had pencil boxes and notebooks with Potter imagery. Reviews and articles relating to this phenomenon were found in papers, radio and television. Various fashion accessories built on the popularity of Harry Potter: pockets for mobile phones, toy cameras and phones, backpacks and sweets, children's clothes and jewellery – all these were not themselves as such media commodities but they were media-related commodities that certainly testified to the unavoidable popularity of the phenomenon and were drawn into its wide circle of use. Such a phenomenon seemed to cross all intermedial borders, highlighting the interconnectedness of the whole media world.

The Danish book market expert Hans Hertel, among others, has found tendencies towards a media symbiosis, suggesting that cultural circuits are increasingly closely connected by a 'media lift', which transports specific works, characters, narratives and genres up or down across various borders and hierarchies that previously seemed relatively stable.[7] Late-modern tendencies toward media convergence are not limited to digital media, though these form a push factor in that process. Coding in digital form enables technical, institutional and textual fusions, creating new multimedia but also new intermedial connections. We saw numerous kinds of interplay among media in the shopping centre.[8] Some were intertextual, others extratextual, depending on whether two textual units or two material apparatuses were related to each other. A Harry Potter novel could tell about fateful phone calls or mention a specific film narrative, but it could also just happen to be placed beside a Harry Potter postcard in the bookstore window. Textual connections could in their turn relate to aspects of either form or content, in that either stylistic design or semantic levels were activated. Harry Potter films thus both follow similar formal storyline as the books, but also narrate similar contents about the same characters and events; in other cases it may be only one and not the other aspect that links two texts. A further distinction is between those intermedialities founded on (substantial or formal) similarity and those based on (spatial or functional) proximity between the two media. In practice, however, real media relations are impure mixtures of these main types. For instance, similarity often makes proximity possible – and vice versa.

The interplay between media can occur with a varying degree of intensity and activity, from simple connection, over some kind of exchange, to a more thorough transformation of the media involved. Another distinction may be made according to how symmetric the relation is between the two. The multiplication of these two dimensions results in six main types of intermediality.

1. When two media or media texts are only passively compared to each other without being affected or transformed themselves, there is a relatively simple relation of *grouping*. Media and/or texts may be treated as similar or related in some way, based on their perceived similarity or proximity, or a mixture of them both. One example is when texts are combined into genres according to some principle of affinity, for instance on the shelves of a CD store, a library or in the consumer's home.

2. When both media are activated in a combined action or joint use practice, which still respects their distinct identities, there is some form of multimedial *cooperation*. One example is when texts accompany and fuse with other texts, such as prefaces, commentaries and covers to videos or records, or when films, books, papers, radio and television programmes work as a joint ensemble to push each other in promoting a certain phenomenon, with Harry Potter and Disney film characters as well-known examples.

3. An even more radical (but still symmetric) combination of two previously separate media forms and practices fuses them into a single multimedial hybrid unit. Obvious examples of such *fusion* are of course offered by digital technologies (computers, web phones) in which several previously distinct forms may be seamlessly combined.

4. If fusion is an intense but symmetric combination of two media, *substitution* may be regarded as an equally radical but asymmetric one. CDs may not fully have replaced vinyls, but computers have almost superseded typewriters, and who uses old kinds of duplicating machines when there is the photocopier? On the other hand, several typefaces for the computer mimic those of the old-fashioned typewriter, and the memory of the old techniques thus linger on in the design of the new ones.

5. Cooperation may be regarded as an active kind of grouping, where different media (texts) still remain relatively separate and unchanged as such. It may, however, also include some form of *transfer* where one medium or text more actively engages with, integrates and transforms forms and/or contents from another one. (a) This kind of intermediality may take the form of intertextual references – direct quotations, pastiche works or hidden allusions – to texts deriving from some other medium. (b) A second sub-type consists of translations of whole works, of specific narratives or of more general themes and genres between media: Dracula or the detective genre moving from novels to films to computer games, or images moving from photos to posters. (c) A third category is the remediation processes whereby new media forms imitate older ones, borrowing intratextual (formal) or extratextual (material) characteristics (rather than semantics or narratives) from an older medium.[9]

6. Finally, *thematization* is a kind of asymmetric, hierarchic or reflexive transfer where the active medium explicitly thematizes another medium, based on a symbolic representation of that medium, rather than an imitation of its aspects. There is a range of genres here, from essays of cultural critique and book reviews

in magazines to representations of phones and television in ads or literary fiction, or as material artefacts (sweets, key chains).

The six types are interrelated in that they combine two axes: symmetry and activity. Symmetrical combinations can be radical as in fusion, active but respecting distinctions as in cooperation, or passive as in grouping. Asymmetrical relations can likewise be radical substitutions, active transfers where both media remain distinct, or thematizations where what is transferred does not basically affect the other medium in which it is incorporated. Fusion, cooperation and grouping are symmetrical combinations of media side by side. Substitution, transfer and thematization are asymmetrical relations, where one medium acts on another rather than the reverse.

TABLE 7.1: A Typology of Intermedial Relations

	Symmetric Combinations (A + B)	Asymmetric Relations (A → B)
Transformation	Fusion	Substitution
Exchange	Co-operation	Transfer
Connection	Grouping	Thematization

These six intermedial forms – fusion, substitution, co-operation, transfer, grouping and thematization – are in practice often combined. A border case is when a medium is used to store or spread texts for another medium. When televised films are recorded on video, or when Internet or postal services distribute all kinds of media texts – either as physical units (like books or records) or in digital form for use in various machines (MP3 files or e-books) – this is both active cooperation and a transfer of one media content through another mediating channel. Remediating transfers may further include moments of explicit thematization. And when media texts are accompanied by follow-up stories, advertisements and related commodities like toys or T-shirts, this supplementary circulation extends and intervenes in the reception process, thus affecting the meanings constructed around the primary text and implying a dialectical play of articulation where transfer and cooperation merge. The boundaries between media are continuously crossed in everyday practices; but then, they are also continuously reinforced by more or less subtle demarcations of old or new differences between media circuits.

One should thus not conclude that all intermediality blurs distinctions between media circuits. Some do, but others do not. Magazines and television programs can publish reviews or reports on Harry Potter books and films, without in any way challenging the distinction between these various media circuits as such. On the other hand, a long-term fusion of previously separate communication technologies in the form of computers may possibly erode the boundaries between them – culturally, socially, functionally and institutionally. The transfer of Harry Potter narratives between books and films may for instance make it hard for some readers/viewers to distinguish between them and identify the narrative and its character as either of a literary or a cinematic kind.

Media convergence and media lifts imply an intensified transfer and cooperation between media. When such cooperation is more or less permanently institutionalized, new 'multimedia' arise out of a symbiosis of previously separate media. These multimedia are not new, and neither is the discussion around them. Media have always tended to interact and fuse. Since borders between media circuits are flexible and diffuse, all talk of intermediality is necessarily provisional and spatio-temporally situated. New media are often first perceived and used as hybrid combinations of their predecessors, until the new forms have gained independent status. And all such relations can either be general and typical for whole media groups or genres, or be particular characteristics of individually staged media encounters. The connection between television and video is, for instance, a much more general rule than a specific quotation of a poem in a particular computer game.

On the other hand and at other points in history, one particular medium tends to be differentiated into subsets that may develop into their own full-blown media circuits. The networked computer was first often conceived as one single new medium, whereas nowadays it is increasingly common to conceptualize it as comprising a set of different media, including websites, e-mail, digital games, etc. The historical patterns of transference from one medium to another are often in practice very complex, in that different media influence each other in partial, generically and regionally specific ways at different points of time, so that new media remediate a whole set of older ones, rather than just imitate one particular predecessor.[10] Through historical processes, symbolic modes are articulated with technologies, industries, genres and uses. The connection between printing presses, publishing houses, novels and reading has thus been so institutionalized that it is often perceived as natural and eternal, but it is upheld by a social and material suppression of other combinations that might in principle have created a different kind of media circuitry.

There are practices that differentiate between media circuits and construct them as separate. Such practices of separation counteract other practices of intermediation. Intermediality does not necessarily imply fusion and erasure of borders. Cooperation and transferences may well preserve differences. For instance, distinctions between modalities are upheld in multimedia like film and television through trades union and other institutional forces, and also in digital media and the www, where music, images and texts are carefully kept apart in technical solutions, in spite of their shared reliance on zeros and ones. Schools and universities are one such separating institutional force.

BETWEEN MEDIA

Media circuits thus intersect and interact. Each medium is in itself intrinsically mixed, incorporating elements of others. Media also work closely together in all production and consumption phases, including shopping and use, as well as in their textual formats (CD covers including lyrics and photos, etc.). And they are distributed, sold and used together in bookshops, libraries, and so on. An expanded media concept shows how media circuits are kept apart but also interconnected in communicative practices of various kinds. By not taking received media types for granted, it is possible to see those mechanisms through which media circuits are produced as separate, and then again intermedially combined at all stages and levels, from production to use and from single texts to whole industrial branches.

Cultural studies explore the borderlands of culture and cultural research: between disciplines, universities, countries – and aesthetic fields. Culture and media are increasingly interrelated in late-modern societies, due to mixed processes of culturalization, mediatization and digitalization. These processes also blur established boundaries between media types, creating new and hybrid forms of communication and cultural genres. In particular, digital media technologies have pushed forward trends of convergence between industries, between genres and between forms of media use and cultural practice. In response to such developments, and parallel to the spread of the concept of intertextuality, concepts like multimedia, hypermedia, multimodality and intermediality have triggered new forms of cultural and media research that crosses inherited disciplinary and generic borders. Both culture and cultural studies thus increasingly move between media.

8. LAYERS OF TIME

Media are primarily tools for communicating across time and space. Media practices are structured along temporal and spatial orders, but they also structure time as well as space, making them into meaningfully ordered sociocultural coordinates of human experience. Let us begin with time, investigating both several kinds of temporal frames to media use and the modes in which it creates and recreates temporalities.

First, media use is always located in time, bound to time. It is organized in daily, weekly, annual, generational and life-span cycles, slightly different for each kind of medium – and for each individual. I read the paper for breakfast, start working at the computer in the morning, listen to radio news at lunch, make some afternoon phone calls, listen to a CD and watch evening television and then read a book at bedtime. Media correlate to my daily life rhythms, and even help organize them so that I am in phase with the surrounding world. Also, each act of media consumption takes its definite time. Watching a poster or postcard image may take just an instant, while reading a book, watching a movie or following a soap opera occupies a very different time span. Media consumption acts are processual practices that cannot be reduced to those focal acts of reception alone. They are prolonged and dispersed chains of encounters between people and media, comprising at least four consecutive phases of shifting length, character and location, and which might be broken off at any stage, from selection over purchase and use to disposal. Some phases are fast and brief, others are slow and prolonged or deferred.

Second, the processes of media consumption that form multifarious temporal chains of acquisition and use also affect time at all levels, from present moments to historical memories that shape identities. Media represent and recreate different times: depict night and day, summer and winter, past and present, as virtual times. Nostalgia is only one obvious example of this mechanism whereby mediated and mediating texts colour and reconstruct memories, history and individual as well as collective identities. There is no sharp limit here (as elsewhere) between reproduction and production. Media not only represent 'real' time and afford it specific meanings by reinforcing certain cultural associations. They clearly also construct and invent time, in particular through the collaboration between media time (the temporal processes of media use) and mediated time (temporalities represented in media texts). One example is the way Solna Centre constructed the annual seasons mentioned in Chapter 1. This indoor place was not strongly tied to the external seasons and weather conditions, but could at least stretch the temporalities of the surrounding world within its own walls, with the aid of ventilation, light, decoration, ads and events. For instance, public communication from the centre constructed the seasons in such a way that winter hardly existed at all, while instead Christmas was treated as one long season of its own, from mid-October to early February.[1]

HISTORICIZING TIME

Definitions of space and time are always interdependent in social life, as is reflected in the modern notion of 'time zones' which divide the common world time – created by the agreement to impose Greenwich Mean Time in 1884 – into spatially separated local times. But as contemporary conceptions of digital real time – or 'timeless time', as Castells designates it – testifies to, even the spatial borders between these time zones are easily transgressed by the time–space comprehension of contemporary media.[2] From such a perspective, time is literally nullified and becomes more and more independent of spatial distances. However, media have always contributed to both preserving and reducing time. Script was the first media in which time could be stored and hence became a prevailing site of historical memory. This is still reflected in the double meaning of the word 'history', referring to both the lived past and its form of representation, from stories to historiography. As time incessantly moves, it demands a medium to 'preserve' it: a technology for the storage, transmission and processing of information. In this way media also contribute to the repetition of the past, which becomes particularly obvious in currents like postmodernism that resurrect art formulas that have been considered out of date.

Our combination in this project of contemporary ethnographic fieldwork and an historical perspective inspired by Walter Benjamin and Paul Ricoeur is an interdisciplinary attempt to better understand the temporal dimensions of media use. To Benjamin, time and history were central but also highly problematic concepts. He did cherish 'that anamnestic intoxication in which the flâneur goes about the city' as well as the arcane practices of collecting as 'a form of practical memory' by which the collector 'takes up the struggle against dispersion'.[3] But these acts of precious remembering serve mainly to rescue past phenomena 'from the catastrophe represented very often by a certain strain in their dissemination, their "enshrinement as heritage". – They are saved through the exhibition of the fissure within them. – There is a tradition that is catastrophe.'[4] It is the institutionalized forms of cultural heritage that critical remembering resists, and it can only be done in flashing moments. 'The true picture of the past flits by. The past can be seized only as an image which flashes up at the instant when it can be recognized and is never seen again.'[5] Benjamin sees history as a fatal struggle:

> Whoever has emerged victorious participates to this day in the triumphal procession in which the present rulers step over those who are lying prostrate. According to traditional practice, the spoils are carried along in the procession. They are called cultural treasures, and a historical materialist views them with cautious detachment … There is no document of civilization which is not at the same time a document of barbarism. And just as such a document is not free of barbarism, barbarism taints also the manner in which it was transmitted from

one owner to another. A historical materialist therefore dissociates himself from it as far as possible. He regards it as his task to brush history against the grain.[6]

Media practices are deeply involved in this struggle. It is through media of storage and transmission that the victorious cultural heritage is canonized, but it is also there that it may be attacked. This has key implications for critical practice. 'Progress has its seat not in the continuity of elapsing time but in its interferences – where the truly new makes itself felt for the first time, with the sobriety of dawn.'[7] With affinities to philosopher Ernst Bloch, Benjamin worked like a detective, tracing suppressed utopian germs of a better future to the dead past. In a striking passage, he juxtaposes the trace with the aura – a central concept in his analysis of how modern media technology erodes traditional art values: 'The trace is appearance of a nearness, however far removed the thing that left it behind may be. The aura is appearance of a distance, however close the thing that calls it forth. In the trace, we gain possession of the thing; in the aura, it takes possession of us.'[8] This alludes to a set of superimposed dialectics of distance and proximity, of dream and awakening and of past and future that may be further elaborated by using Paul Ricoeur's ideas of how traces in the form of documents and monuments bind historical narratives to the prefigurations of past events and differentiate them from fictional stories.[9]

Benjamin conceived of time as a passage – of time itself and of the human effort to grasp it, which can only be accomplished in passing, that is, in a sudden and indirect way. This notion of passage leads on the one hand to the decline of the art-work aura, a phenomenon encompassing presence, nearness and distance in time as well as space, and on the other hand to the repetition of history in the midst of the evolution of modernity. Benjamin gives media a crucial role in both these processes, although more prominently so in his writing on the former than the latter subject.

Photography and film incorporate time into the production of the work of art in a more direct way than the preceding visual arts, according to Benjamin. Film in particular introduced new spatio-temporal orders by releasing visual perception from the limits of the human eye, speeding up or slowing down action sequences in time and assembling 'multiple fragments' of reality 'under a new law'.[10] Benjamin used film as a primary example of how media display and structure time and space. Technical devices like mechanical reproduction and digitalization have an overall effect on media as well as on socially anchored spatio-temporal orders, not least by creating new opportunities to store and reproduce the past. The past available to the present has successively grown and expanded by the storage capacities of successive media inventions like script, photography, film, phonographs, video, DVD and computers.[11] Although those media for a time stand as symbols for modernity and change (and in some cases even for the future) they also function as impediments to forgetting the past, actually recording every trace of visual and oral sense data from it, leaving only subordinate sense memories like smell and taste to oblivion. In this way the development of media technologies fosters a sense of the past that is consistent with Benjamin's definition of the modern as 'the new in the context of what has always already been there'.[12] From a different perspective, Bruno Latour has suggested that 'we have never been modern', since reality has never adapted to the contours of a universal rupture dividing historical time into pre-modern and modern times. Rather, modernity works as a conceptual tool dividing the present into a now and a then, that is, defining which parts of it belong to the modern and the pre-modern world respectively.[13]

'It is the present that polarizes the event into fore- and after-history,' writes Benjamin.[14] He regards modernity as an endless renewal of 'primal history'; where traces of archaic and pre-modern practices survive even in the most modern times, but in a way that often marks a radical break in their form and content.[15] This is reflected in the conception of time itself. Since the advent of contemporary modernity in the nineteenth century, the social control of time has expanded rapidly and established the universal spatio-temporal order of the homogeneous and empty time of the clock. Within this order, time turns into an eternal passage, without internal meaning or goal. Hence the need to fill it with 'dream-images' or 'collective wish images', often expressed by archaic or pre-modern symbols that are like mirrors in which modernity sees itself. Through these dream-images, the empty 'space-time' (*Zeitraum*) of modernity becomes a 'dreamtime' (*Zeit-traum*), a time one can awaken from but also project upon times to come.[16] Things that are comprehended as lost or buried in the past feed dreams of tomorrow. Paradoxically, the collective wish images of modernity that break with its recent past are themselves derived from a more distant archaic or pre-modern past. Hence there is no utopia without nostalgia, and vice versa.

This makes the concept of the present equally paradoxical, since it does not coincide with the now-being or the presence of the now: 'One could speak of the increasing concentration (integration) of reality, such that everything past (in its time) can acquire a higher grade of actuality than it had in the moment of its existing.'[17] To Benjamin there is a dialectical relationship between now-being (*Jetztsein*), the presence of the now (*Jetztzeit*) and the present (*Gegenwart*), that breaks the atomic character of the 'now' and makes it to something other than a simple or uncomplicated moment in the unfolding of time and history. But Benjamin also stresses that the embodied now-time or 'the now-being of "the present time"' is more important to the modern time-consciousness and its conception of history than the homogeneous and empty clock-time: 'History is the subject of a structure whose site is not homogeneous, empty time, but time filled by the presence of the now (*Jetztzeit*).'[18]

THE TEMPORAL DUALISM OF MODERNITY

Benjamin is not alone in pointing to this temporal dualism of modernity. Since the end of the nineteenth century, the gap between standardized world time and individual time experience has been a recurrent theme in the philosophical and sociological discourse on modernity. The modern sense of time is organized by a basic dualistic structure of abstract versus concrete time. Contrary to the abstract world time, concrete time is heterogeneous and determined by social practices, filling the empty form of abstract time with content, at the same time as the latter directs and frames the former.

The embodied now-time of each corporeal human being is constantly integrated into different layers of abstract and concrete time. For instance, work is separated from leisure in terms of time, structuring time and imposing a spatio-temporal order onto everyday life. It is also crucial for consumption and media use, since they are primarily regarded as leisure activities, though people do not always experience them as such, since they often become routinized habits.[19] For instance, 'prime-time television' refers to the time when most people have the best opportunity to watch TV, but also testifies to the way they can experience their habitual media practices as a break with the ordinary duties and routines of everyday life. 'Prime-time' shows how media are both structured by and contribute to structuring people's comprehension of time. That structuring process is far from uniform. The uncoupling of time from space is a salient feature of contemporary media like mobile phones, portable computers and CD or DVD players, that allow people to be reached by mediated contents anywhere and at any time, in a way that also makes it easy to transgress the long-established spatio-temporal borders between work and leisure.

But media also structure time on what might be called a basic syntactical level. At this level it is often hard to distinguish the material or technical properties of a medium from its cultural impact. Media could roughly be categorized as either linear or non-linear. Many forms of mediated communication rest on a linear order of time, where some things have to precede others. Script has the same basic linear character as speech, but at the same time opens for non-linearity, in that it is possible to go back and forth when reading. The latter opportunity is also indirectly present in speech, for example by referring to what has been said earlier. This shows that the distinction between linearity and non-linearity in media communication is better conceptualized as a question of more-or-less rather than either-or. Nevertheless, it is quite obvious that, for example, a book has an intended beginning and an end, whereas a photo or a painting does not. A photo does not impose an equally imperative syntactical time order on those who watch it as does a book on its readers. Computer media in particular tend to mix linear and non-linear syntactical time structures by combining different forms of symbolic communication: texts, pictures, film, sound and music.

The linear syntactical time structure of speech and script is also reflected in narrative, in terms of the episodic dimension that unfolds itself between its beginning and its end and that one has to follow to reach its conclusion. This linear representation of time can be inverted in the appropriation of the narrative, in the sense that it is possible to look at it retrospectively when it has reached its conclusion and recollect its beginning in the light of its ending, but it remains a basic structuring principle in much human communication. Narrative is a basic human form for representing and comprehending the past, the present and the future. Hence it is also a basic tool for transcending the present, either backwards to the past or forward to the future, in line with a linear or 'natural' order of time. This function is mainly fulfilled by media, whether in documentary or fictional genres. But narrative is also crucial for the mediated representation of the present. For example, media news requires a narrative mode in order to be comprehensible. Although this mode may be rudimentary – possibly promoting a fragmented view of reality – it is always present in mediated displays of news, up to the point where newspapers, tabloids or television channels promise to disclose 'the full story' to the public.

'We tell stories because in the last analysis human lives need and merit being narrated,' writes Ricoeur.[20] According to Ricoeur the relationship between time and narrative is circular and accomplished by a threefold mimetic process of prefiguration (mimesis I), configuration (mimesis II) and refiguration (mimesis III), in which a prefigured time 'becomes a refigured time through the mediation of a configured time'.[21] The key to narrative refiguration of time is the 'emplotment' – the opening of the world of the plot – constitutive to the second moment (configuration in mimesis II) of the transfiguration. The refiguration of time results from the plot's capability to organize dispersed actions and events into a unified course and thereby transgress the order of 'natural' or 'real' time. In this way, a creative process of mimesis is at the heart of the perception of time, where the prefigured understanding of the world and the composition of a work are confronted with a reader, whose reading is a refiguration of the configured work.

All temporalities represented in contemporary media are in one way or another mediated by narratives. In this sense mediated time, that is, the temporalities represented in the media, becomes an instant of the historical time Ricoeur designates as a 'third time' and a bridge between lived and universal time.[22] Historical time 'cosmologizes lived time and humanizes cosmic time' and thereby re-inscribes 'the time of narrative into the time of the world'.[23]

The past must be mediated if it is to become history. Ricoeur mentions the calendar, the successions of generations, archives, documents and traces as 'connectors of lived and universal time', mediating and refiguring the past into history. Calendars, archives and documents are clearly media for the storage of time. But also human bodies function as media in the transmittance of memories of the past to ever-new generations, while traces of the past in monuments and ruins also work as mediating signs for something that has existed, but no longer is.

Media constantly contribute to create and maintain 'the third time' of history as a bridge between concrete (lived) and abstract (universal) time in modernity, on the one hand by their capability to store information, and on the other hand by being major vehicles for narratives. Both these capacities are in turn dependent on and change with the historical development of the media themselves. One important trait of this development is that the degree of reproducibility that media allow has increased considerably since the nineteenth century. This increase has had far-reaching implications, not only for the commodification and opening of new consumer markets for symbolic goods, but also for the reproduction of the past in the present and thus for the mediation of history.

The representation of the past and the future in the present is a central concern for Benjamin's reflections on time and history. As first pointed out by St Augustine, the human conception of the present is actually threefold, since it also harbours the presence of the past and of the future.[24] The present is threefold, combining the now of the past (*memoria*), the now of the current (*attentio*) and the now of the becoming (*expectatio*). It holds together three directions of time, equivalent to the capacity of the human mind to have memories (of the past), be attentive (to the present) and have expectations (of the future). History and its future course are always seen from the horizon of the ongoing present. Even if historical time works as a 'third time' that bridges the dualism between concrete and abstract time, it is thus itself fettered to an ever passing and ongoing present; or 'filled by the presence of the now', as Benjamin writes.[25] Therefore, history is always a construction, albeit not a totally arbitrary one, and every representation of it becomes a 'text written in invisible ink'.[26] One way of making this ink more visible is to look at how history is used and works in the present. Benjamin hoped to accomplish this by making the 'thirst for the past' of the modernity of the nineteenth century the 'principle object' of his *Arcades Project*.[27] This 'thirst' is still present in contemporary modernity, not least in consumption and the media.

Before turning to this subject, the main time layers can be depicted as in Figure 8.1.

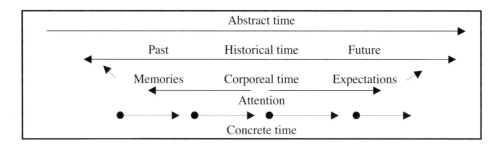

FIG. 8.1 Layers of time.

Media are related to different time layers in contemporary modernity. Their relationship to time is further complicated by the fact that they both structure and are being structured by time. This two-directed process of structuring is at the heart of the human conception of abstract or universal time, as the clock could be regarded as its basic medium. But the most important temporal function of contemporary media in a more narrow sense is to mediate between abstract and concrete time. This makes the modern notion of time dualistic and heterogeneous, so that different kinds of 'time arrows' criss-cross each other in late-modern everyday life. Abstract time, conceived as 'real' or 'natural' time, has the character of a straight linear 'time arrow' pointing to the future, while concrete time – the time inscribed in the social order of action – though having the same irreversible linear character, is punctuated by changes in social practices. Memories and expectations of now-being unlock the doors to historical time, which gives a sense and meaning to abstract and concrete time but cannot be approached without the mediating role of media narrative. It is narrative and media that give the 'time arrow' of history a double direction, pointing both backwards to the past and forwards to the future. The embodied now-time opens itself up to the remembrance of the past and the expectation of the future. Attention to the present 'here and now' is a corporeal time perception, but always filtered through memories of the past and expectations of the future.

Whereas *media time* – the temporal processes of media use – is primarily related to the concrete and abstract time, *mediated time* – the temporalities represented in media texts – is mainly related to the historical time layer. Whether based on facts or fiction, media narratives are the main contemporary entrances to history, but also give a direction to the future course of history, which in a sense is always fictitious since it is genuinely unknown.

Mediated time is related to the material, technical and syntactical traits of different kinds of media. These traits primarily work on the immediate experience of the embodied now-time that may be perceived as 'long', 'short', 'slow' or 'fast'. Raymond Williams has given a good example of this capability of media to influence the ex-perience of time by pointing to the flow created by broadcasting and especially tele-vision.[28] Altering the temporal sequence from an emphasis on programme to flow, which became a common feature with the start of MTV in the early 1980s, brings the time-experience of television close to some aspects of the conception of abstract and concrete time. De-emphasizing the discrete time units of programmes gives the time-experience of television approximately the same flow as the perception of pure abstract time, passing without being punctuated by qualitatively changing contents. But contrary to the slowness and emptiness of abstract time, the television flow rather speeds up and fills up time. This makes the viewing of television less dependent of any single time layer, since it is possible to join in and float with it at any time, day or night.

In summary, there are at least five important ways to approach the relationship between time and media. First, media contribute to the coupling and uncoupling of *time and space*. Second, *abstract time* works as a steering-medium for when and where media are used. Third, *concrete time* concerns the way media time is correlated to other time structures in everyday life, for example the alteration of work and leisure. Fourth, media narratives are used to refigure *historical time*. And fifth, the material, technical and syntactical traits of the media shape the experience of *corpo-real time*.

CONSUMPTIVE AND MEDIATED TIME

Consumption and media use belong to the routines of everyday life. Habitual routinization underpins a cyclical notion of time, grounded in the repetition of activ-ities or events. Although basically linear, both abstract and concrete time can easily be adapted to cyclical notions, for example through the way clock time repeats itself within a twenty-four hour cycle. There is no fundamental contradiction between linear and cyclical time.

Routinization often gives day-to-day practices a mundane or even dull quality. This is in stark contrast to when historical time repeats itself, whether in the form of nostalgia, ceremonials or regular outbreaks of war. The comprehension of historical time is to a large extent a product of rehearsal. This is manifested by the celebrations of historical jubilees, memorials, festivals and anniversaries that stabilize collective memory, but also by a more general 'thirst for the past' in contemporary modernity, for instance in medieval role-playing games or historical theme parks for tourism, which offer fictionalized ways to relive the past. 'History' has become a profitable target of the so-called experience economy in recent years, as a strategy to 'enrich' and 'theme' the experiences that it offers its customers.[29] This is not a brand-new trait in the social sphere of consumption, but it is today unfolded in more conscious and organized ways than before.

One example is the architectural construction of Solna Centre, which according to its architect was partly inspired by the nineteenth-century arcades in Paris. The arcade building style, once developed from ancient prototypes to represent modernity, have nowadays turned into references for historical places of consumption, used as retrospective anchorage in department stores and shopping centres all over the world. 'The first structures made of iron served transitory purposes: covered markets, railroad stations, exhibitions,' noted Benjamin. 'What was once functional and transitory, however, begins today, at an altered tempo, to seem formal and stable.'[30] By such historical references, a shopping centre inscribes itself in a historical context. But this way to '*cite* history' also tears the historical object 'from its context', as Benjamin puts it.[31] As mentioned in Chapter 1, these citations rewrite local history within an overall frame of popular culture and nostalgia. In Solna this even includes an historical relocalization of the city's well-known soccer team, AIK, which has its own supporter shop in the shopping centre and whose legendary players are depicted in its wall paintings. Originally founded in the middle of Stockholm in 1891 and considered a Stockholm team for a long time, the club relocalized itself in 1937 when the newly built Råsunda stadium in Solna became its home field. This relocalization, which will be further discussed in the next chapter, is buried in the images of local history that flash by in the centre and its supporter shop, according to an account of AIK as always having been a local team. This reconstruction of local history shows how consumptive practices contribute to reconstruct the experience of time and history, embedded in larger social, cultural and political contexts. It is a matter of reconstruction rather than construction, since there remain bounds to pre-existing, sometimes conflicting, historical narratives.

One basic element in the construction of consumption time is marked by the opening and closing hours of the shopping centre. The city centre, on the other hand, never 'closes', although individual shops and other activities all over town have varying opening hours. The fixed opening times in Solna Centre therefore install a strong temporal regime in the city, dividing concrete time into two distinct layers, shopping time and city time, which do not completely overlap, although both are related to the abstract time of the clock. The shopping centre also constructs its own calendar of seasons that deviates from the 'natural' seasons, but resembles the ecclesiastical year. This resemblance stems from the importance that both Christian religion and commerce attribute to feasts like Easter and Christmas, and may be interpreted as a commercial reconstruction of the ecclesiastical year. Commercial reconstructions of traditional calendar time are widespread around the world, but also locally specific, depending on a combination of natural and cultural conditions.[32] For instance, the sharply marked changes of seasons in the Nordic zone make midsummer a highly celebrated feast, with historical connections reaching far back to the days of hunters and gatherers, and to the old agrarian calendar that has partly been incorporated into the ecclesiastical year.

Christmas, Easter and Midsummer Day are the focal points of the seasonality displayed in Solna Centre, as in most other commercial spaces in Nordic countries. However, from these focal points the seasonality of the shopping centre deviates from the culturally defined and officially proclaimed 'natural' or meteorological seasons of the year. The most striking deviation is the absence or marginalizing of the winter season in the calendar of the shopping centre. According to the astronomical definition of the seasons in the Nordic hemisphere, winter starts on 21 December and ends on 20 March. There are, however, few traces of this annually recurring three-month cycle of winter within the shopping centre, where it is replaced by Christmas and spring as symbolic focal points of commerce and consumption. Christmas tends to start by the end of October in the shopping centre, when expectations of the Christmas holidays are displayed through Christmas trees, gifts, greetings cards, carols, advertising, and so on, and lasts approximately until mid February, when Christmas sales, after-greetings and the collecting of disposed Christmas trees come to an end. When that happens, spring has already begun its symbolic entry into the shopping centre, with the display of phenomena like the new spring fashions, advertising slogans that proclaim that the brighter season of spring has arrived, and expectations of the summer to come.

In this way the astronomical calendar, with its four equally long seasons of spring, summer, autumn and winter, is reconstructed as a commercial calendar, where spring lasts approximately four months, summer three months, autumn two months, and Christmas three months. Here, the dark, cold and snowy or slushy winter tends to disappear from the customers' views, with delimited exceptions in retail stores for winter sports, games or clothes. The fact that this commercial calendar is supported by advertising, and especially the overall and trans-national mediation of Christmas, points to its universality in the late-modern world, even though different societies and cultures perform it in particular versions.

This is just one instance of how the corporeal experience of shopping is surrounded by mediated reconstructions of consumption time that derive from layers of abstract, concrete and historical time, in ways that make those reconstructions unnoticeable and quasi-natural. The commercial calendar of consumptive seasonality is a remediation of time, juxtaposed to many other mediations of time that affect contemporary practices of media consumption. Media are at the core of late-modern time comprehensions, as technologies mediating syntactical structures and narratives, and as founders of everyday routines. Their tools for time management range from filofaxes and digital electronic almanacs to media equipment with timesaving properties, including DVD recorders with time settings. Such tools give a sense of an increased flexibility in the management of abstract time, increasing people's capability to adapt their media time to other time layers, at the same time as the homogeneous quality of the abstract clock time loosens some of its grip. The 'time-shifting' property of DVD recorders is also a good example of how media use is both structured by and structure time and space. At a more basic level, this dual-time structure of media use on the one hand lets media impose a certain order on daily routines, but on the other hand makes media use dependent on such routines.

Media use is habituated through the daily, weekly, monthly and annual periodicity of media contents: the morning and evening papers, the weekly and monthly journals, the seasonal TV serials and annual televised events. *The Donald Duck Christmas Show* broadcast by Swedish public service television at precisely 3 p.m. on Christmas Eve for the last forty years is an example of the latter. First broadcast in 1963, the programme has established itself as an intrinsic part of the Swedish Christmas tradition – a true 'invention of tradition'.[33] Some older traditions are less obviously 'invented' and commonly regarded as stretching back for many centuries, but even though the Swedish Christmas Donald Duck tradition is commonly understood as 'invented', it nevertheless serves as a binding tradition. Traditions are increasingly dependent on communication media.[34] Although often seen as a threat to traditional ways of living, media contribute to maintain, reconstruct and 'invent' new traditions. The same goes for history in general, which must also always be transmitted from each generation to the next in order to become part of collectively preserved memories, with media as essential tools. Media prolong the past into the present and save it from vanishing.

New media technologies make possible new ways to actualize history and collective memories in the present. An example is the recycling of voices of deceased popular singers on recordings with contemporary artists, for instance Natalie Cole singing duet on recordings with her long-since deceased father Nat King Cole. But media also constantly revive collective or public memories of the recent past, illustrating Benjamin's effort in the *Arcades Project* to 'fix the image of history in its most insignificant existence, at the same time keeping its refuse'.[35] Collective memories that fade when gone out of fashion live on unnoticed and refused, balancing between recognized public history and mere private memories, until they are revived by media retrospectives or flashbacks, whether in nostalgia or as 'new' retro-styles. Fredric Jameson has critically argued that the electronic media and the commodity culture of late capitalism have founded 'a new and original situation in which we are condemned to seek History by way of our own pop images and simulacra of that history, which itself remains forever out of reach'.[36] Benjamin instead emphasized the possibility of awakening from recent history. If rejecting what Jameson calls the simulacra of history, Benjamin feared that one also rejects an important source of utopian energy in the present. One has rather to 'pass through and carry out *what has been* in remembering the dream! – Therefore, remembering and awakening are most intimately related. Awakening is namely the dialectical, Copernican turn of remembrance.'[37]

By reconstructing and recycling 'what has been', the dream world of popular culture media and commodities creates a potential gap between memories of the recent past and the way it is depicted, which may give rise to what Benjamin referred to as a 'flash of awakened consciousness'.[38] The same holds for the fantasies of the future that become a part of the contemporary dream world. Strivings for change, emancipation and real progress are constantly projected on the future in the present and become something one would eventually wake up from in due time. In this way, the corporeal 'here and now' of media consumption is constantly intersected by a 'dream time' that harbours dreams of the past and of the future. This 'dream time' has also got the structure of a threefold present and direction of time, towards what has been, what is, and what will be. These directions of time are reflected by mediated time – the temporalities represented in the media – but also in the marketing of commercial 'dream time'.

NARRATING THE PRESENT, PAST AND FUTURE

In the same way as we perceive ordinary dreams as narratives, the dreams on display in contemporary media are narratively structured. Narratives are at the core of human existence, making sense of people's lives and giving meaning to events. They tell people who they are, where they come from, where they are going and what is happening in the world. The ability to tell and understand stories is a basic existential for humans' comprehension of themselves, others and reality. This involves a temporal understanding in the form of 'and then', where the present is understood in terms of what it has become and where it is on its way. The past is constantly being reworked and ascribed different values through narratives that give sense to people's lives in the present, and on which they project their future being. Such narratives unfold a threefold direction of time – a temporality that distinguishes between past, present and future, and links them with the formula 'and then'.

Every story is narrated by somebody, and there is always a distinction between the time of narrating and narrated time. Hence, there is always more than one time layer present in the telling of a story or the narrating of a narrative. A film may last two hours but tell a story that stretches over two centuries. On the other hand, a book like *Ulysses* by James Joyce takes several days to read, but tells a story about one single day in the life of the main character, Leopold Bloom. Even when the time of narrating and narrated time may almost coincide, they nevertheless differ in terms of linearity. While the time of narrating has to follow a linear order, narrated time can move forward and back, or in a time circle, like for example in Quentin Tarantino's film *Pulp Fiction*, or even go backwards as in Christopher Nolan's *Memento*.

The separation between the two times of narrative mostly demands some kind of coupling or bridge to be trustworthy. The narrator can be positioned either within or outside the story: homo-diegetic or hetero-diegetic.[39] And the narrator need not even be a person, as in films and visual narratives where the camera without any narrating words defines the point of view of the narrator for the audience. Where there is no explicit narrator at all, or the originators of the narrative are unknown or non-identifiable, there might still be an implied author.[40] This is often the case in advertising, docusoaps and reality TV.

Mikhail Bakhtin used the concept of chronotope – 'time-space' – to refer to a system of time and space coordination in novelistic writing.[41] Chronotopes exist in any narrative media genre, confirming or reworking the time of corporeal reality and its location in historical time. Chronotopes work by unifying specific characteristics of historical time and space into condensed figurations or articulations of the past, the present and the future. They are at the heart of many media genres like news, historical melodrama and science fiction, and approach what Benjamin discussed as images of history. Even historically periodizing terms like 'modernity' function as chronotopes – or tropes – of political, theoretical and historical narratives. The advent of postmodernist dismissal of utopian thought in Western culture indicated a crisis for these grand narratives in recent history. In the late 1970s, Lyotard proclaimed that the autonomous multiple language games of postmodernity had displaced the grand narratives of modernity.[42] In fact, master narratives have broken down or eroded earlier in history, disrupting its unity and direction in the minds of people, as for example happened to the grand narratives of religious absolutism and feudal monarchy in seventeenth- and eighteenth-century Europe.

Grand narratives offer basic answers to questions of continuity and discontinuity in history, and thus of the unity of historical time itself, serving as comprehensive frameworks to which people can relate and make sense of their own particular narratives of themselves. Although there is hardly any universally accepted master narrative in the contemporary world, the mutual interplay between grand, smaller and personal narratives still persist within political, religious and social movements. This is especially true of sectarian radical or conservative movements, where media narratives that do not confirm the self-apprehension of the members and their worldview are rejected. Converting into a new worldview goes hand in hand with recasting one's life in a new narrative and changing one's view of other mediated narratives, whether fictitious or historical. In a similar way, common-sense worldviews are also based on more or less conscious and consistent narratives that connect the self to a greater scheme of things.[43] It is impossible to make sense of life without some kind of narrative framework for individual stories and media plots. Grand narratives work as frames for more petty narratives, in the media as well as in the stories people tell in everyday life. Some of these grand stories have even been told and developed since ancient times, as shown by Michael Walzer's exploration of the story of the Exodus and Northrop Frye's analysis of the empowering stories generated from the Bible throughout Western history.[44]

Benjamin had something similar in mind when he pointed to the secularization of theological thought by Marxism, but at the same time was sensitive to the way modernity and its new media transformed the conditions for telling stories and mediating them – and, as a consequence, contributing to what he saw as 'the decline of storytelling'.[45] However, that conclusion seems to have been precipitate, since storytelling and narratives seem to continue to thrive on all levels in late modernity. Although the act of narrating undergoes changes, narratives undoubtedly live on in various forms through the ages. For instance, the modern narratives of progress and democracy, as well as pettier narratives like the murder story that originated in the mid nineteenth century, have all regained their popularity.

The last two centuries have generated widespread narratives of commercialism and mass media as a form of modern decadence or fall from grace. Usually, such 'mid-size' narratives of modernity come in competing optimistic and pessimistic variants, one with a 'happy' ending and the other with an 'unhappy' one. Thus in the 1990s, the new computer-based Internet technology gave rise to utopian hopes, but also to dystopian fears. As Latour notes, modernity comes in many versions, some optimistic, positive or utopian, some pessimistic, negative or dystopian; some grand, some petty; but all afford meaning to the passage of time.[46] This process mixes disenchantment with re-enchantment or re-mythologization that point to continuities between archaic times and the most radicalized late modernity.

Like any other narrative, utopias work on the border between the real and the fictitious, and the possible and the impossible. Any utopian thought must break with the past and the present, or proclaim a transcendence of the present state of reality. This makes it necessary but also difficult to determine what is real and unreal. The same goes for the notion of the death of utopianism, which is often depicted as a return to reality or an awakening to the facts of life. It is true that the mentality of utopian thinking and the efforts to emasculate it do change, but if historical time is comprehended as both real and illusory, utopias in general cannot be dismissed as social dreams that could be clearly distinguished from realistic views on the unfolding of history. History appears as simultaneously real and illusory: 'fiction is quasi-historical, just as much as history is quasi-fictive,' as Ricoeur puts it.[47] Neither history nor fiction could do without narrative; which is also true of utopias, that are about the future, but nevertheless are told or mediated in a retrospective form, similar to the way a science fiction story that takes place in a distant future is always told in the imperfect, as if what will happen has already happened and reached its conclusion.

Jean Baudrillard has argued that contemporary media tend to blur the line between reality and simulation, in a way that makes the simulation of reality seem more real than reality itself.[48] Certainly, the last twenty-five years have given rise to new concepts and words – likefor instance, 'virtual reality', 'hyper-reality', or 'real time' – that seem to either sort out what is left of an ever-shrinking common reality or distinguish one kind of reality from another, thereby contributing to the insight that any conception of reality is symbolically mediated rather than totally destabilizing the borderline between the real and the unreal. However, an overdose of simulation seems to feed a thirst for reality, as exemplified by the current popularity of documentary soaps, role-playing games and blogs. Contemporary media paradoxically try to break with the sense of simulation by bringing audiences closer to reality, but this only replaces one kind of simulation by another, since media function as mediators, not as mere intermediaries, between people and their surroundings. The same goes for the relationship between media and time. Media contribute to the polytemporality and dualism of time in late modernity, but are also dependent on socially or naturally established borders between different kinds of temporalities – borders they cannot all transgress or delete. In the present state of modernity, people are always brought back to the ever-present time layer of corporeal time – the anchor of any notion of real time. The refiguration of time by media narratives is always confronted with corporeal or real time by the act of reading, listening or viewing.[49] These acts become a 'necessary mediator of refiguration', as Ricoeur puts it, but without being able to completely tear down the distinction between the time of narrative and the time of real life – or, for that matter, between fiction and reality.[50]

Media produce as well as abolish both time and space, but are also dependent on them in order to function. This is hardly surprising, since society to an ever-increasing extent consists of and is maintained by media. Hence, the separation of society and media nowadays seems antiquated to the same extent that the notion of human beings as cyborgs less and less seems a narrative of the future.

9. TRANSLOCAL SPACES

All shopping malls are alike, it is said. Rob Kroes has paraphrased the phenomenon, 'If You've Seen One, You've Seen the Mall'.[1] Considering that the proliferation of this retail form in the United States alone (the so-called 'malling of America') reached an astonishing 39,000 in last century's final decade, it is not surprising that entering Solna Centre feels like stepping into a place where one has been before.[2] Even the first-time visitor enters an environment that in many ways is already familiar. The wide covered walkways, the mixture of daylight filtered through the glass roof with the light from shop windows and signs, and the omnipresence of advertising logos together form an indoor shopping space that is easily recognizable from elsewhere. The common tendency to design the retail environment around a specific set of themes (the town square, Main Street, etc.), paradoxically generalizes the shopping centre even further by tying it to other themed retail environments, including not only malls, but also restaurants, airports and tourist sites. Solna Centre's narrow, dimly lit Post Walk, designed to resemble the arcades of 'old Europe', and its main walkway, with its large square floor tiles, street lamps and soundscape intended to connote an urban street, are in fact reminders of other shopping centres across the globe.[3]

In this chapter we look more closely at Solna Centre as a place that is both local and global, and specifically how these aspects of proximity and distance are layered onto each other in the shopping centre. The concept of a 'global place' is a contradiction in terms, since globality is understood as precisely the opposite of the local, rooted in a specific place. There are nevertheless specific places that cannot be characterized without referring to processes that transgress local, regional and national borders. Yet even these processes rarely encompass the entire globe, but follow previously established lines of power and communication as they link together people and places across ever-greater distances. Hannerz has proposed substituting 'transnational' for the term global, in order to keep in mind the varying scale and spread of these border crossings. Despite the fact that the transnational can be a misleading term for processes that often transcend the nation state, it has the advantage of being somewhat more humble, and even more important, lacks the ideological baggage the term globalization carries. Following Hannerz, we refer to the processes that connect Solna Centre to an infinite array of elsewheres as transnational, although depending on the context, we also find the global deeply inscribed in this shopping centre.[4]

As touched upon in Chapter 1, the tension arising in the many-layered relationships between local and global or transnational characteristics of contemporary spaces of consumption has several dimensions. There is first a geographic dimension; and a tension between on the one hand the local context, where we find a shopping centre located in the town of Solna with its specific history, and on the other hand its economic dependence and structural relationship to transnational organizations with centres far removed from this locale. Secondly, this dimension has implications for Solna Centre's social character, where public and private uses of space are intertwined at the same time that they are strictly regulated. A shopping centre is undeniably a public space, yet private commercial interests exert an increasing influence on its form and use. It is further a public space that borrows and shares many characteristics of the domestic and intimate spheres of home and family. Whereas in Chapter 1 we considered the history of Solna Centre and the implications the rewritings of history have had on the identities of the shopping centre and the people who pass through it, here the focus is on the local and transnational dimensions of this place.

Before entering the shopping centre, however, we begin the chapter with a general overview over some basic coordinates of media spatiality, parallel to what was said on temporality in the previous chapter, but moving more rapidly towards the communicating spaces of the shopping centre. We then continue by examining the complex mix of diverse geographies and social dimensions of place manifested in Solna Centre. This forms the background for a more detailed examination of two phenomena – football and film – both closely identified with the town of Solna, and we look at how these two forms of popular entertainment have been caught up in transnational developments, transforming their relationship to Solna Centre in distinctly different ways. In the final section we return to considerations of media and their social uses as a means of both confirming and transcending place, specifically how people change their relationship to the place where they are through their uses of media. At that point we also use some ideas from Paul Ricoeur to connect back to the temporal dimension of the previous chapter, showing how time and space are interlaced in media and cultural practices.

MEDIATING SPACE

The previous chapter went into some detail to discuss the multidimensionality of time experience and its relations to mediation and narrative of history and fiction. There is a strong parallelism between the dimensions of time and space, and analogous arguments could therefore be made about the general phenomenology of spatial experience.[5] It is for instance useful to make a distinction between, on the one hand, abstract geometric space as a system of linked 'sites' and, on the other, the concrete lived spatiality of 'places'. Paul Ricoeur points at a 'kinship between memories and places', indicated by the linked phenomena of dating and localization that testify to 'the inseparable tie between the problematics of time and space', and sees the 'act of inhabiting' as 'the strongest human tie between the date and the place', where the date is the lived temporality just as the place is the lived spatiality.[6] Just like historical time results from the intersection of objective time and lived time, so does geographic space result from the joining of geometrical space and lived space. There is a chronotopic 'system of places and dates' that frame all the events and actions in lived space and lived time, a system further elaborated by the sciences of geography and historiography.[7] He traces 'analogies and overlappings' in the parallel workings of 'constructed' space and 'narrated' time, arguing that inhabiting and constructing are correlated in a third space of localities mediating between geometrical and lived space, corresponding to the idea of a third time of history with the dates on the calendar mediating between cosmic and lived time. This third space can be interpreted as 'a geometrical checkering of lived space, like a superimposition of "places" on the grid of localities'.[8]

Reminiscent of Walter Benjamin's readings of nineteenth-century Paris as a text, as well as of our own reading of Solna Centre, Ricoeur describes the particular relationships between space and time in the city:

> Narrative and construction bring about a similar kind of inscription, the one in the endurance of time, the other in the enduringness of materials. Each new building is inscribed in urban space like a narrative within a setting of intertextuality … The city gives itself as both to be seen and to be read. In it, narrated time and inhabited space are more closely associated than they are in an isolated building.[9]

It is important to note that in modern societies, this combined narration of time and inhabitation of space is normally mediated through communication technologies that are used in everyday life to link subjective experiences to sociocultural communities. Ricoeur then offers the following condensation of his argument: 'To the dialectic of lived space, geometrical space and inhabited space corresponds a similar dialectic of lived time, cosmic time and historical time. To the critical moment of localization within the order of space corresponds that of dating within the order of time.'[10] Localization marks out certain nodes in space as special, linking them to memories of social acts and symbolizing them in representations that invest sites with meaning.

Before reading the urban space and inhabited places of a shopping centre, let us first scrutinize how communication links media and space. The interplay between people and media is always spatially contextualized, in spite of the inherent transgressional character of communication. Places frame and delimit media uses, which at the same time create spatial formations as meaningful geographic places and social worlds. Media texts represent places and spaces, and afford them meaning. Media use also creates social spaces through structuring interaction between humans and the built environment. This is true of all media spaces, as they overlap shopping spaces in particular and urban spaces in general. They are all spaces of communication and consumption.[11]

(1) First, all media use is spatially located, framed and determined. On the one hand, there are material and technical limitations related to access of electricity, network coverage, etc. Books and papers tend to dissolve under water and cannot be read in the dark. Before transistors, lightweight batteries, microelectronics and the establishment of

far-reaching radiation networks, radio, television, records, telephones and computers were all strictly bound to fixed and mostly indoor stations, and there are still geographic or climatic conditions where they normally do not work. On the other hand, there are functional and social limitations as well. It is hard to watch films on the dance floor or the football arena – at least for the dancers and players in question. It is considered impolite to let your cellphone ring while attending a lecture or making love. Likewise, when media can be (and are) used, the place of use interferes with that use, affecting the interpretations made. The place of reading, listening or viewing is not neutral to the meaning or pleasure that media texts offer. Having read a text at home, at school, in the subway or while on vacation makes a difference to how it is experienced and understood – even when such links are not consciously remembered.

(2) Second, media represent places and spaces, and afford them meaning. In our project, we found many examples of mediated 'place identities' – media texts representing a location and associating it with historical, cultural and social meanings. In fact, no place or space can ever be thought or experienced in a pure way, without such symbolic meanings attached. We may try to experience a building or a street in a raw, physical and 'meaning-less' manner, but we are doomed to culture, bound to always make interpretations and to pull everything into meaning-making, so that our experiences will always immediately be coloured by signifying associations. The shopping centre itself was in one respect a nontextual structure of cement and glass, framing material movements of things and organisms, but it was always also more or less consciously understood and experienced as a kind of text – read by management and visitors alike to mean different things. And this faculty of making meaning was actively played out in its architecture and design. In the other direction, all media texts repeatedly refer to spatial forms and symbolically reconstruct them as virtual spaces.[12] The spaces narrated, depicted or implicitly referred to in computer games, posters or film music interact with the spaces in which these media are used. This interaction is sometimes rather arbitrary, but at other times deliberately planned and utilized in order to modify spatial identification. The shopping centre used web pages, ads, signposts, placards and mural paintings to remind people of historical events that located the centre as a unique place and invested it with intentionally positive meanings, in order to attract visitors and entice them to become consumers. Solna Centre identified itself by referring to Solna's popular soccer team AIK and to its history as the cradle of Swedish film production. Such references in and around the centre marked out its identity and distinguished it from competing centres. Some visitors were attracted to that local identity, identifying with the place and its history, while others might reject it, for instance if they favoured a rival team.

(3) Third, media uses create social spaces. Mobile phones form 'talk spaces' that intersect geographical space: bind physically distant places together while inscribing a circle around the talking individual, separating him or her from the surroundings and those who cannot hear the distant voice or participate in the dialogue. People reading

papers in a public place are likewise surrounded by a kind of invisible and silent halo that socially prevents others from disturbing their reading. Social communicative rules for media use sometimes change abruptly, for instance when crossing entrances to the centre and to various stores and other spaces. The Solna Centre library was, for example, full of little signs forbidding mobile phone talk, and the books and papers found there could be read and borrowed but not sold, in contrast to those in the bookshop. Places of and for media use (street, library, magazine shop, etc.) were dialectically intertwined with places which were virtual arenas constructed through media use and connected to distant places. Talking on a phone, looking at a photo or reading a paper you could connect to people and events far away, for instance in your home town if you were immigrant from a distant part of Sweden or another continent. Certain places in the centre were like doors that opened up for such transitional and often transnational connections, and echoes from those distant places sort of vibrated in the various media shops, through sounds, images and memories reminding one of somewhere else.

A shopping centre is a complex kind of 'mediascape'. A mediascape can be defined as a configuration of media forms and texts that surround and are available to specific people at specific times and places; just like any 'scape' in general is a particular set of phenomena in a given spatial and temporal setting, analogous to how a 'landscape' is a style and shape of some geographical place in space, a 'soundscape' is a configuration of aural components in a given setting, and an 'ethnoscape' is made up by a particular local mix of ethnically identified persons.[13] As such a mediascape, Solna Centre is a fascinating crossroads of long- and short-distance connections.

Visitors relate to media while passing through the centre, using them to link to (spatially or temporally) distant others through texts of many kinds. The management and the businesses of the centre also use media to communicate internally, thus unifying it into a single functional entity. This is achieved through digital webs for telephones, radio, television, broadband and financial transactions (for instance ATMs), but also for those stencilled notes, posters and meetings that connect the centre management with the trade association and the individual businesses of Solna Centre. Another linking device is the system of guards, cameras and charge cards that registers customers and guides them towards preferred behaviours and targeted marketing efforts. Yet another example is those 'inscriptions and signs on the entranceways' that Benjamin found had 'about them something enigmatic'. Through their laconic and catchy formulations, store names and other insistent letterings seem to 'want to say more'.[14] Not only the items on display but also these signs are rebuses to decipher, with a kind of poetic surplus of meaning inviting cultural interpretation as forms of symbolic communication. Informative signs, advertising displays and store names are interwoven into a polyphonic hypertext where intertextual dialogues between visual landmarks create sometimes carefully planned but often also unexpected associations – as in the narcissistic encounter between shops like Ego and Ecco.

Headed by its management, the centre consciously acted as a communicator. The local Solna Centre manager saw his centre in its entirety as a communication medium, where visitors corresponded to the readers of a newspaper. What the centre more precisely intended to mediate was up to its resident businesses. As a material and spatial as well as an organizational and economic unit, the centre had a communicative power: a force to influence visitors. The ultimate purpose of this power was to maximize the profits of its corporate owners. The means to reach this final aim was by a form of communication that primarily conveyed a wish and a promise of profit: to the shops that were enticed to make good profits, and to the customers who were enticed to make good deals in comfortable settings. In order to succeed in the competition for shops and customers with all other shopping environments with identical goals, each centre has to create and display an image of itself as a unique and attractive place. It communicates its *place identity* through websites, advertisements, signs, decoration and architecture.

A visitor to Solna Centre is struck by the impression of a lucid expanse, with a wide modern city street with shops and houses under an elevated, suspended glass roof.[15] But the internal space soon reveals a series of ambiguities. Not only is it, in Walter Benjamin's words, both street and house, both outdoors and indoors; it is also both bright and dark, open and secret, transparent and opaque, ultramodern and archaic, futuristic and nostalgic. Typically, modern shopping environments try to create an urban feeling, and mall architecture therefore also directly connects to city planning. Alongside the 'high-tech' urban style, Solna Centre offers plenty of historizing elements of the 'old town' type.[16] The former constructs of steel, glass and plastic materials an abstract city of metropolitan greatness and geometric openness, with open elevators running up and down, producing a feeling of three-dimensional rapidity and a soundscape crafted to give a sense of grand technological expanses. The latter uses kitsch and nostalgic traits in stone, wood, brick and paint to simulate a traditional, dense and intimate town labyrinth. In Solna, this was made by explicit (but to most visitors and even the management not consciously registered) references to the winding and enigmatic passages of nineteenth-century London and Paris – precisely those arcades described by Benjamin. Together, they are balanced to offer an impression of *safe excitement* – a secure place to 'feel at home' and pursue one's daily routines, but also an attractive centre of events and entertaining experiences.

To achieve such effects, architectural design is used as a means of communication, but also decorative elements. Solna Centre made direct references to the Paris arcades in its design of walls, windows, roofs and lamps. It also had a couple of mural paintings made when the centre was constructed in the late 1980s, reminding us of old Solna town houses. A unique feeling of the particular place was then further elaborated in Solna Centre ads published in the daily papers and frequently exhibited in the centre itself, meant to link a clear image and character to the body of the buildings and inducing a positive mood. The material body and the symbolic soul of the centre were developed jointly, using all conceivable kinds of communication, from glass and stone to print and electronic media.

In Chapter 1, we mentioned the Solna Centre ad that placed a young family on a living-room sofa in the middle of the centre, with the slogan 'Feel at home in Solna Centre'. The image recalls Benjamin's comparison of city and home spaces, where he likens the arcade to the drawing room: 'More than anywhere else, the street reveals itself in the arcade as the furnished and familiar interior of the masses.'[17] Solna Centre's campaigns connected to the homey feeling as a means to create the safety required for maximal consumption but also to foster an emotional identification with the centre.

The management also saw Solna as a particularly 'popular' centre. The first manager we interviewed had a kind of essentialist perception of the centre as an organism with a pre-existing soul to which all commercial efforts had to adjust in order to be maximally successful. His task was therefore to discover the unique character of his centre, referring not to the building as such, but rather to the people who filled it. As Solna was populated by a rather average set of Swedes, the centre had to make itself 'ordinary', accessible, middle-of-the-road, neither snobbish nor sluggish. Ideas of authenticity were crucial for the manager, as he detested how some other centres were abstractly constructed from nothihg, and instead expressed a deep fondness for the sometimes troublesome popular 'soul' of his centre, to which he had to adjust. This idea of authenticity was legitimated by loose references to the specific history of Solna city, which appears to be infused into the walls of the centre, as well as painted on them.

These aspects of the shopping centre have parallels in the way each mass medium and text communicates its identity – its style and genre. Just as Solna Centre projects its specific self-image through a wide set of communicative tools, so does any record company or weekly magazine. In the other direction, this also parallels the manner in which cities are identified through complexly evolving sets of markers: names, slogans, monuments, rituals and accidental or engineered events. Together with other political, economic and cultural factors, a wide range of media texts contributes to make certain places into 'hot spots' for both social practices and symbolic representations. The production of urban centrality can be set in motion by a combination of dramatic events, performances and conflicts, a constantly evolving set of collective rituals, social practices and textual representations that reproduce the centrality of city sites. The representation and construction of place is a central theme in a period of 'glocalization', where global flows mix with localized 'place identities'.[18] The double image of the city as specific and universal is mediated through monuments, guidebooks, news reports, works of art, songs, poetry, novels and other narratives, artefacts and images. In such processes, media, consumption and urbanity work together, as media events are strong attractors for shopping centres as well as for city centres, and media texts offer representations of place identities.

These place identities are not just scripted 'from above', by management and politicians. They are the result of a negotiation between many different groups and interests, including inhabitants from 'within' and 'below', as well as from visitors and strangers from 'outside'. Identification – of people as well as of places – is always a process of interaction between selves and others. And the different kinds of identifi-cations mirror each other. 'People and places script each other,' as Ash Amin and Nigel Thrift put it.[19] Physical sites and cities are read and named by people who in turn are identified with these places. Solna Centre is interpreted by its manager, shop owners and customers, who simultaneously also place themselves there, borrowing parts of their individual and collective identities from this particular location, and being mapped and labelled as 'Solna people' by political and commercial practices, in a circular process.

FROM LOCAL TO TRANSNATIONAL SPACE

In previous chapters we have described how Solna Centre, dating from 1965, was glassed over in 1989 and subsequently extended in 2001 to enclose additional shops and the local hotel. This expansion was largely possible because of the commercial success of the centre, and a long cooperation between the Solna city council and the Swedish investment company Piren, which paved the way for corporate ownership of increasing segments of the city centre. By 1989, the City Hall and the local library remained the only municipally owned properties in what had previously been an urban mix of commercial and public space. Solna Centre was in turn one of a large number of shopping centres in the Stockholm region owned by the same investment company. As the marketing and advertising campaigns of these malls were increas-ingly integrated, Solna Centre attained in a sense a more 'regional' profile. In the year 2000, Piren was bought out by Rodamco, a multinational corporation with head-quarters in the Netherlands. Solna Centre has thereby undergone a series of devel-opments that make it a textbook example of the transformation from community control and local ownership to being increasingly subjected to the expanding inter-ests of ever more distant centres of power and control. In Lash and Urry's terms, this transformation renders the community no longer sovereign.[20]

As the ownership of the land on which the shopping centre was located shifted, the shops and brands represented in the mall also changed. Individual shop owners who could not afford the rent increases nor meet the management's demands for longer and standardized opening hours vacated their spaces, and national and transnational chains moved in. Exceptions included the family owned newsagents and the several cafés located in the open 'street' down the centre of the mall which appeared to maintain a stable business and clientele despite competition from the two McDonalds. National and international brands and their logos took over larger segments of the buildings' façades, often against the protests of local interests who argued for less commercialized uses of the space.

The aggregation of transnational influence in the space of Solna Centre has not, however, replaced all traces of the local. The wall murals with their specific references to local places and events remain, even if many of them are overshadowed by the large colourfull graphics of brand names. There is still the painting of a camera filming Greta Garbo, referencing the nearby studios of Film City (Filmstaden), once the cradle of Sweden's proud film industry. And the line of soccer players remains as a reminder that Stockholm's largest stadium lies just across the street. The imposing Hollywood Stairs is a central architectural feature of the shopping centre, intended by the architect as a double reference both to Solna's importance to the Swedish film industry and to the wide staircase in the Stockholm City Hall which the Nobel prize winners descend each December.

As the mall has expanded around them, these and other features built into Solna Centre in the late 1980s have lost their prominence. It is further not likely that they have retained the specificity of their references to Solna that they once had for mall visitors. They now belong to the older and less flashy part of the mall. The recent expansion is far grander and more spacious, and makes no pretension of locality. There is a broader staircase, which leads nowhere but forms an excellent arena for various performances and events, and a wide, bright passage from the new entrance, connecting the original shopping centre to the hotel. This new space is devoid of details that would detract from the expanse of shop window that line each side. It is difficult not to interpret the latest renovation and expansion as an expression of Solna Centre's place within a transnational enterprise. Structural and visual reminders of this shopping centre's relationship to a specific geographic and demographic place on the outskirts of Stockholm survive primarily as archaic references to the past.

A few steps from the bench where Ronald McDonald sits cross-legged looking out on passers-by is the entrance to the municipal library, where we find a stark contrast to the transnational character dominating major sections of Solna Centre. On the wall opposite the library's checkout desk hangs a large tapestry depicting Hagalund, the neighbourhood most closely associated with Solna. Passing the tapestry and turning right, the visitor enters a small gallery where a range of work is exhibited. The exhibits, which are changed at regular intervals, have included the work of school classes, evening art classes and local artists working in a range of media. Another popular exhibit was a series of historical photographs of Solna. The primary requirement for displaying work is that it has a connection to the community. A documentary photographic exhibit on Black Army, the controversial supporter club of a national league soccer team, was displayed here: a link to Solna's 'home team'. Not surprisingly for a municipal library, there is also a collection of reference works about the town, and at one time a small collection of historic postcards could be purchased at the checkout desk. The library is not only local, of course; its collections of books, periodicals, records and videos, and its Internet access, provide visitors with the means of transcending the local community – a point to which we return in our consideration of translocal media use. Here the point is that the library looks as it does to a large extent because it is located in Solna. At other sites of media consumption throughout the shopping centre, including bookstores, newsagents, video rental shops and card shops, the goods are much the same as those found in other shopping centres across Sweden, packaged and presented to a great extent like similar goods in similar environments around the globe.

Geographically, Solna Centre is neither global nor local. Rather, it is constituted through a successive layering of references to specific places, both near and far, and increasingly, to non-places that remain abstract except in their influence on the structure and appearance of the shopping environment. It is an example of the deterritorialized space that is created through the complexity of cultural flows that challenge simple notions of a cultural centre and a subordinate periphery.[21] The familiarity the first-time visitor feels in Solna Centre cannot be traced to a specific geographic location, but is based on the generalized experience accrued while passing through other equally non-specific places.

Let us now turn from geographic to social dimensions of place and consider how the changing physical landscape affects Solna Centre as a meaningful site. What impact does the experience of specific and non-specific geographies have on the forms of sociality that take place here?

To the extent that Solna Centre can be considered a social space, its sociality is based on movement. People are continually on the move through this environment, passing through the shopping centre to make a quick purchase, between destinations. The fact that it is a place where goods are bought and sold also determines the forms of sociality that dominate here, that is the small exchanges that characterize these transactions of selecting and purchasing desired items. These social practices are organized in ways that structure space according to a dominant polarity of *front stage* and *back stage*. These concepts have been used by Erving Goffman to analyse social life in general, and in a shopping centre environment such dramaturgical terms clearly make sense.[22] It is easy to see how salespersons perform various professional roles to connect optimally to the audience of visiting customers, and stage encounters between consumers and the commodities on sale. Compared to more old-fashioned types of shops, those found in a shopping centre are often experienced as transparent and open, but there are in fact lots of hidden and forbidden back regions. Advanced architectural and decorative design serve to hide from the consumer the system of places for deliveries, staff breaks, and so on that are needed to make everything appear lucidly efficient. In a steady process, commodities are moved from back to front regions, where they are put on display for potential buyers. Typical for such commercial places is the rapid pace of interactions, since visitors tend only to pass by for a very short moment and have to at once understand the basic principles of how the shopping space is organized, and preferably be enticed into spending some money there.

There are of course many other interpersonal encounters taking place in the centre, such as asking for information, a chance meeting with a friend, an appointment in one of the shops or services, but the vast majority of these are also brief, transitory encounters. In this sense the dominant social dimension of a shopping centre, like its geographic dimension, shares many characteristics with other translocal spaces of late modernity, including centres of transportation such as airports and train stations, as well as other spaces of consumption around the globe.

From the management's perspective, movement is a highly desirable characteristic of the shopping centre as a place. Attempts are made to locate shops and services strategically, in order to encourage the flow of visitors through major parts of the mall. The many benches placed throughout the centre were found to interrupt this desired flow, for people quite naturally used them to stop and rest or chat. At one point the management removed most of the benches, which brought on a conflict, particularly with the seniors who frequented the mall. One of their arguments was that, despite their relatively low buying power, by sitting on the benches they performed the important function of keeping an eye on things and thus helped keep order in the mall.[23] Eventually, the benches were returned to the central passageways.

Some forms of socializing are prohibited in Solna Centre, including for example political activities and demonstrations that are ordinarily permitted in public places. Political campaigning is relegated to the small square outside the shopping centre. The regulations of the centre also exclude local groups and fund-raising activities, such as the sale of lottery tickets. Rollerblading and roller-skating are prohibited, and the mall is also designated a smoke-free environment. The full list of regulations, posted at the mall entrance, maintains order at the same time that it gives a clear signal that certain social groups and social activities are not permitted on the premises. These regulations are an expression of the power structures that govern Solna Centre, and at which we will soon take a closer look. Here we see that these regulations have clear implications for the social space. The list tells the visitor not only whether he or she is welcome in the shopping centre, but also who one is likely – and not likely – to meet here. Other activities, while not expressly forbidden, have nevertheless been excluded in practice by the management's policies and priorities. For example, previous promises to provide space for youth activities and a theatre have been abandoned. Similarly, a proposal to install a 'speaker's corner' was rejected at an early stage of the shopping centre's development.[24]

The line of cafés in the centre of the shopping centre provides a much-appreciated and convenient form of social space, particularly in inclement weather. Many people who work in the mall eat lunch here. Several of the cafés serve food with origins in another part of the world, including Mexican, Middle Eastern and sushi or stir-fried specialties. Others have followed the international trend of serving a dizzying range of coffee-based drinks. The social space of these cafés is located between public and commercial space. Although some customers have complained that not being allowed to smoke restricts how long they are willing to sit over their cup of coffee, the cafés obviously serve as meetings places for many different social groups. It is not unusual to see a small group of men sitting for hours in one of the cafés, conversing in Arabic over long empty cups of tea.

Solna Centre, like other malls in other parts of the world, has occasionally arranged quasi-public events under its roof. The Swedish tradition of the annual Lucia Day celebration is one such event, when children, usually from a local school, sing carols and carry candles as they parade slowly through the mall. An 'AIK day' was organized, celebrating the team that had won the Swedish premier league in 1998. The event attracted a crowd of 200–300 people of all ages, many dressed in the team colours. They came to see the team and get their autographs, to hear speeches by the coaches and star players, and some particularly enthusiastic fans were even photographed with the trophy. Such an event, because of its popularity, never-theless runs the risk of keeping buying customers away from the mall. This was the case with the afternoon of children's entertainment when 'Bananas in Pyjamas' performed, and the shopping centre management decided to limit future such events.[25] Once used to draw customers to Solna Centre, these local performances and events have since disappeared from the shopping centre's home page.

A complementary communicative aspiration for contemporary shopping environ-ments is to market themselves as arenas where memorable experiences take place. The late-modern rhetoric of the 'experience economy' engages a wide set of 'creative industries' that think of themselves as producing and marketing experiences rather than products or services.[26] This implies a culturalization of the economy, in the form of an aestheticization of marketing practices, but it also indicates a correspon-ding economization of culture and a commercialization of artistic practices. Both high-tech and nostalgic styles can be drawn into that process. In recent years, hardly any shopping ad text can be found that does not include some variant of words like 'experience', 'feel', 'explore', 'discover' or 'event'. It was by no coincidence that one of the slogans we found was: 'Solna Centre – the centre of events!' Another expanding centre in the Stockholm region, Kista Centre, has a similar slogan on its website: 'Experience Sweden's smallest metropolis!' What is communicated is an invitation to a place that combines the receiving appropriation of shopping with an emotional subjective intensity exceeding the cool rationality of pure purchase and consumption.

One such event was the official opening of the new section of the Solna Centre, held in August 2001. The ceremony established the shopping centre's relationship to place as simultaneously local and transnational. This construction was accomplished differently by different participants in the event, however. In the speeches held by the centre's manager, the town mayor and the visiting Swedish CEO, Solna Centre's success was described as resulting from local government's cooperation with transna-tional corporate structures.[27] For one local resident we interviewed about the opening, it was not the ceremony but the entertainment that provided the link between this local context and distant places. Because she recognized aspects of the event – forms of music, dance and performance – from her travels abroad, she saw these imports from afar as enriching the local, the place where she lived.

As many of these examples illustrate, there is no clear distinction between local and transnational or global phenomena in the space of the shopping centre. The slogan which invites visitors to 'feel at home' in Solna Centre is formed as an invitation into a social, domesticated space. Yet the space of the mall has more in common with other commercial spaces – regionally, nationally and transnationally – than with the private space of home and family. It is not difficult to locate signifiers of the shop-ping centre's geographic location, if one knows where and how to look. But these recede into the past, losing their currency as the mall becomes reconfigured according to a norm that is determined elsewhere and nowhere. Like the faces of the mall employees who smile down on visitors from the banners hanging from the glass roof, they no longer represent themselves. They are serving a constitutive function, the construction of a translocal space.[28] This is consistent with all media that open up (visual or audial) virtual representations of foreign places, from newspapers to phones, destabilizing the concept of locality and the border between the public and the private.[29]

We turn now to three cases that illustrate some key distinctions in the ways places are mediated. First, we take a closer look at how the local sports team strives to uphold a local identification even when participating in wide spirals of mediations. Second, while having a physical location, film and cinema appear to be interpreted as less strictly tied to the particular place of Solna, providing examples of relatively more deterritorialized activities. In the last section, we present individual visitors who in everyday life use various imaginative tactics to bridge the gap between anchorage and mobility.

THE LOCAL TEAM

Solna Centre's location near the Råsunda soccer stadium, home arena for the AIK team, has been an important ingredient in building a profile for the shopping centre.[30] Sport has always had a strong connection to place, as seen in the pride invested in a home-town team, the loyalty of many alumni (at least in the US and England) for the school they attended, and national allegiances that come into play in international sports competitions. Well aware of this loyalty and the commercial possibilities it carries with it, Solna Centre was designed to encourage the connection between shopping and sport. We have already mentioned some of the efforts expended in that direction, the wall paintings of soccer players along the main passage through the mall, and the special 'AIK day' event the year the team won the national cup. Here we consider in what ways the shopping centre's connection to sport and to the AIK team in particular serves to particularize Solna Centre's relationship to place, identifying the shopping centre with a specific locale. We examine what Appadurai describes as the production of locality, in which the efforts expended in this production are more important than the particularities of local knowledge.[31]

AIK won the Swedish premier league in 1998, and the player who scored the winning goal was the first to be designated 'Solna's Person of the Year'. At the victory party following the match, Alexander Östlund gave the mayor the left shoe he had worn when he scored the goal (1-0 over Örgryte). After consulting some local business representatives, the major appointed a jury to make the award, and the 'golden shoe' was put on display in a glass case next to the information desk in Solna Centre. The following year Östlund's shoe was moved to a larger case in front of the City Hall where it was displayed together with pictures of the Person of the Year and Club of the Year for 2000, and a text explaining its significance. The commemoration of this victory survived as a continuing point of local pride.

Management has a grand vision of glassing in the entire area between the shopping centre and the stadium. In 2005, Solna decided to build a large 'national' arena, inspired by the new Amsterdam Arena that happens to be in the same city as Rodamco's main office. Solna won the competition with a similar proposal for a new arena proposed by Stockholm city, near the Stockholm Globe Arena. The competing proposals illustrate the fierce struggle over centrality that goes on between city areas, with sites for culture, sports and shopping as weapons. It is interesting to note that neither of the local teams involved want such a large 'national' arena: AIK as well as the Stockholm clubs instead preferred a smaller one that would fit their own needs and be based on 'club feeling' for a 'home field'. There was thus a tension between local and national interests among politicians as well as sports organizations.

Certainly since the late 1980s, Solna Centre's management has made concerted efforts to establish a sports profile for the mall. A large sporting goods store is the anchor business at the main entrance, and Solna Centre is the only shopping centre in the Stockholm region to have all the major sports chains represented under its roof. The plans for expansion and the presence of large sports shops may seem to have only a tendentious connection to AIK; the sports shops only sell national and global brands such as Nike, Adidas etc., and exclude the team's own products. National sports chains and global brands nevertheless fit into the framework created by the conjunction of a high-profile local sports team and the local shopping centre.

AIK does have a large product and souvenir shop in the mall, the only one of its kind in Sweden, where fans can buy clothing and other team memorabilia. These products are available elsewhere, in a small shop at the Råsunda stadium, over the net and at Derby, a shop in downtown Stockholm that AIK started together with two other Stockholm teams. But the AIK shop in Solna Centre is the only equivalent, if on a smaller scale, to Manchester United's Megastore, built next to the team's home arena, Old Trafford. The active merchandizing of the club brand near the spot the club calls 'home' marks out the place as a potential tourist site. This raises the question of similarities between tourism and sport, specifically in their relationship to place. A tourist souvenir has a direct connection to the place it was purchased; it symbolizes the place itself and its value resides in the memories it carries of the tourist's visit to the place. A souvenir of a sports team may have the same function, if the fan's trip to the site can be seen as a sort of pilgrimage to the place his heroes have their home pitch or have won important victories. But the sports souvenir's primary significance is as a marker of identity rather than place. The purchase and display of items bearing the club brand are acts of consumption that confirm a social rather than a geographic identity. The sports fan's relationship to place is more indirect and, at least in the case of AIK fans, more complex.

In order to understand this relationship and its ultimate connection to Solna Centre, we must make a brief detour into the history of the AIK sports club, briefly touched upon in the previous chapter. AIK (Allmänna idrottsklubben = Public sports club) was formed in 1891 to support an array of amateur sports. The club was initially located on Östermalm in Stockholm, and soccer matches were played on a number of different arenas, including the sports field in Råsunda before the stadium was built. In 1912, the soccer team had the newly built Stockholm Stadium as its home ground and played there until AIK moved to Solna. Most players were recruited from the Stockholm region, and although players occasionally moved between Stockholm teams, it was the exception rather than the rule (and remained the case until the professionalization of the sport paved the way for purchasing players from other teams). By the 1930s AIK had become Stockholm's most successful team, drawing crowds that tested the capacity of the Stockholm Stadium. Spurred by its own success and the rapid rise of soccer's popularity in Sweden, in cooperation with the Swedish soccer organization, the club initiated construction of a new stadium in Råsunda in 1936. AIK moved its entire organization to Råsunda when the stadium was completed, in time for the 1937/38 season, and the team won the Swedish championship, outclassing its competitors on its new home pitch. Six years later, the town of Solna was incorporated and AIK became increasingly identified as a Stockholm team from Solna. The club flag and the town's flag were created at the same time, look much the same and are often seen flying side by side at matches and other events. The date 1891 remains on the AIK flag and logo, making it easy to forget that forty years passed before AIK became Solna's home team.

There are several complex developments that account for the historical path of the club from its origins in the popular culture and working-class base of amateur sport prior to the turn of the twentieth century. Against a backdrop of urbanization and industrialization, sport combined conservative values with the democratic ideal of competition, and became a bridge to new social structures and the building of new masculine identities. A central aspect of this was the channel sport provided for the rise of local patriotism, which in turn was easily expanded and mobilized as nationalism in the context of international competitions and world cup tournaments. Another key aspect of the complex mix was the increasing professionalization and commercialization of sport. The organizations of clubs on an amateur basis with significant civic support changed as the composition of the clubs' boards and steering committees progressed from their previous base in popular movements to include representatives from the world of business and finance.

Early in 1999, Solna Centre hosted an event in front of the town hall that brought together this history and AIK's victory in the Swedish championship play-offs. The crowd of visitors that afternoon included people of all ages, and although men with their young sons (eager to get autographs) seemed to dominate, there were also clusters of young women in their twenties, families with small children and elderly men in their eighties, all wearing the team colours, black and gold. Solna Centre, across from the home stadium, was the self-evident location to celebrate the team's victory. The crowd gathered in front of the platform heard speeches by the coach and key players, lead by a presenter who carried on an enthusiastic dialogue with the team and the crowd. He reminded everyone that the first game of the season was just a few weeks away, and 'You'll all be there?!' The crowd shouted its response in the affirmative. The team's 'gold video' was for sale from the stage and at several shops throughout the mall. The team then divided into two groups and signed autographs and answered questions from the fans who lined up outside McDonald's and one of the sports shops. In another sports shop, a photographer had set up a simple studio where fans could pull on a football shirt in their size and be photographed next to the trophy.

The professionalization, commercialization and mediatization of sport permeate Solna Centre in the global branding and personalities that are evident throughout the mall. In this sense, Solna is not so different from other shopping centres. The global economic structures of sport are a clearly defined dimension of late modernity, lacking any link to a specific place. What distinguished this particular consumption space from the general pattern is rather the ways that specific events and artefacts work to activate local pride among some mall visitors. During these events the two dimensions of place – the geographic and the social – are tied together. In such moments, Solna becomes a football town, finding its expression in the local loyalties that coalesce when visitors reread the story of how the golden shoe came to be displayed in the mall, browse in the AIK shop or gather to celebrate the team. Without such events and in the absence of the specific artefacts that anchor the social to the geographic, Solna Centre loses its geographic specificity and becomes part of the generalized culture of sport. This pattern of generalization and loss of specificity of place can also be found in other cultural phenomena, as we see in another local dimension: Solna's tie to the Swedish film industry.

FILM CITY

Film City, the former headquarters of the Swedish film industry's production studios, is also in Råsunda, quite near Solna Centre. Film City dates back to the early years of silent film and is the place where many Swedish film classics were produced. In 2001 Swedish Film (Svensk Filmindustri), the country's largest film producer and distributor, and owner of the largest chain of theatres, moved its headquarters 'home' to Råsunda. The renovated Film City Råsunda now includes a new theatre with three relatively small viewing spaces, each named after famed Swedish actors and the additional 'Bergman Salon', renovated in the style of the 1940s, where films made during the period 1919–1970 are shown.[32] It is possible to book tours of the old facilities that now include a café and souvenir shop, and 'Old Film City' has become a site for events commemorating the studios' history.[33]

Like Solna's history as a soccer town, the town's place in the history of Swedish film would not be obvious to the visitor entering Solna Centre for the first time. The small mural of Greta Garbo is obscured behind an elevator, and the Hollywood Stairs can at best be seen as an obtuse reference to the nearby film studios. Also like sport, however, film as a major cultural phenomenon is evident throughout the mall. There is a large video and DVD rental shop, the library has a video rental section, and many stores sell videos and DVDs of popular films, including Disney classics. Film stars and characters appear in advertisements for a range of products, an aspect of the previously mentioned intermedial use of characters and themes from popular films. Characters from blockbuster films and Disney classics are found on posters and products in virtually every shop in Solna Centre. Until 2002 there was also a small film theatre that showed current popular films most evenings. Despite the prevalence in this space of consumption of these many references to film in general, specific films and film characters, these do not refer to any concrete place, but only to the generalized world of contemporary film in all its transnational dimensions.

Sagittarius (Skytten), the small film theatre in the mall, might have been such a place.[34] Shopping and going to the movies have much in common, and for over a hundred years cinema has had a place in the major spaces of consumption. Early department stores often included movie theatres, at first to attract customers and eventually where children could be entertained while their mothers shopped.[35] It was not until cinemas began to establish independent viewing palaces that the connection was severed, but then only temporarily, as we have seen with the resurgence in the 1980s of film complexes in close proximity to shopping centres, even under the same roof. Sagittarius was built some time around 1965 and thus can date its origins to the early years of Solna Centre. It was part of the community centre (Medborgarhuset) and included, in addition to the theatre itself, five conference rooms of various sizes and a number of additional smaller areas. The theatre itself also functioned as the town stage, and theatre performances and meetings of various kinds were held there. SF (Svensk Filmindustri), which ran the theatre followed the possibly unique practice of not showing films on Wednesdays and Thursdays, in order for theatre and other events to be held there. In other words, Sagittarius functioned as a kind of open house for local citizens where a variety of public events, including film showings, were held.

In early 1983, Eurostar took over the rental contract from SF. Sagittarius thus became part of this smaller chain, one of twenty-two cinemas located mostly in small towns and suburbs of larger cities. Popular current films were shown three days a week, with family film outweighing action film and thrillers, and a children's matinee on Sundays. On the other weekdays the facilities continued to be used for a variety of community activities. Because it was open only in the evenings, when the rest of the shopping centre was closed, the community centre and its cinema had little contact with the rest of the mall. When Rodamco purchased the shopping centre, the community centre was included in the purchase. The conference rooms were remodelled as office space for businesses, leaving only Sagittarius, which Eurostar now rented from Rodamco. The hotel was responsible for booking film showings as well as other community and business activities in the theatre on evenings when films were not shown. This arrangement continued for several years, but Sagittarius's visibility in Solna Centre continued to decline. In the last few years the only entrance to the cinema was through the bookstore, and it became increasingly difficult to find information about the film programme. Eurostar was aware of SF's plans to open a new cinema in the old Film City, which would reduce Sagittarius's customers by at least 30 per cent. The local cinema/community centre was caught in a downward spiral.

Solna Centre's local manager said he was interested in the advantages a larger cinema would have for the shopping centre. But it was difficult to find a solution to the impractical location and an area that prohibited any expansion. In addition, Solna Centre and its owner Rodamco were in need of more office space. By 2001, when the new theatre opened at Råsunda Film City, Sagittarius had closed and the former manager had moved on to a higher post in the company.

Parallel to the twenty-year decline of Solna Centre's small theatre, other developments were taking place that might further explain the outcome. The changes in film viewing practices that had given rise to the video industry and watching film at home were being countered by the building of multiplex theatres.[36] These new vehicles of film consumption, while not excluding the possibility of small local and suburban theatres, made it harder for these endeavours to survive. One vehicle for smaller and independent theatres was to structure an appeal to the cultural importance film had once had, and forge a link either to the 'glamour' of film-going or to a public interested in the culture of cinema. The more secure alternative nevertheless remains tied to the large complex, and the possibility of drawing a suburban public 'who don't get in to the city' in sufficiently large numbers to support the megaplex.[37] A related development during the period of Sagittarius's decline is the growth of the block-buster, which organizes other media and in a sense jumps over the local movie theatre. Even more influential than its impact on theatres is the ways the blockbuster overshadows the possibilities of other kinds of film, including European films.[38] Together these factors account for how a theatre complex could open a mere stone's throw from Solna Centre – since SF is privy to the showing of the blockbuster and runs megaplexes that are supported by urban and suburban audiences, and can therefore afford the luxury of a small 'Bergman Salon' for the occasional viewing of original films not available in other venues.

The Swedish film company has engaged in a form of 'place marketing', offering a taste of the glamour of the old small movie theatre by opening a theatre on this historic site, even though the audience is coming to see the latest blockbuster film. It's admittedly not on the scale of the tourism described by Couldry's study of Granada film studios, perhaps only because Bergman's audience is still not on the same scale as *Coronation Street*'s.[39] The constructed environment of locality which the visitor to Granada studios or Film City experiences is undoubtedly one of place, but more importantly is also an aspect of fandom. Film itself, as a medium, operates in a deterritorialized spatial landscape.[40] The Bergman fan could equally well go to a viewing of his or her favourite film wherever it happens to be shown, or rent or purchase it to view at home. It does not require a place or locale in order to work as media consumption. Renting a video at the shop in Solna Centre or watching a film at the newly opened theatre with its romantic tie to the 'old' film city are two distinct yet compatible forms of media consumption. Neither of them is tied to a specific local place.

Film as a medium, despite its historic relationship to a locale quite near Solna Centre remains too deterritorialized to actualize a geographic relationship in the space of the mall. Soccer, on the other hand, remains highly territorialized, not only through its geographic connection in close proximity to the shopping centre. Even when viewed on television, a match is seen in a particular stadium, and the team retains its local, if constructed, identity. The local soccer team has in this case the critical possibility of actualizing Solna Centre as a social space for enacting the local identity and team loyalty, a tie that has a symbiotic economic advantage for local merchants, chain stores and the team itself (assuming the event- marketing equation remains weighted on the marketing side and the event does not get out of hand.) On face value, the history of Swedish film production would appear to have a more 'authentic' connection to the town of Solna. Early films were after all actually made on the site of Film City, whereas the soccer team has a forty-year history prior to its move to Råsunda Stadium. This affirms Appadurai's distinction between local knowledge and the production of locality, and shows that geographic proximity must be made meaningful by the active production of a social dimension, in this case by fandom. Only when Solna Centre becomes a social space does it emerge as local. These instances become less frequent as events in the shopping centre refer less often to a local context, and as centres of power and control became increasingly distant from the local community. The local survives as a series of fading paintings, signs that become less meaningful as they recede from memory.

BECOMING TRANSLOCAL

Our sports example illustrated the strength of local ties, whereas the film example showed the importance of transient flows. All media and people in practice have to combine these two aspects. This is true for all media circuits, and it is also a necessary condition for the lives of the centre's visitors as well as of its staff. As mentioned above, the first manager of Solna Centre was enchanted by the 'soul' of his centre, to which he felt a strong but ambivalent tie, at once respectful of its authenticity and irritated by its stubbornness. His successor was brought in from a previous position at the Eurostop Halmstad centre in another part of Sweden. He was a newcomer to Solna and thus had not yet any personal relationship to the place. However, he moved into an apartment in the centre itself, and soon become an integrated inhabitant of Solna. Yet he saw his career as a series of moves upwards and outwards, perhaps to work for Rodamco somewhere else in Europe. The company typically moves its staff to where their qualifications and experience are needed, without regard for where they are from or their connection to the locale. As the manager of Solna Centre, he was supposed to represent its core values, but simultaneously was one of the more 'transient' persons we encountered. Through his accumulated experience of inhabiting and managing the centre, he also became quickly entangled in its local networks, and the fact that he was still there years after testifies to the inescapable balance all people have to strike between local links and transient flows.

Cultural production is never exclusively place specific, but is increasingly accomplished in situations where global and local dimensions of place are present simultaneously. The movement and permeability that characterize contemporary cultural phenomena have provoked theorists into new ways of thinking about place, in particular how people relate to place differently today than they once did. Appadurai was among the first to link migration and media as the two principal factors accounting for the contemporary plasticity of people's conceptions of place and changing notions of what local means.[41] The migration of people and the changes in media forms and use increasingly point to ways that different locations, however disparate they may be, are nevertheless linked together. Media in particular challenge the idea of culture as place-bound. And, if culture is no longer bound to place, the study of culture must also relinquish its tie to place as a concrete and bounded space where culture is located. This has in turn pointed to the necessity of translocal studies of how disparate places are related through the movements of people and their use of media (and vice versa).[42] Tracking what Gemzöe identified as the centrifugal trajectory of media use was from the outset a central focus of the present study.[43] Here we alter that perspective slightly by holding place constant and examining how people use media to connect to other locales. Although quite aware that a shopping centre is a transitory place, populated largely by people who are only passing through, it is also a place where people come and use media to connect them to other places. If in the previous sections of this chapter we were looking at the production of locality, and the limits of that production, here we focus on how translocality is produced in the shopping centre, specifically through media consumption. We find a number of media-specific ways people have developed to accomplish the task, in effect, of being in two (or more) places at once.

The cellular phone is an obvious case of the way contemporary media transform media users' relationship to place.[44] Whereas a few years ago we answered the phone and asked whom we were speaking to, today the most common question is 'where are you?' In making or answering a call, or reading a phone message, the caller creates a new space, defined by gestures and body movement, tone of voice and topic of conversation, clearly separating the caller from his or her surroundings. Nevertheless, the conversation becomes a public performance that others in the caller's immediate vicinity cannot avoid noticing, even though it is directed at someone at another location. Kaijser interprets this complex transformation of space with the help of Goffman's dramaturgical model of front- and backstage aspects of performance, demonstrating how this relatively new form of media consumption simultaneously dislocates and relocates the caller.[45]

The Internet user is also two places at once, either in real or virtual time. Solna Centre had no Internet café at the time of our study, but the library's so-called 'public' terminals were in nearly constant use. Users could either book a terminal, or use one of the computers available on a drop-in basis. For people who did not have access to Internet through a home computer, this public place provided an important connection to other sites. Many of the library's regular Internet users were first- and second-generation immigrants who looked at media from their former homeland and in their first language. A typical example was two recent Columbian immigrants who visited the library several times a week to read the Internet newspapers from Columbia (which the library did not subscribe to) and other Spanish news services, and then exchanged emails with friends and family located in different countries. Immigrants did not confine their Internet use to information services in their first language, however. Camauër found that many used the library's terminals to access the Internet editions of a range of newspapers, including the *Financial Times*, *Le Monde*, *International Herald Tribune*, *New African*, *The Economist* and *Die Zeit*. Their choices were motivated either by a general interest in a variety of perspectives on world events or by a desire to be informed on a particular country where a family member or friends was living. In many cases, the Internet was used to complement private newspaper subscriptions and the newspaper one read at home.[46]

According to the population statistics for Solna, 20 per cent of its residents were born outside Sweden, twice as many as for Sweden as a whole. If one includes in addition those Solna residents who have 'a foreign background', that is with one or both parents born in another country, the figure rises to one-third of the town's population. The largest migrant groups come from the Nordic countries, followed by other European countries. Asian is the most common non-European background, followed in turn by African, Latin American and North American. At the time of our study, the percentage of residents with backgrounds in Iran, Poland and Ethiopia were significantly larger in Solna than in Sweden as a whole.[47] To this complex pattern of migration one should also add the large number of Solna residents who claim their origins in other parts of Sweden, further complicating Solna Centre as a place with connections to other places.

Nowhere in the shopping centre is this complexity seen more clearly than in the library reading room. At the time of our study, the Solna library subscribed to around 400 periodicals. These included local newspapers from all over Sweden, and newspapers and magazines in over twenty languages, including all the languages represented in the community's population statistics.[48] While the computer terminals are used primarily by younger visitors, many of whom have a foreign background, in the reading room these media consumers mix with older migrants who also have come to read their hometown newspapers.[49] Most people are regular visitors, coming in after school or on their lunch breaks, or are waiting at the entrance when the library opens on the day 'their' newspaper arrives. Most come to read newspapers from the country or town they come from and to be able to imagine what it is like for people who still live in the place they once knew as home. Recent migrants are interested in reading about people whose names they recognize, but for older and retired migrants who no longer know many people, it is the connection to the place that is primary. They want to read not only about what has happened, but where, in order to keep their local knowledge alive.

Like the Internet users, many frequent reading-room visitors read a range of other periodicals in addition to their hometown papers in order to stay abreast of events elsewhere in the world. The availability of newspapers in a range of languages is also a resource for readers who want to improve their competence in another language. Particularly important for many of the reading room's visitors who have immigrated to Sweden are the Swedish newspapers available there. As one older Turkish man described his perspective, Turkey is a long way away and he no longer has any influence over what happens there. Swedish papers give him information he needs to influence the life he is living today. The Swedish periodicals serve a double function

– as information source and aid in language learning – for many of the reading room's visitors.

Among the diverse group of people whose background is not Swedish, two distinct ways can be identified of using media to maintain and re-establish a relationship to place. First, the selection of transnational media – periodicals and Internet sources – in order to maintain a link to the place which was once home, and a continuity of local knowledge about that place. Second, the ways that local media – in this case Swedish newspapers and magazines – provide a way for transnational people to establish links to the place and perspectives that constitute the new environment of the local. In these two aspects of media use, translocality is produced in a doubling of the dynamic between places that are simultaneously global and local.

TAKING PLACE, MAKING SPACE

Some media practices tend to emphasize and continually (re-)construct place identities, symbolizing collective memories that link specific people to specific places. This is exemplified by many sports – not least team sports, where a sense of local anchorage is upheld as a key to authenticity and fan identification. On a larger scale, it is also true for international athletics championships, where each country's participants form 'troops', geographically linking the 'team' to its national space, even though connections to any particular town are much weaker than in team sports. Television and other media partly act to erode such spatial positionings, by enabling cross-local and transnational identifications as well.

In other cases, it is the transient side that dominates. Films are certainly viewed in certain places, for instance a specific cinema theatre that may be remembered as special by those who spent a part of their youth there, and there are also some few examples of recording places that are developed into tourist sites. But such connections tend to be secondary to the experience of taking part in an enacted narrative whose main place is virtual and not strongly territorialized.

No strict lines separate these two extremes, and individual practices criss-cross between them, as people shift between fixating particular places by inhabiting, naming, using and remembering them, and transcending them by moving between sites – physically through travel or virtually in media use. In this way, people become transnational through local and localizing practices, making use of a wide range of media circuits in order to connect to many different places, thereby linking them to each other, in dynamic and polycentric networks. Some individuals and groups may lean towards the 'localist' side, preferring media practices that strongly link them to a specific place. Others tend towards 'cosmopolitanism', favouring forms of communication and consumption that enable them to become maximally mobile.[50] However, while there are people who can be identified as 'locals' or 'cosmopolitans', the two sides are in most cases rather seamlessly blended. People ambivalently move between the two positions through multifaceted media uses where they for instance develop identifications with many different yet specific localities, and where local spaces like the shopping centre itself is full of echoes of and openings towards a wide range of other places.

At the beginning of this chapter, we cited Paul Ricoeur's parallels between temporality and spatiality, where spatial localization within the dialectic of lived, geometrical and inhabited space corresponded to temporal dating within the similar dialectic of lived, cosmic and historical time.[51] Our informants' media practices offered many examples of these dialectics, as they used media to locate themselves in the world and simultaneously to interpret the particular moment of the present, in relation to a past somewhere else and a possible future where elements from different places could be combined and inhabited in new ways.

In the spatial dimension, this is often depicted as a dialectical process between space, on the one hand, and place on the other, where space is conceptualized as abstract geometric coordinates in constant tension with concrete, meaningful localities. Doreen Massey criticizes this 'persistent counterposition of space and place', as the abstract vs. the concrete, and frequently linked to 'a parallel counterposition between global and local'. 'The couplets local/global and place/space do not map on to that of concrete/abstract.'[52] Ricoeur's model avoids this fallacy by specifying different levels of spatiality, parallel to the corresponding levels of temporality. It is important to avoid projecting the dialectics of abstract structure and concrete agency onto the interplay between space and time in general. Instead, as we have shown, a dialectics of abstract, subjective and intersubjective develops within each of these dimensions.

Massey recognizes space, first, as 'the product of interrelations', from the global to the minute as always 'constituted through interactions'; second, as the sphere of 'multiplicity in the sense of contemporaneous plurality' where 'distinct trajectories coexist' and thus of 'coexisting heterogeneity'; and, third, 'as always under construction', i.e. as 'a simultaneity of stories-so-far'. For Massey, space 'is no more than the sum of our relations and interconnections, and the lack of them; it too is utterly "concrete"'.[53] This is an excellent corrective to the one-sided negative view of space as an abstract and restricting structure. If time is a dimension of change, it is indeed important to understand that space is a dimension of coexisting multiplicities. However, it is difficult to ascribe any particular characteristics to either dimension in splendid isolation. The simultaneous multiple trajectories Massey speaks of can hardly exist without their simultaneous combination, since trajectories presuppose their mutual intersection. It serves little purpose to project any critical burden or emancipatory hopes onto any of these basic dimensions as such, since one can never exist without the other, and each should rather be understood to have a wide range of aspects, from the abstract to the concrete, as well as from the restricting to the liberating. If the thinkers who may be called the 'temporalists' tend to overestimate the revolutionary role of time and reduce space to a confining geometric grid, then the opposite 'spatialist' position makes an equally problematic reverse projection of utopian values onto space. Here again, Ricoeur's analysis avoids reducing the rich complexity and ambiguity of both time and space, pointing instead to different ways each of them may be used and understood, and how they are interlaced in social practice.

As nodes for trade across geographic distances, market places have always been places where transnational currents of communication intersect with transnationally mobile people.[54] Today, shopping centres are such nodes, key locations for the development of cosmopolitan cities and identities. Social intercourse in such places is often volatile and transient in character, though visitors and staff carve out niches of relatively stable belonging even in these passageways. People thus balance and oscillate between, on the one hand, provisionally identifying and inhabiting certain places, naming them and investing them with meaning based on memories of personal experiences, and, on the other, moving rapidly between places across space and sometimes also time, either materially and physically, or virtually in their minds and mediated social interactions.

Interacting with people, media and other commodities under late-modern conditions puts great demands on the ability to make meanings: to read and interpret the flood of signs and multimodal texts approaching from every corner of these passages. There is a similar pressure on the capacity to explore, express and shape identities: both individual and collective, both those of persons – of the self and of others, and those of places – of the centre, the city and the nation through which one moves. The increasingly complex and transient mixtures of late- modern lifeworlds finally also involve shifts in power relations, to which the last chapter will turn.

10. COMMUNICATIVE POWER

On the basis of our ethnographic findings, the previous three chapters have cut across media circuits, in order to fully develop the three main themes of the Passages project mentioned at the start of our inquiry. In Chapter 7, we explored the widening of the media world and the increasing interplay between media circuits of our age. In Chapter 8, we developed a multidimensional understanding of temporality in media consumption. In Chapter 9, we analysed the spatially situated processes of communication. At various points, all these themes touched upon the forms of power and resistance that were outlined at the end of Chapter 2. In this concluding chapter, it is now time to focus on this theme. Based on the power plays found in the spatial setting of a contemporary shopping centre, this chapter discusses the main forms in which media power is formed and contested. Three co-existing front lines are identified: (1) the *political* front lines, primarily related to the public municipal institutions dependent on the state system; (2) the *economic* front lines, involving the centre's management and shops, based in the market system; and (3) the *cultural* front lines, engaging civil society and anchored in the lifeworld. This leads to a consideration of issues of cultural citizenship and communicative rights. The chapter then ends by summing up the main insights developed throughout this book.

Media power is always spatially and socially situated, and the individual and institutional agents involved interact closely and in different ways with the contexts in which texts and subjects – media and people – meet and produce meaning and identity. While some strive to control media spaces as resources of social order, others explore their contradictory fissures as openings to radical change. Different social and geographic spaces offer different constellations and opportunities in both directions.

Shopping spaces are not only crossed by people and media, but also by structurally anchored interests and practices. Shopping centres are spaces where the different forms of power intersect and frame everyday life and media use in an extraordinarily complex and dense manner. Although primarily market places, they are actually a mixture of market and municipally organized spaces, involving a number of stores, offices, administrative institutions and public services. Hence, people visit the centre both as consumers and clients of public services. There turn out to be continuous struggles between individual shops and chains, centre staff and management, producers and distributors, and visitors and customers of different kinds.

Historically the ownership of the grounds on which Solna Centre is located has shifted in ways that reflect the overall trends in Swedish politics and economy.[1] From 1943, when Solna became a town on its own, to the beginning of the twenty-first century, the ownership has shifted from what can be called 'landlord capitalism' (up to 1945), through 'state-controlled capitalism' (up to the 1980s) to 'globalized neo-liberal capitalism'. Since 2000, the centre has been owned by the Dutch company Rodamco, which owns shopping centres all over Europe. The political efforts in the 1960s and 1970s to regulate and counteract the influence of the market forces on the city centre as a public sphere have weakened, but still remain active in the political life of the city.

Just as economic and political power is spatially ordered in the centre, so is symbolic power. For example, although the shopping centre at large appears as a place of popular culture, distinctions between high and low culture are not quite absent. The centre is decorated with art and references to high culture are built into its architecture, borrowing and transferring the uplifting flavour of celebrated high cultural standards to the overall popular image it displays of itself as a place where everyone can 'feel at home'. Solna Centre is a place where popular culture reigns and high culture is marginalized, but where the esteem of consecrated art values can at certain points be used to legitimate and affirm its own existence. Many examples of value conflicts between high and low culture can also be found within each of its media shops, in the hierarchical ordering of books, records and videos, and in various taste tensions between different categories of customers and staff.

When people encounter each other as sellers and buyers, the dominant forms of power and resistance tend to be economic. Such encounters are guided by what Habermas calls strategic as well as communicative action.[2] Basically, seller and buyer pursue oppositional strategic or goal-directed interests, but at the same time draw on a common stock of communicative competence. Mediated by money, the encounter between seller and buyer also functions as the most concrete encounter between systemic market forces and the understanding-oriented interaction of the lifeworld. It is a sphere of action where economic macro-powers and everyday cultural practices linked to the micro-powers of the lifeworld converge. It is important for sellers and buyers not to violate the symbolic order of everyday life. They are bound to both conceal and accept each other's strategic interests and actions.[3] Their relationship therefore rests on a delicate balance between trust and distrust. The latter kind of suspicion makes customers interpret sellers critically and is thus a form of potential resistance in shopping customers' rules of conduct in relation to sellers, or in a more general way to the consumer market's offerings and advertising. This mistrust can be grasped by ethnographic studies, but is rarely expressed in explicit acts of contestation. Resistance may also manifest itself in many other ways in media consumption, for instance in the manner in which audiences more or less consciously question or dismiss the ideologies diffused through symbolic media forms and contents. The popular culture of consumption is no pure product of 'the culture industry', or of 'the people', but the outcome of their interaction, in an ongoing dialectics of power and resistance.

In a specific social setting like Solna Centre, economic, political and symbolic power-resistance formations intersect in multifarious ways. The following three sections will exemplify some such struggles that came to the fore in our ethnographic study, corresponding to the three main dimensions of power and resistance presented in Chapter 2. (1) The first section concentrates on the political front lines and struggles that specifically point at the role of the state system. The main focus is on the inter-systemic relations between local municipality institutions for public services and the shopping centre as a commercial market actor, but internal tensions between different levels and institutions in the state sector are also mentioned. (2) The second section focuses on economic struggles mainly related to the market system, in particular the intra-systemic interest conflicts between the management of Solna Centre and the individual enterprises and shops that operate within its walls. (3) The third section discusses how cultural front lines primarily involve civil society actors who as customers, visitors and users of the city centre space collide with the owners, management and sales companies that together represent the shopping centre at large. This section explicitly thematizes relationships between the market system and the lifeworld, but it also briefly touches upon tensions between civil society and the state, as well as the many internal divisions that cross civil society itself. It leads to a discussion of cultural citizenship and communicative media rights. (4) The chapter then concludes by summing up our arguments in the form of a new agenda for cultural studies of media consumption.

POLITICAL FRONTLINES: STATE AND MUNICIPALITY

The state controls a wide range of institutions with administrative power that is based on (and legitimated by) the political power developed through the parliamentary system. There are several internal tensions within this hierarchically ordered state system. One such front line runs between the national level and the local municipality, where national laws, taxes and political measurements are balanced and sometimes compete with local and regional regulations and actions. Solna had a stabile conservative majority, while Sweden has for most periods had social democratic governments. Solna's markedly market-friendly policy can therefore sometimes collide with directives from the national state level. Still, there has been a surprisingly strong consensus between the social democrats and the conservatives around the issues of privatization, and no really strong opposition to the selling out of Solna city centre have been voiced even within the local council. But there are certainly internal differences and struggles running between – and within – different local institutions, for instance in the debates in the local council around freedom of expression issues in Solna Centre, or minor frictions between different unities within the local community. These could also involve individuals and groups in civil society, in ways that will soon be further discussed.

However, in our empirical material, the power struggles between the local state representatives and the shopping centre were the most striking ones. They related to the centre's ambiguous position on the border between private and public. In some respects, all spaces are ambiguous or ambivalent, only to varying degrees. Just like Benjamin's Paris arcades, Solna Centre is both house and street, with glass roof and entrance doors, but also named street and shop entrances. A further ambiguity concerns its status as combined shopping centre and city centre, and thus as both private and public space.[4] It is the municipal square and main streets that have been placed within glass walls and under the control of a private property owner, Rodamco. This peculiar mixture of public and commercial interests relates to basic societal contradictions between state, market and civil society. The commercial interests of market agents intersect conflictually with state interests administered by municipality institutions and with private and public interests seated in civil society, defended in the public sphere by individuals, groups, associations and the media.

There were still several traces of the public character of space within Solna Centre. One such trace was the signs with street names left on the corners of buildings: 'Solna Square', 'Town Hall Walk', etc. Another was the Hollywood Stairs in the middle of the centre, used for various events, including both commercial sales events and certain communal celebrations where the room fulfilled a more traditional function as the true common and public centre of the town, for instance at certain seasonal festivals like Christmas or the typically Swedish Santa Lucia celebrations. The name of the stairs was supposed to remind people of Solna's honourable history as the cradle of Swedish film-making, and there was also a wall painting with Greta Garbo, who was first filmed there.

The privately owned space also contained certain public utilities. There was a big and active public library, in which citizens could dwell, read and listen, with no demands for payment. There was also a town hall that also offered certain public services for citizens. A small cinema didn't manage to survive, but it was the last remnant of a communal Citizens' House, with rooms for conferences, meetings and theatre activities. This was gradually taken over by commercially run shops and offices, as part of a general trend towards privatization and commodification of the public spaces of communication in Solna.

The interplay between commercial and municipal interests includes both cooperation and competition. The local centre manager clearly saw the advantages of having non-commercial public and cultural service institutions integrated in the centre:

> We want a good co-operation with the municipality. It wants to keep a high level of general service in Solna Centre. And thus Solna Centre becomes the evident choice for Solna city to arrange various activities. Which attracts people … We have a very good library that draws lots of people. There is a job centre; there is a citizen forum, a regional social insurance office. And all that generates people, which in turn after a while generates trade. And we do have a rather big traffic with visitors here.

The museum curator who was responsible for the visual design of Solna city in her turn explained that the municipality had 'a mighty good co-operation' with Solna Centre, which allegedly understands that 'the combination of the commercial and the cultural' is 'a rather wonderful mixture', while it is important 'to give and take from each other, that it is important for business to also have an artistic or visionary outlook, to have this mix'. She repeatedly referred to art in terms of 'enrichment':

'you actually get enriched by looking at visual arts.' The striking parallel to the market striving for economic enrichment is ensuring productive cooperation between the two systems, local state authorities and the private market interests. People need to buy, 'but also to get a chance to enjoy,' said the curator, explaining how shops and public cultural spending happily combine. Art was readily integrated in a consumption-promoting experience industrialism.

At other times, however, the curator instead stressed the division between the systems that is the basis for their mutual exchange to be at all meaningful. For instance, she said, 'the municipality has a small free zone' in front of the town hall, where 'it owns the ground; therefore it's free'. She also mentioned instances of a 'cultural clash with the commercial', so that art had to be protected against the intrusion of marketing. Here was a conflict between symbolic and economic power, where state-employed civil servants as representatives of political power defended cultural interests against the commercial ones. In front of the town hall was a large square area with a mobile sculpture hanging under the roof, made by an established Swedish artist. The curator did her best to prevent advertising posters to interfere with this public art space, thus trying to safeguard a non-commercial zone in the centre. The open view became a sign of publicness in an ideological attempt to embody the democratic ideal of free exchange of ideas.[5]

Another state-dependent pocket of resistance was the public library that through its very existence as a cultural institution on the most central square of the place could be seen as a challenge to economic power. It had sparse collaboration with the local centre management, who had talked about sponsoring certain cultural events, but refused to do so inside the library building, for which they received no rental income. As was shown in previous chapters, libraries are no longer exclusively for borrowing and reading books. Nearly half of Solna library's visitors neither borrowed nor returned any books there.[6] Instead, they read papers and magazines, borrowed CDs and videos, studied, or used computers and the Internet. Books remain the medium that dominates the library (from which it derives its name: *liber* is Latin for 'book'), but many other media are found there too. Today's libraries tend to function like mediatheques.[7] The traditional image of libraries as seats of official high culture of the cultivated upper classes has also changed. The chief librarian was very conscious of the library's role as servant of the people in the cultural sphere. She defined their task to stimulate people to look for knowledge and experience, to offer all citizens free access to information, to improve literacy and general education, and to seek to eradicate all social and physical hindrances for people to use the library services, and more specifically to meet the needs for reading among young people. She regarded the library as 'a resting-place from the commercial, this demand to always have to pick up a wallet as soon as you enter a door in this centre'. The need for alternatives to commercialism within the centre was particularly strong for children and the elderly, who often lack sufficient economic resources. The library also serves many other needs besides free reading: it is a quiet and restful place, a calm oasis for reflection and concentration in the midst of the cross-currents of marketing and sales. In this old institution for symbolic power, visitors may make themselves temporarily invisible for the overwhelming strategies of surrounding economic power.

In practice, all spaces of consumption are mixed spaces. Visitors shop but also stroll around and pass right through without even recognizing that they have crossed a delimited area, borrow books or read papers for free in the library, rest their legs on a bench, chat with friends on some corner or look at people over a cup of coffee. Some do experience the centre as a pure shopping space; others use it as a public, social or aesthetic space as well. But there is no doubt that commodity consumption is the activity preferred by the controlling space owners. Ownership of the grounds and buildings is a key factor for securing commercial hegemony. The progressive selling out of city centres to multinational shopping centre enterprises shifts the power balance from the public sphere of the state system to the private sphere of the market. The private property owners must give maximum dividends to their share-holders. If art or public services can assist in this, they may be accepted, but as soon as urban space is sold to private owners, there is no general chance to consider other values than those of sheer profitability. Nor is a private company responsible to public deliberation: as long as it adheres to the law, Solna Centre need never defend its actions in any public arena.

Mostly, the centre company and the city council seem to thrive in perfect harmony. In August 2001, the Swedish Rodamco manager and the local council chair and mayor jointly inaugurated an extended part of Solna Centre. The mayor started by describing Solna city as a pioneer in making the political and private sectors coop-erate to create a modern and expansive urban environment. The Rodamco manager congratulated Solna Centre on its enormous success, and said that he remembered with warm feelings the first time he had met the mayor, fifteen years ago. He explained that Rodamco was a European-based company with an international network of shopping spaces, owning twelve shopping centres in Sweden. The foun-dation for its success had been laid squarely in Solna, he testified, expressing his gratitude to all who had contributed to this success story: politicians, architects, consultants, building firms and the owners of enterprises and stores in the centre. He ended by offering, last but not least, 'a big thanks to the most important ones: the shop-happy consumers!' Then came the usual clipping of red ribbons with both men happily smiling and shaking hands in front of the eager cameras.

The municipality has sold all ground and property in the city centre to Rodamco, except for the town hall and the library. This privatization has induced some resist-ance from left-wing parties who proposed motions in the city council to create prem-ises for activities for children and young people, as well as a theatre stage, and protested against the selling out of municipal space to the core company. These protests have so far all been in vain. The private property owning company won the definition wars that raged from 1986 to 1993 concerning which social praxis should apply in the new, glazed-in centre. In a 1986 motion, the opposing left-wing party feared that 'an indoor square also presents a threat to democracy, since it may result in restrictions of the freedom of assembly and of demonstrations.' This fear has been repeatedly justified. Amnesty International and other NGOs have been denied the right to place a table for information and books there, 'because the property owner did not accept political activities in that part of Solna Centre', according to a social democratic interpellation in 1988. The property owner said he didn't want to make the place a 'refuge for ayatollahs and political pundits'. Soon, political parties were also denied the right to have lotteries and information stands under the glass roof of the municipal core site.

Paradoxically, several state regulations have supported the property owners in their struggle to win power over public space. According to Swedish law, the area occupied by Solna Centre is defined as a 'common' public place, although in practice it is only a half-public space, since the state law and the local statutes leave room for the regulations of the shopping centre to overrule the public regulations, motivated by the fact that the municipality does not own the ground. These regulations are posted at all entrances to the centre. Among other things, they explicitly state that it is forbidden to advertise and organize demonstrations. Solna's citizens may have lost their town centre, but have gained a thriving shopping centre, just like millions of people all around the world. Even though the political agencies seem to have capitulated to economic power, some pockets of resistance do remain within the state sphere. As mentioned above, they are primarily located among civil servants within the cultural sector who tend to represent symbolic power.

The speeches of mutual admiration at the 2001 inauguration mentioned above show how state and capitalist interests worked together to reconstruct increasing parts of the city as a gigantic and thoroughly surveilled and planned shopping centre, with total service for all inhabitants. Many towns and suburbs walk the same way. This forces shops and visitors who do not fit in further and further away to marginal places. Some welcome this development, others feel sorry about it, as when the shopoholic Edina, during a visit to Paris in the British television comedy series *Absolutely Fabulous*, sighed to her critical daughter Saffy, with a gesture of resignation: 'The world is becoming a shopping centre – and you are looking for an exit?!' Another Stockholm shopping centre, Kista Galleria, has been described as 'a small town, nicely wrapped up in a glass case'. 'Inhabitants will simply never have to leave Kista, since all they can wish for and need will be there.'[8] Such are the visions for city centres to be transformed into shopping centres.

Issues of communication relate to issues of public and communal versus private and commercial space. The border between private and public is notoriously blurred, and the precise rules for what is one allowed to do in the shopping centre were unclear. Political manifestations are allowed on streets and squares in other city centres, but hardly when these have been put under glass roofs and fenced in, with doors locked at night. That would disturb business. The commercialization of public space therefore clearly shifts the power balance in urban centres. Such developments have provoked a growing awareness of the fragility and importance of public communication in society. When material space is transformed into pure consumption spaces, public spaces are increasingly virtual and mediated. But even the most advanced media use remains bound to specific localities, and there is a continuing need for physical meeting places where people can do things other than selling, selecting and buying commodities.

Consumption sites, on the other hand, are never pure market places. The more they grow and swallow up their surroundings, the more practices they have to accommodate. There are reasons to fear the growth of a totally administered panoptic surveillance society where state and market institutions integrate all sectors in maximally profitable structures. But contradictory moments remain active within these structures, where even the most commercial shopping centre is still an ambiguous space.

ECONOMIC FRONTLINES: MARKET AND MANAGEMENT

The relationship between the municipality and the shopping centre clearly has an economic side of taxes, ownership, rents and commodity exchange. There is also economic power involved in the exchanges between individual customers and the shops. However, one particularly striking lesson from our ethnographic fieldwork was that the market sphere is far from unified, so that economic power needs to be differentiated into forces that not always go hand in hand, even though they all confront consumers as belonging to a capitalist and profit-driven sphere of society.

Solna Centre was directed by a local management team consisting of the managing director with an assistant, officers responsible for marketing, the letting of premises and the operation of daily routines, and two property technicians. Such a local management unit is posited at an intermediary level in the hierarchical structure of this whole organization. At the top level resides the management of Rodamco Sweden, together with the highest international Rodamco management, located in the Netherlands. The ground basis of the organization is the operative level of shops, cafés and restaurants in the centre. They supply commodities and services to consumers and are thus the most visible level to ordinary visitors. To match the centre management, those corporate tenants that rent stores, restaurants, cafés and offices in the centre have formed a business association that functions as the partner but also counterpart of the management. This business association has regular meetings to make decisions for the tenants' collective about how to deal with demands and rules set by the management, for instance concerning opening times and other issues of mutual interest. As a matching party to the local management, this association inserts a kind of horizontal division into the strictly vertical hierarchy of the centre. This opens up potential tensions between the two, in rare cases where the shared profit interests do not automatically decide the outcome of decisions.

But things are even more complicated, since the shops at the lowest level often have other loyalties other than to the centre they inhabit. Several of them are integrated into larger regional, national or even international chains such as the international Expert chain referred to earlier in Chapter 6. Most of the single shops thus have a double loyalty: towards the local centre, and towards the branded chain to which they also belong. This creates a kind of double identity. Such a shop may be considerably less interested in contributing to creating a distinctive image for this particular centre, and more prone to emphasize that which connects it to the many other similar stores found in almost every Swedish shopping centre. In Chapter 4, on media images, Kodak and Fuji exemplified two different strategies in this respect. This implies a superimposition of two kinds of vertical hierarchies that cross in Solna Centre, so that shops, while placed at the base of the Solna Centre/Rodamco pyramid, also have a position as a link in their specific chain of stores. This makes room for potential gaps in communication and conflicts of interest that are normally handled through peaceful negotiations but may sometimes lead to disputes that can result in some important actors deserting the centre.

Like most international shopping centres, Solna Centre is built around a set of anchor stores, i.e. big, well-known chains and department stores that tend to be placed near the entrances. Solna Centre has H&M, the Åhléns department store, Stadium, Intersport and a couple of other famous national clothes shops. These big stores are mixed with smaller local retailers. The wide definition of a shopping centre is as a set of stores, restaurants and other commercial services organized within a shared framework. This 'shared framework' is provided by the centre management, which sometimes has to go against single units at the operative level in order to secure the most profitable totality for the centre as a whole (and its business association). The management talks about the centre as a home-like, popular centre, motivated by data on the average income in Solna. They think of people living in Solna as 'ordinary people', with average characteristics among the Swedish population. They visit the centre on an average three times a week, so that these visits are generally a popular frequent experience.

In our interviews with the management, some recurrent words came to specify their notion of the 'popular' in Solna Centre: congeniality, authenticity and accessibility. (1) The notion of 'congeniality' originated from the fact that the centre was built as a small town, which gave a feeling of comfort, according to the manager, who also described the typical Solna Centre shopping experience as 'relaxing' and 'pleasant', which in turn was related to security and feeling safe. (2) 'Authenticity' was also mentioned several times, especially in relation to other, competing shopping malls. Solna Centre was supposedly not 'knocked up' on a field but was instead 'a natural part of people's everyday life and surroundings'. Built over the old town square and decorated with images from Solna's history, it was allegedly more 'authentic' than certain other centres, and the natural daylight that flowed down through the glass roof also contributed to this claim. (3) The notion of 'accessibility' can be broken down to three more specific components: (a) opening hours – the centre must be open at least 360 days a year and as many hours a day as all shops would agree to accept; (b) easy access – by car to the many parking places, for pedestrians from the adjacent tube station and from surrounding housing areas; and (c) the mix of shops, characterized by the non-exclusivity that supposedly 'fit' the average Solna consumer.

Most discussions between the levels of the centre concerned opening times and store mix. The rental contracts stated that tenants had to attend the jointly fixed general opening times, or else pay high fines. Some small shops found it difficult to be open anything like 360 days a year, whereas the management and the big stores wanted to extend opening times to summer Sundays and all main weekends. Another discussion concerned rental levels, which were increased rather steeply, in spite of tough negotiations with the business association. Fewer and fewer small companies could afford to pay these rents, with the result that big chains were gradually dominating and the store mix was becoming progressively more uniform. This homogenization runs the risk of making people bored with shopping centres that are everywhere filled with roughly the same content. Another problem was that the commitment of shops to the centre as a whole would diminish if their main allegiance was to the large chains. The Academy Bookstore did not, for instance, show any particular interest in communal activities such as the Christmas celebration in the centre. The Academy Bookstore chain centrally organized their marketing, which had very few items specifically targeted towards the visitors of this particular centre. All this added up to an erosion of the shared, unique framework that characterizes each single shopping centre. On the other hand, Solna Centre was also a part of the multinational Rodamco chain of centres, which to some extent counter-balanced this centrifugal tendency to decreasing internal cohesion.

These examples indicate that power and resistance is not just a matter of conflicts between big economic and political institutions on one side, and common people on the other. Economic power and resistance are also executed within the market sphere. It is often hard for ethnographic fieldwork to document such conflicts, since managers and staff in the private sector tend to be reluctant to discuss openly those kinds of antagonisms. While public institutions may feel they have some kind of duty to be publicly responsible for what they do, and therefore let researchers in, private companies have no such obligation. We experienced that when, for instance, trying to talk to mobile phone stores and being refused entrance. Other than a considerably longer kind of undercover fieldwork, passing hints and slips of the tongue may be the only ways to access some of these intrasystemic tensions.

CULTURAL FRONT LINES: VISITORS AND CUSTOMERS

If the detailed workings of economic power are concealed behind the closed doors of private ownership, the interaction between the shopping centre and its visitors are more accessible. There are striking parallels between this interaction and, on one hand, that between media industries and their consumers, and, on the other, the relationships between urban planning and city dwellers. Ambiguity radiates from all parts of modern society, where on every level rational strategies of production and control encounter diffuse tactics of evasion and unintended uses that disturb the given order. The media world may easily seem to be a very homogenous sphere, under total control by a few major cultural industries that rationally divide up markets and steer their audiences, but when the multifarious activities and interpretations made by media users are taken into account, goal-directed rationality breaks up into much more complex patterns of interchange. This is equally true of the carefully streamlined shopping environments, as soon as people start inhabiting them. It is also true of city planning at large, and Solna Centre clearly combines features from both shopping centres and urban centres.

Walter Benjamin depicted how city planners had already tried to tame and control the chaotic city and its inhabitants in the nineteenth century.[9] 'Haussmannization' hit Paris when Baron Georges Eugène Haussmann, the prefect of Emperor Napoleon III, reconstructed the city in 1852–70, creating a geometric structure of boulevards, parks and 'pleasure grounds'. This transparent city planning answered several demands: hygienic, economic, as well as political. Benjamin showed how the modern project was constantly undermined by its own unconscious dreams – the other, magical shadow of its rational and enlightened side. 'Arcades are houses or passages having no outside – like the dream,' he argued. 'These gateways – the entrances to the arcades – are thresholds', leading down to dark, secret and labyrinthine worlds connected to the collective unconscious of the masses, 'the dreaming collective, which, through the arcades, communes with its own insides'.[10] In Benjamin's world of ideas, a map over the city should therefore not only reconstruct streets, churches and houses, but also 'the more secret, more deeply embedded figures of the city: murders and rebellions, the bloody knots in the network of the streets, lairs of love, and conflagrations'.[11] In fact, the modern dream of transparent rationality has a double shadow, both in the form of these secret dark elements that linger on in the interstices of the Haussmannized city, and in the fact that this dream of transparency is itself a kind of magic, materially inscribed in institutional practices of construction and panoptic surveillance, but nonetheless filled with unconscious desires of omnipotent control and purity.

For Michel de Certeau, too, the modern city is more unpredictable than the planners and those in power want to admit: 'Beneath the discourses that ideologize the city, the ruses and combinations of powers that have no readable proliferate; without points where one can take hold of them, without rational transparency, they are impossible to administer.'[12] Benjamin's and de Certeau's ideas of how power is built into the urban environment feel highly relevant for a shopping centre like Solna Centre, as does the latter's ideas of how pockets of resistance are opened up within such a strictly controlled place. At the end of Chapter 2, we mentioned how Michel Foucault described the dispersed character and immanent relationship of power and resistance. In spite of important differences, this approach has certain affinities to de Certeau's ideas of strategies of power and tactics of resistance. A shopping centre tends to build such relationships into its very architecture and design, and while the polarity does not so well describe the front lines discussed in the previous sections, it seems to suit rather well when depicting the way in which individual visitors relate to the centre's management and shops.

While strategies 'produce' and 'impose', tactics 'can only use, manipulate'.[13] (1) *Strategies* have three specific traits. First, they tend to be spatially fixed, bound to specific territorial place. Second, they strive to control that place through sight: panoptic efforts to survey, overview and predict. Third, they build upon specific types of knowledge, linked to the power to supervise its own territory. (2) *Tactics* are the way dominated groups oppose power by temporal and flexible counter-moves that through unique actions make use of gaps, fissures and the unexpected to momentarily transgress normative orders. Tactics are mostly unconscious and scattered acts that arise in the fleeting moment, but they can also be developed in a reflexive way, for instance by alternative social movements. According to de Certeau these tactics are present when consumers appropriate media-produced texts and can be discerned in what he calls 'textual poaching', in which 'readers are travellers; they move across lands belonging to someone else, like nomads poaching their way across the fields they did not write.'[14]

Panoptic practices abound in the shopping centre. Surveillance in the form of cameras or security officers is an obvious example. It is motivated by a wish not only to prevent theft and other crime against the shops, but also to make customers feel safe. They want the centre to make sure that the threat of criminality from 'other' visitors is eliminated, and can often accept to pay the price of a certain sense of self-surveillance, provided it is unobtrusive enough. The security officers safeguard both the physical and the social borders of the centre. The social border is that 'you mustn't shout out loud and disturb customers, you mustn't steal, you must behave in a civilized way', as one security guard told us. In this work, they are supported by the local regulations mentioned previously. The simplest punishment for misbehaving is to be expelled from the centre, i.e. moved outside its physical boundaries, by being asked to go away voluntarily, or by being physically removed. These physical boundaries must however not be too marked, so that visitors are not scared away by an implied sense of danger.

The panoptic topic is not only present in the work of Michel de Certeau or Michel Foucault.[15] Benjamin, too, makes many references to the panopticon as a metaphor for a modern visual regime. Mirrors are another aspect of surveillance that were found everywhere in the Paris arcades: 'One may compare the pure magic of those walls of mirrors which we know from feudal times with the oppressive magic worked by the alluring mirror-walls of the arcades, which invite us into seductive bazaars.'[16] This mirror theme links consumption and commodity to desire and pleasure. Mirrors expand and multiply the perspectives of a space, but they also enable surveillance and control, both by staff and other visitors. Reflecting surfaces in every nook and cranny signal that someone else might be watching you, just as you might be watching them.

Yet another aspect of the panoptic strategy is the frequently used transparent architecture and design of the shopping centre, which avoids the dark and mysterious spaces that so fascinated Benjamin. While older forms of sale hid commodities behind doors and in boxes, forcing consumers to enter through doors and ask staff for help to discover the hidden secrets, the twentieth century has privileged forms in which all desired objects are immediately exposed on the surface to all who pass by.

This transparency of commodities is built into the architecture, with big glass windows and mirrors that also make customers visible. This was however not the whole truth in Solna Centre. There existed some winding alleys and hidden places where it was easy to get lost. In our fieldwork, we experienced one such area as a 'black hole', into which the people we tried to track as they strolled through the centre tended to disappear, apparently without a trace – making themselves invisible not only for the panoptic strategies of marketing actors, but also for the ones of social science.

Mediated forms of communication were also employed in the panoptic strategies. Surveillance cameras were one example, though they were not yet very common in Solna Centre when we made our study. A more indirect form was through credit cards and other forms of registration of customer behaviour, enabling retailers to customize their marketing and target specific individuals. Current developments in networked microelectronics provide a radical expansion and refinement of such techniques, as expressed in Steven Spielberg's film *Minority Report* (2002).

All these control mechanisms are designed to reproduce the centre as a safe environment primarily for shopping. They also steer people in and out of the centre, organizing its physical place as a social space that mirrors the dominating power relations in society at large. And individual visitors can usually only respond by accepting and internalizing the power structures, or by developing certain marginal and secret kinds of resistance. These latter are then of the evasive kinds that de Certeau described as 'tactics', as when people look for interstices where they can enjoy their own pleasures outside the dominant shopping order. Shoplifters are an extreme case, but there are also groups of young kids or senior citizens who hang around forever, transforming commercial sites into spaces for social intercourse. Solna Centre prefers visitors who spend money and has problems with flâneurs who just wander around. But according to its own figures, there are 'too many' who buy too little. Some cannot afford to, others just happen to prefer to window-shop or look at people. Many teenagers, senior citizens and unemployed belong to these categories. The ones you do not see are the middle-aged career men who are too busy and the subcultural bohemians who prefer less mainstream places.

This reminds us of how Walter Benjamin, inspired by the nineteenth-century French poet Charles Baudelaire, described the flâneur as a male bohemian position from which it seemed possible to experience and study mass life. The way in which the flâneur moved around in cities was simultaneously a reflexive process characterized by a dense oscillation between strong presence in the here and now, swimming with the crowds, and a more solitary, distanced observation.[17] 'The flâneur still stands on the threshold – of the metropolis as of the middle class. Neither has him in its power yet. In neither is he at home.'[18]

> The flâneur seeks refuge in the crowd. The crowd is the veil through which the
> familiar city is transformed for the flâneur into phantasmagoria. This phantas-
> magoria, in which the city now appears as a landscape, now as a room, seems

later to have inspired the décor of department stores, which thus put flânerie to
work for profit. In any case, department stores are the last precincts of flânerie.

In the person of the flâneur, the intelligentsia becomes acquainted with the
marketplace.[19]

The flâneur was certainly no man of open resistance, but a deviant individualist and
a border creature, and as such akin to the critical intellectual and a challenge to the
organized order of both the city and the shopping sites. 'Preformed in the figure of
the flâneur is that of the detective,' writes Benjamin, thinking of how Edgar Allan
Poe and Arthur Conan Doyle constructed detectives as similarly bohemian
outsiders.[20] The figure of the flâneur partly fits de Certeau's description of resistant
tactics, but also hints at its limits. This chameleon evades certain urban control techniques, but is every such avoidance really a resistance in Foucault's terms? There
seems in any case to be a need for distinguishing kinds and levels of resistance along
this social and cultural front line.

Doreen Massey finds most other theoreticians guilty of privileging time over space
and misrepresenting space as lined up with structure and power. One of her main
targets is indeed Michel de Certeau, whose dichotomy of strategies and tactics is
accused of reproducing that of structure and agency, and projecting it onto that of
time and space. Massey prefers to free space from this link to structure, immobility
and power. Instead, she argues, 'for time to be open, space must be in some sense
open too' – a 'simultaneity of open-ended multiplicities' that is 'as impossible to
represent as is time'.[21]

This criticism can be supplemented in two directions. Firstly, it is problematic to
link power strategies to space and resistance tactics to time. In the previous two chapters, we delineated a model where both time and space must be seen as developing
on several levels, from abstract to concrete, with a cultural level in between: narrated
or historic time mediating between cosmic and lived time, and inhabited or social
space mediating between geometric and lived space. For the panoptic power strategies of the nineteenth century, there might possibly have been some truth in that they
tended to emphasize the spatial aspects of vision and geometry. But in late modernity, surveillance and control are as much implicated in the temporal dimension, in
strategies for containing everyday time management and manipulating the forms of
historic remembrance that underpin constructions of collective identities. It is therefore better to release power/resistance from any fixed links to the space/time polarity.

Secondly, de Certeau's and also Foucault's concepts have invited certain cultural
studies scholars to reinterpret them in terms of rather fixed dichotomies, where a
closed camp of power is set against an equally reified and homogenized configuration
of popular resistance. We discussed this in Chapter 2, apropos John Fiske's ideas of
the people versus the power-bloc. Another example in the same direction is when
Michael Hardt and Antonio Negri oppose 'the Empire' to 'the multitude'.[22] Many
share a wish and longing for a situation where all good resistance stands gathered
against all evil power, and revolutionary politics may well strive in that direction,

trying to articulate different counter-forces and blend them into successful alliances. This may well be a fruitful and often necessary tactic, but there is a great danger that this kind of thinking falls prey to what Stuart Hall once (referring to the ethnic dimension) described as a combination of stereotypization and polarization.[23] Critical social and cultural studies need to be aware of the unruly intersections of many different axes of power/resistance, each of which is also ridden with internal ambivalences.

There are thus many different cultural front lines in media consumption. Let us return to the flâneur. While Benjamin's flâneur found the arcades exciting, the bourgeois avant-garde of the early twenty-first century is less fond of shopping centres. How much can this figure be bound to a particular classed and gendered position, like the male bourgeois avant-garde? Janet Wolff and other feminist critics have observed the obligatory maleness of this flâneur, while public women tended to be identified with prostitutes.[24] Women were active in public space, not least in department stores and arcades, but dominating male discourses preferred to reserve critical agency to men. Elizabeth Wilson and others have preferred to look for instances of female flânerie, with resistant gazes and attentive walking movements.[25] Women were certainly present and visible in the modern city, in several social roles, but this induced defence reactions from male writers who tried to hide them away or degraded them to objects of male lust.

Department stores were once built around the female consumer, who was the main target for spatial design, marketing and choice of commodities for sale. Men were supposed to shop fast and efficiently and thus got a separate entrance from the street, much smaller than the 'female' main entrance.[26] Mica Nava and others have shown how the earlier department stores targeted women and constructed a female consumer paradise.[27] Women are still strongly present in shopping, but there has been an historical change in its dominant gender regime. The shopping centres of the late twentieth century have no clear gender-specific spatial outline, instead striving for 'accessibility for all'. And though there exist plenty of gendered marketing, for instance in the strongly dichotomizing weekly magazines, the marketing produced by Solna Centre does not specifically target women at all, but rather the heterosexual nuclear family. According to statistics, women still tend to dominate family shopping. Men spend as much money on shopping, but focus on larger and more expensive products such as cars and machines, whereas women still take the main responsibility for the time-consuming procurement of daily provisions like food and clothes. Seventy per cent of Solna Centre's visitors were women.[28] Comparable figures are reported in many countries, for instance by Daniel Miller in the UK.[29] By implication, the average customer cannot be the traditional nuclear family, but is rather one solitary woman, or possibly a couple of women. The marketing focus on the nuclear family was thus more a result of prevailing family ideals and norms than a realistic mirror of who really makes the shopping. The realism instead lies in the sociocultural dominance of the family as consumption unit. Miller asserts that even though women make the daily purchases, they are made in a family context. The goods bought are generally not for individual use by the women, but for family use. The family *is* thus a basic unit of consumption – though not its main agent.

The older department stores' explicit focus on the female consumer was an acknowledgement of her economic power and cultural taste, and of her right to a social space in a public world otherwise dominated by men. In comparison, today's shopping centre tends to push her back again, in spite of the fact that she remains its most frequent visitor and customer. The step from gender-split department stores to bi-gendered shopping centres implies a kind of *heterosexualization* of commercial space.[30] Vernacular buying, managed by women, has been confined to supermarkets and stores in housing areas, whereas leisure-oriented shopping is concentrated either on city centres (particularly in Europe) or spectacular shopping malls on the fringes of the city, far from housing estates. Their emphasis on leisure, pleasure and desire, far from the unsexy, boring everyday with its diapers and recycling, is meant to attract *both* genders to increased consumption. And today's marketing is either aimed at the family, or trying to attract the heterosexual male gaze, as exemplified not least around Christmas when posters are regularly filled with glamorous models in minimal underwear.

There can thus be discerned in the organization and marketing of shopping sites an historical displacement from the dimension of gender to the dimension of sexuality, corresponding to trends in the media. This amounts to a restructuring of dominant identity orders and their relative hierarchies. There are also strong age, class and ethnic regimes of power in the centre, some of which have been touched upon in previous chapters. All these also point to the existence of lines of power and resistance cutting through civil society itself. The identity orders constructed by the centre are not only imposed from above, but also in most cases shared by a majority of its visitors. It is a matter of hegemonic social structures, rather than of external manipulation.

The contradictions between different citizen groups are of several kinds. There are for instance taste gaps that may induce fierce debates and even hate between different customers in the media shops. A hip-hop aficionado may despise a typical lover of mainstream pop, jazz or opera, and a young feminist in the video rental store may want to protest loudly against those middle-aged men that drool at its porno shelves. Another example is when different social movements sometimes collide, for instance racists versus anti-racists, or fundamentalists versus freedom rights movements. A series of *intersectional* relations between orders of identity and difference makes room for complex front lines in civil society. However, the shopping centre is a strictly regulated environment that tends to minimize the open expression of such conflicts. Explicit anti-commercial critique is pushed outside its confines, as are the activities of subcultures and counter movements. This makes the internal tensions between civil society interests less visible there than elsewhere in the city.

There are also tensions between visitors/citizens and political/administrative state institutions, and these may as well relate to issues of media and communication. One example is when there is dissatisfaction with public broadcasting, or popular opposition to high culture in general. However, these front lines are less specific to this particular environment, and it seems therefore more relevant to look at how visitors/customers may react against the panoptic strategies of economic power, by way of rudimentary forms of resistance to the commercial sphere of the centre and its media retailers.

Power and resistance are mutually dependent on each other, and the counterpart to the regulating measures may therefore simultaneously also point at embryonic forms of resistance. The security officers in Solna Centre unofficially believed that youngsters and gypsies were particularly prone to shoplifting; it may therefore also be argued, in the reverse direction, that young people and certain ethnic groups either have forms of practice that are not tolerated by the centre, and that may in themselves be understood as forms of symbolic resistance to these groups' subordinate positions in society, or that perhaps in response to the prejudiced suspicion of the centre staff, they had to develop counteracting tactics of various kinds, including simply staying away from the place.

Senior citizens and shop owners also quarrelled about the number of benches for resting. During one period, bench after bench was removed from the centre, as a deliberate strategy to keep customers moving, exposed to the temptations of the shops. The official explanation was that benches with resting visitors would block the view of the shops and their advertising. Solna's senior citizen association, with 850 members, strongly protested against the lack of free sitting facilities: 'We do not want to sneak a seat in the many cafés, and we neither should nor can stand eating ice-cream, pizza, or having a coffee and a cake each time we need to sit down and rest our old bodies,' they complained in a letter to the city council. Assisted by the ombudsman for disabled persons, they won that struggle. The centre management obviously didn't dare to go against one of their most rapidly growing groups of customers.

The centre management was considerably less interested in caring for the rights of free expression. This caused a more explicit form of resistance, as public and political debates sporadically occurred concerning the amount of freedom of expression for non-commercial organizations on the squares and streets that had been made indoor spaces with the adding of a glass roof in 1989. This front line related not only to the formal regulations, but also to the practices and rules concerning how to use the few premises existing for meetings in the place. Even the Lutheran Church had difficulties obtaining access to meeting facilities, since taxation reasons made the centre unwilling to rent them and other NGOs the available meeting areas. In December 2003, this made the church organize an open hearing on 'the power over public space', to which they invited the Bishop of Stockholm, the managing director of Rodamco Sweden, the conservative chair of the local council and the Swedish state minister for culture. At this hearing, the Rodamco managing director ensured that they could willingly supply meeting premises for the church and other NGOs, but that the local authorities should then pay the rent costs. The council chair responded that in that case they could not rent such premises in Solna Centre, since they were far too expensive. The structural result of the commercialization of central city space is thus that non-profitable public activities are effectively pushed outside the centre's glass cage.

In his study for the Passages project, economic historian Martin Gustavsson gave ample evidence of struggles between media stores and customers in Solna, and in Sweden at large.[31] Customers may individually or collectively act against single media stores or chains of stores by simply talking to salespersons or other representatives; by writing letters to the press or to Internet sites; by setting up critical home pages; by hacking companies' websites; or by organizing boycotts and other critical protests. Demands may be raised for adding more goods to the stock, or on the contrary for omitting media texts and genres that are found in some way problematic (pornographic, sexist, racist, or violent genres, for example). Demands may also concern the quality or the price of products.

The diversity – or lack thereof – of media forms and genres belongs to the most common topic of controversy, in particular as it is linked to historical trends towards centralization and concentration in the distribution and retail systems. The computer and the mobile phone today are the media tools most commonly associated with the 'new social movements' where activists attack aspects of global capitalism.[32] There was, for instance, some opinion critical against the increasing uniformity of stores for home electronics. In such cases, some critics used the state as a mediating instance to solve various problems, by raising complaints to the National Board for Consumer Policies. The number of such complaints grew steadily from the mid 1990s, and companies selling home electronics (computers, hi-fi equipment, television sets, CD and DVD players, cameras, etc.) were the most frequent targets of dissatisfaction. People used their new PCs and Internet connections to file complaints against the companies where they had bought them. E-mail started to be used for such purposes around 1997, and this convenient channel to the authorities had become the dominant one by the turn of the millennium.

Among the 2,702 home-electronic complaints filed in 1995–2000, 25 per cent came from institutions (private companies, local municipalities or state departments), 55 per cent from male individuals and 17 per cent from women. The fact that private firms also sent in complaints to this state office – for instance criticizing competing firms' marketing as unfair – indicates the paradoxical interplay between the two systems, in that commercial actors make active use of the state authority to regulate market competition. Local municipalities were the largest group among institutions. In Solna, one citizen went to the town hall citizens' office with an ad from the Expert chain, complaining that its information about the costs for cellphone subscriptions was not satisfactory. He thus made use of his competence to convert from consumer to citizen. Solna's consumer guidance officer first went with the citizen to the shop in Solna Centre, but no agreement was reached, and the criticism was therefore forwarded to the National Board for Consumer Policies. In this particular case, no action was taken in the end. Most complaints (more than 70 per cent) came from private citizens, predominantly men, who are the major consumers of home electronics. One third of all complaints dealt more generally with consumers' rights, mentioning no particular company or brand name. Among the total of 523 companies targeted about those complaints that did implicate another company, ten (2 per cent) had received more than thirty complaints each, and still did not meet up to customers' demands. They were all big corporations and nationally famous chains of retailers in home electronics or network supply: the five worst ones were, in descending order: Telia, Tele 2, Onoff, SIBA and City Stormarknad. The firms organized in unified branches attracted considerably more critique than the chains that were built up as voluntary associations of individual shops.

It is not surprising that the number of (satisfied or dissatisfied) customers increases with the size of company sales, although these figures do not concern dissatisfaction with bought products, but with misleading marketing. A large distribution network need not by definition produce worse information than a smaller one. Complaints could concern both the form and the content of an advertisement. A common criticism was that ads promised much more than the shop could actually fulfil, for instance by pushing attractive offers that in practice could not be found anywhere, thus fooling consumers to visit the store in vain. Very few complaints (only 1 per cent in all) resulted in some kind of legal action from state authorities.

Other dissatisfied customers had taken the matter into their own hands, discussing the problems with the power of large corporations in letters to the press or on alternative web pages. Articles in the daily press could, for instance, debate the habit of media companies to talk of 'sales' when prices were in fact not considerably lower than normal. A growing number of websites make comparisons between different suppliers of the same services, in terms of prices, offers and/or test results. There are also channels for complaints, with blacklisting of companies that have refused to follow the decisions of the National Board for Consumer Complaints. Two such independently organized websites are 'Crush the Low Price Giants' ('Krossa lågprisjättarna') and 'The Black List' ('Svarta listan'). Many critical voices sharply criticize the big corporations and instead praise the smaller, local, independent retailers who can supply better support and more personal service to their customers. A woman, for example, wished there were more female sellers of computers and cellphones, so that she could be treated with greater respect. On these websites, people share experiences and good advice as to how to deal with difficult shops, forcing them to live up to their promises. In all cases, they are forums for educating and empowering consumers.

Still more radical critics frankly copied products of large corporations with their own PCs or DVDs. Media piracy today is a mass movement in most media circuits and world regions, and a fierce battle rages between the big corporations and the underground movement of hackers, crackers and pirates, some of which are just after money, others having idealistic motivations. Walter Benjamin once argued that the technologies of reproduction added by each new medium tend to erode the 'aura' of the unique work of art, pushing art from the sphere of religious rituals to that of mass politics.[33] Copying techniques have since then been multiplied and perfected, in particular with the refinement of microelectronic digital techniques. This has widened the sphere of criminal transgression of copyright law, but the Internet has also fed a growing 'open source' movement, striving to transform commodity economies into networks of collective sharing and mutual gifts. For instance, back in 1998, a 26-year-old man was convicted in Solna for having sold 371 illegally copied Sony PlayStation games. In between these two poles are the many individuals who just make use of the opportunities offered by new media machines, with no particular economic or ideological motives. To this development, corporations have responded with lawsuits and scaremongering. Anti-piracy departments of the trade associations for computer games, video films and music organize campaigns to hunt down pirates and restrict their field of action, but big proportions of the population – the young in particular – find it morally justifible to copy these kinds of media texts for private use or for sharing with friends. Besides copying practices, there are also globalized networks of online 'hacktivists' who break corporate codes and place critical counter-messages on their websites.[34]

These struggles involve tensions between different groups in civil society as well, as witnessed by individual music and film artists' efforts to defend their works from piracy, in order to secure their personal incomes. Front lines of power struggle do not just concern the two societal systems, but can as well criss-cross the lifeworlds of everyday activities and identities. It must further be mentioned that social movements do not only lean on the state to defend the lifeworld against deficiencies of the market. It may also be the other way around. Especially in totalitarian states like the People's Republic of China, or some Eastern European countries, protest movements make regular use of free market resources to undermine censorship and other forms of authoritarian media control. But with the neo-liberal trend towards deregulation and privatization in most countries, during the last couple of decades it has been the commercial sector's constraints that have been the focus of critical practice and debate.

The various alternative media movements raise many important questions for the politics of media consumption. The piracy and copyright wars have legal, technical and economic as well as ideological dimensions. They question the role and function of commodity exchange, copyright, private ownership, freedom of expression and the relationship between producer and work in late capitalism.

COMMUNICATIVE RIGHTS, CULTURAL CITIZENSHIP

The media are consumed, but they are also consuming – of time, space and resources. People need all these resources in order to use media, and media use has its costs. This doubleness is implied in the title of this book: 'Consuming Media'. The chapter on media hardware argued that many communicating machines are today necessary tools for citizens to implement their rights of participation and communication in complex, late-modern societies. This is confirmed by certain state regulations, though there is no consensus about precisely which media belong to the basic necessities of life, or which forms of provision should exist for them. These basic issues on the infrastructure of how power and resistance interact in the mediating and mediatized public sphere connect media use to issues of citizen rights, which are fought for by social movements in civil society, mobilizing lifeworld networks and using resources of the public sphere. In such struggles, citizens put pressure on the state system to legally codify basic rights on a national, international, or even global scale.

Sociologist T.H. Marshall divided citizenship into three elements: *civil citizenship* (freedom of expression and assembly, belief, ownership and equal juridical rights), *political citizenship* (rights to vote and thus have a share of political power) and *social citizenship* (basic economic and social welfare, work and education). Graham Murdock and many others have added to this list *communicative* or *cultural citizenship*, including rights to information, experience, knowledge and participation in culture and public communication.[35] It should be noted that it was precisely these rights that the librarian in Solna wished to safeguard, as was mentioned above. In 1958, Raymond Williams was among the first to explore the links between communication and community, arguing for the need of a 'common culture' that is no 'equal culture' but leaves room for 'multiple transmission' that encompasses all citizens and 'is not an attempt to dominate, but to communicate, to achieve reception and response'.[36] These ideas had similarities to Jürgen Habermas's 1962 thoughts on the public sphere and – much later – on communicative versus strategic action. Williams understood that this common culture in modern times can 'not be the simple all-in-all society of old dream. It will be a very complex organization', and needs to be combined with increasing specialization.[37]

In *Communications* (1962), Williams proposed a new, democratic system of communication, grounded on basic rights to transmit and to receive that together formed a basis for free speech, participation and discussion. These rights must be guaranteed by public-service institutions not directly controlled by governments, so that 'the active contributors have control of their own means of expression'. Instead of censorship of irresponsible expressions, he preferred 'to let the contribution be made, and let the contributor take responsibility for it', in order to achieve the need for a democratic balance between 'freedom to do and freedom to answer, as an active process between many individuals'.[38] More specifically, he proposed that public responsibility in the area of education included teaching speech, writing, creative expression, contemporary arts, institutions and criticism.[39] The reforms he proposed in the area of institutions aimed to 'make sure that as many people as possible are free to reply and criticize', which demanded 'the right to reply, the right to criticize and compare, and the right to distribute alternatives'.[40] To this purpose, he listed specific proposals for reform of the press, books and magazines, advertising, broadcasting and television and theatre. Finally, he called for developing alternatives to the two systems of state control and commercial markets.

Williams outlined a program for a democratizing reinforcement of the public sphere that could better guarantee 'genuine freedom and variety'. This plea also had clear affinities to Habermas's roughly simultaneous work on the public sphere.[41] Since then, technological, economic, political, social and cultural transformations have modified the picture. Still, the basic impetus remains valid, and related ideas have been formulated in many parts of the world.[42] The discussion of citizen rights may be criticized from a position inspired by Foucault's preference for conceptualizing power/resistance in terms of struggle and war rather than contracts and rights.[43] However, we have already questioned that substitution, arguing instead for a need to see power and resistance as multidimensional and thus allowing a place for the rights dimension, too. If a cultural dimension is acknowledged, seated in the intersubjective lifeworlds, then it may need to be secured by certain communicative rights.

Culture is constructed and reproduced by processes of communication. In his early work, and in opposition to an elitist conception of culture as confined to the fine arts, Williams had chosen to define culture as 'a whole way of life'.[44] This formula soon became widespread in cultural studies. By the end of his life, however, Williams became convinced that this definition, 'derived primarily from anthropology', was not really useful, at least not for 'highly developed and complex societies', in which 'there are so many levels of social and material transformation that the polarized "culture" – "nature" relation becomes insufficient', and where culture has been differentiated and 'embedded in a whole range of activities, relations and institutions'. Instead, he preferred to see culture as a *realized signifying system*.[45] This is in line with the concept of culture that since the 1960s had already been used in hermeneutics by Paul Ricoeur, among social anthropologists by Clifford Geertz and others, and also in cultural studies by Williams's successor in Birmingham, Stuart Hall.

Culture is thus a matter of signifying processes, through which people making and using texts in contexts shape meaning, identity and power. It is the capability to enter such interaction that is the key, rather than the resulting forms of meaning, identity or power as such. Cultural citizenship should therefore not be too strongly bound to cultural identities. Identities are constructed in communication processes that are the mediating linkage mechanism of culture. Identities are always provisional, relative and transient products of identification practices, anchored in intersubjective processes of interaction. Partly in response to the implied Western ideology of linking rights to single individuals, various forms of identity politics and 'communitarian' theories strive to base civil rights in traditional customs, self-understandings and collective identities of social groups such as families, clans, nations or subcultures.[46] However, this tends to freeze and reify social groups or 'cultures' into rather fixed units whose borders are taken for granted, thus giving rise to a problematic kind of 'culturalism'. It is difficult to subsume individuals under such collectivities automatically and treat them as given entities. In modern societies, collective identifications are increasingly dynamic and polymorphic. Homi K. Bhabha has, for instance, criticized that Article 27 in the Universal Declaration of Human Rights 'emphasizes the need for minorities to "preserve" their cultural identities, rather than to affiliate across emergent minority communities. For all its good intentions, such rights neglect the "inter-cultural" political existence and ethical imperative' that are crucial to a glocalized post-colonial situation.[47]

Nancy Fraser has argued against the culturalist model of identity and analysed how demands for redistribution, recognition and participation need to be balanced through a network of public spheres.[48] By acknowledging cultural citizenship, state institutions can strive to guarantee a minimal level of communicative resources for all citizens. It must be remembered: (1) that these communicative rights always need to be defended and developed by civil society actors in the everyday lifeworld of society, and can never be delegated to state administration; and (2) that they are only a condition for securing that the continual power struggle over resources and interpretations can take place in a reasonably democratic and fair way. Thus they are never a substitute for the concrete interaction that takes place within the lifeworld. Fraser, Williams, Habermas and others who support an intersubjective model of society and culture, still regard the individual citizen as the basis for civil society and the public sphere(s). They instead place the emphasis on communicative rights and networks in the public sphere, mediating between individuals and groups of different kinds and on varying levels of society. Canclini has used Ricoeur to argue for 'a politics of recognition over a politics of identity'. He notes that citizenship 'is no longer constituted solely in relation to local social movements, but also through the communicative processes of the mass media', and that critical policies should support 'the sites of consumption where the aesthetic foundations of citizenship take shape'.[49] Since culture rests on communication, cultural citizenship is the form of citizenship that most clearly strives to expand outside any national confines. Citizenship has historically been developed under the umbrella of the nation state, but today there are a number of debates and efforts concerning a widened concept – and practice – of citizenship, including supranational initiatives like the European Union, up to the global level of the United Nations. Cultural citizenship is tendentially global, though its present embryonic forms have largely been created in national forms.

Cultural citizenship thus requires access to tools for full and active participation in communication practices. This demands access to the means to fully use the widest possible range of media in dialogues with others. Communicative rights aim to secure the democratic availability of three main kinds of such means: material, social and personal resources.[50] Each of them is linked to one of the three basic elements of communication and culture: the text, the context and the subject.

(1) The *material* resources for interaction include access to many kinds of media forms – objects with which to communicate. This is linked to political issues of censorship and rights of free expression, as well as economic issues of how the media market pools resources for consumers. Material media resources include access to both software texts and hardware machines, and to technologies for consumption as well as for production. Not everyone has reasonable means to access these material resources in commodity form through the market, and there is therefore a need for provision through other channels as well, including interpersonal gifts and public utilities.[51] This requires a combination of efficient media markets and democratic networks of libraries and other public services. It also highlights the unfair global

distribution of such facilities. Communication rights are blocked by global poverty and totalitarian regimes, and therefore imply demands for a transnational redistribution of media resources.

(2) There is also a need for *social resources*, since communication is a matter of interaction that always takes place in specific social and spatial contexts. Not only must there be access to texts and machines, but also to the social organization of a wide range of media circuits and genres, engaging all human senses and covering both fact and fiction, news and entertainment, information and the arts, and offering access to multifarious spaces for communication, including public libraries widened to mediatheques. There must be appropriate settings for acquiring media through purchases, gifts or loans, and for using these media for a wide set of different purposes. There is thus a continued need for public spheres, linked to public spaces: physically located sites for face-to-face interaction as well as geographically dispersed virtual spaces for mediated interaction. Public space has functioned in virtual forms since the advent of mass media. The interacting citizens who once formed the early bourgeois public sphere did not just meet in salons and coffee houses, but were also united as readers of printed books and newspapers. Today, there are very many more forms of such virtual public space, whether gathered through dissemination of centrally produced mass media messages, or through more or less horizontal dialogues via telephones or computer networks. Still, public space continues to be needed in a material sense as well, in order to enable embodied human beings to interact fully and with all senses.

(3) Third, each individual needs *personal resources* to be able to make full use of the available media texts and machines in the accessible social settings for such media use. Williams belongs to a persistent tradition, in Britain as well as in Sweden, for which this is discussed in terms of popular education and literacy. This position has roots in an Enlightenment project of elevating the masses. From alphabetization and mass education to public service and media literacy, this project has had tremendous effects. It has empowered the working classes and other subordinate groups, but it has also had a problematic paternalistic tendency to evaluate these personal skills according to a biased normative scale, derived from the standards and norms of bourgeois high culture. Populist and neo-liberal relativists have on the contrary argued against all state intervention and tended to collapse civil society and the public sphere into the market, which they falsely trust to offer a satisfactory supply to every existing demand. However, it is now possible to reformulate the model of media literacy without falling back to such an individualist position. Habermas's ideas of the life-world processes of social integration seated in civil society imply a more fruitful perspective. Personal capacities must be related to the specific demands raised by the communicative situation of each individual, each moment and each place. Media literacy thus cannot be a straightforward question of trained experts teaching young people how to listen to music or use the Internet. In many media areas, there is no

effective schooling system, and there will never be one that covers all new genres and modes of communication. Instead, the task must be to create conditions for everyone to develop complex media literacies through participation in a diverse set of education settings, subcultures and interpretive communities. For this, people need access to reliable information on how to find and use different media, but there is also a need for opportunities to develop critical reflection on the existing media world in which everyone takes part. This can never be fully 'delivered' by state institutions, but the communicative rights of cultural citizenship can strive to deconstruct the obstacles that commercial businesses or oppressive social groups raise for such critical engagement.

EXIT?

Our odyssey through the passages of media consumption, with its complex layers, spheres and flows of communication, has indicated some of the difficulties of guaranteeing general access to time and space for communication in late modernity. Uneven distribution of economic resources, leisure time and power over the use of urban space underpin restricting inequalities in access to communication tools, texts, public places and competencies. Since the early and high phases of modernity analysed by Benjamin, historical developments of technologic, economic, political, social and cultural forms have transformed the ongoing and unresolved tensions between potentials of authoritarian oppression and exclusion on the one hand, and of democratic empowerment and emancipation on the other. Late modernity is characterized by an increasing complexity in all dimensions.[52] New media technologies and genres, global flows of migration and travel, transformed institutional bodies on different levels, emergent and subdivided cultural fields and intersectional crossings of identity dimensions add up to a situation for media consumption that is difficult to reduce to any simple theses. At this endpoint of our investigation, some conclusions can be briefly summarized along the three main dimensions outlined in the beginning and running through the whole of this book.

(1) The *structural circuits* of media use are open, dynamic and intersecting. There is no strict, definite and universally valid definition or delimitation of the media world, nor of its sub-categories. A wide range of media circuits have developed through history, and there is no pre-given limit to what may be used or understood as a medium. The various media are interdependent and co-articulated, as they intersect and mix in many hybrid intermedial forms that sometimes give rise to new circuits and at other times retain a borderland character. The existence of double and multiple media, based on the differentiation of software and hardware analysed in Chapters 6 and 7, has consequences for the dominant patterns of consumption for different media circuits. There are many types of media texts and also a diversified set of media machines, and shifting ways in which these are acquired and used. Some uses are mainly for production, others can be classified as consumption, but these two forms of practice are often mixed in intricate ways, for instance in the use

of interactive communication techniques. New, digital media networks and an intensified intermedial complexity require new critical and interpretive approaches. These considerations have consequences for issues of media power and resistance, since access to – and influence on – all these various media circuits is the most central way to get a chance to make use of symbolic and communicative power. Cultural citizenship needs to ensure communicative rights related to the widest range of media: software and hardware both for consumption and for production, and in all possible genres and forms of communication.

(2) The *temporal chains* of consumption are stretched out in time and often intersect with other ways of communicating, for instance through gifts, loans, or the free or subsidized use of public utilities. Looking at the full process of communication makes it possible to combine insights from consumption studies and media studies, and to understand how media power is played out in all phases of the encounter between people and media. Issues of access relate to the acquisition of communicative resources, including the organization of supply on media markets. Issues of use concern social and legal rules for communicating, from censorship to 'netiquette' (the etiquette or norms of social behaviour that have developed around the Internet). Struggles of power and resistance develop around all phases of consumption and production. Media use is also deeply enmeshed in the construction of time, history and future, so that these issues have fundamental repercussions on the basic coordinates of social life today.

(3) The *spatial contexts* of communication put public spaces on the agenda. Public spheres remain linked to public spaces, and it does matter how these spaces are organized, for instance in urban centres and environments for acquiring and using media. Here, city centres play a particular role, and their commercialization in the form of shopping centres poses threats of limiting the scope of what interactions are allowed and possible in those settings. There is in fact a need for a range of distinctly organized physical spaces, on a scale from intimate to open ones: private, semi-public and public places. The shopping centre raises the issue of a right for privacy, in the face of advanced forms of surveillance technologies that tend to intervene in the most intimate settings. Another issue is the need for semi-public spaces for groups of people to meet and interact on their own. The issue of public space is finally put on the agenda by the accelerating commercial privatization of city centres. With Jürgen Habermas, we have argued for the development of dynamic and intersecting public spheres, and against their colonization by either system: that of the state or that of the market. It is important to develop and defend spaces for media use of various kinds, both as commodities and as public utilities, and both for consumption and for production. All these spatial issues are clearly relevant to issues of cultural citizenship and communicative rights. Again, media use is central to basic human constructions of spatiality, as people use them to orientate themselves, to identify situated localities, to emulate virtual spaces for interaction, and to develop transient mobilities that enables lines of escape as well as forges links to distant others.

Media are used as tools for shaping individual and collective identities, histories and places, in communication with the cultural identities, narrative histories and inhabited places of others. Our study has offered ample evidence of how these dimensions are mutually linked. In agreement with Walter Benjamin's view on history as a battlefield where official cultural heritage confronts repressed and transformative counter-histories, we have traced various ways in which people construct personal and local memories to give meaning to their lives. Confirming Doreen Massey's theses, we have shown how spaces are filled with co-existent multiple trajectories and are used in many and often contradictory ways. We have made use of Paul Ricoeur's understanding of parallels and interactions between time and space in such processes of identification, and put an emphasis on the role of communication media for forming modern life. While raising many new questions, our odyssey has thus at least managed to highlight many of the key issues in late-modern society and culture.

This concludes our walk through the passages of contemporary media consumption. But, dear fellow flâneurs, is there really any exit?

NOTES

CHAPTER 1 LOCATING MEDIA PRACTICES

1. Simmel (1909/1994: 10).
2. 'Digital age' and 'information society' have become widespread expressions. Castells (1996) argues that the late modern world is a 'network society', and Hardt and Negri (2000: 294) point out that today 'productivity, wealth, and the creation of social surpluses take the form of cooperative inter-activity through linguistic, communicational, and affective networks'.
3. See for instance Couldry and McCarthy (2004) and Falkheimer and Jansson (2006).
4. A full Swedish translation was published in 1990, the English one in 1999.
5. His famous 1936 essay 'The Work of Art in the Age of Mechanical Reproduction' is itself frequently reproduced, for instance in Benjamin (1969/1999: 211ff). For relevant analyses of media history, see Thompson (1995), Peters (1999) and Hörisch (2001).
6. Autobiographical sketches including combinations of urban and media memories are found in Benjamin (1950/2002) and (1955/1997). His theses on the philosophy of history are included in Benjamin (1969/1999: 245ff).
7. See Ricoeur (1985/1988) on the relationship between historical and fictional times.
8. Benjamin (1982/1999: 544).
9. Benjamin (1982/1999: 4).
10. Gilroy (1997), Bauman (2000).
11. Benjamin (1982/1999: 10).
12. Benjamin (1982/1999: 63f).
13. Benjamin (1982/1999: 540, slightly varied on p. 874).
14. Benjamin (1982/1999: 460).
15. Stallybrass and White (1986: 27–37).
16. Hardt and Negri (2000: 44f).
17. Nava (1998: 188).
18. Nava (2002: 85 and 94).
19. For historical mappings of shopping environments, see Benjamin (1982/1999), Bowlby (1987), McCracken (1988/1990), Goss (1993), Lancaster (1995), Bjurström et al. (2000: 46ff).
20. Caygill (1998: 148).
21. Benjamin (1982/1999: 89).
22. Benjamin (1982/1999: 406; see also p. 839).
23. The Passages project started with a workshop in 1996 and then organized, full-scale field research from 1998, engaging in all eighteen scholars from various disciplines in a large number of studies in and around Solna Centre and its media shops. The project concluded in 2004. It was funded by the Bank of Sweden Tercentenary Foundation and was first placed at the Department of

Journalism, Media and Communication (JMK) of Stockholm University; later relocated to the National Institute for Working Life in Norrköping.

24. Four Swedish volumes have been published: Bjurström *et al.* (2000) on cultural theories of consumption and media use, Becker *et al.* (2001) on media and culture in the shopping centre at large, Becker *et al.* (2002) on the media shops of the centre, and Gemzöe (2004a) with methodological reflections on collective media ethnography.

25. John B. Thompson coined the concept 'mediazation of culture' to refer to the development of media organizations: 'By focusing on the activities and products of these organizations, and by examining the ways in which their products have been taken up and used by the individuals who received them, we can gain a firm hold on the cultural transformations associated with the rise of modern societies' (1995: 46). We use 'mediatization' in a similar sense, in adherence to common usage of the term.

26. Benjamin (1950/1969: 247).

27. Cf. Buck-Morss (1989: 261).

28. Benjamin (1982/1999: 473).

29. Benjamin (1982/1999: 463).

30. Certeau (1974/1988: 93); Donald (1999: 17).

31. Benjamin (1982/1999: 154).

32. Goss (1993: 36f).

33. Jencks (1987: 95); Goss (1993: 20).

34. Stewart (1993: 23).

35. Urry (1995: 160); Miles (1997: 74); Goss (1993: 36); Hewison (1989).

36. Cf. Olofsson (1995). Wood Green, the British shopping centre examined in Miller *et al.* (1998) is, like Solna Centre, the result of close cooperation between city government and private investors, and includes the town's administrative offices.

37. Fyfe (1998), Jackson (1998), Massey (1994).

38. Cf. Gottdiener (1995: 83), Lees (1998: 236ff).

39. Habermas (1962/1989).

40. Gottdiener (1997).

41. Goss (1993: 32).

42. Jackson (1998: 178).

43. Jackson (1998: 189).

44. Cf. Bjurström *et al.* (2000), Husz (2004).

45. Miller *et al.* (1998: 95).

46. It must be acknowledged that the urban street is also increasingly subject to regulation and control.

47. Gemzöe (2004a).

48. Goss (1993: 26).

49. Andersson (1991).

50. Appadurai (1991).

51. Peters (1997).

52. Gupta and Ferguson (1997: 15). See also Ginsburg *et al.* (2002).

53. Hannerz (2001a).

54. Hannerz (2001b).

55. Marcus (1986: 172).

56. The problem is not unique to the Passages project, and has been discussed in the growing body of anthropological literature concerned with globalization and the cultures of late modernity; see for instance Appadurai (1991) and Hannerz (1996).

57. Drotner (1996).

58. Gemzöe (2004: 51).

59. Cf. Appadurai (1986), Mauss (1925/1990), Thomas (1991), Marcus and Myers (1995).

60. Gemzöe (2004a).

61. Gemzöe (2004a).

62. Benjamin (1982/1999: 6).

63. Becker (2004).

64. Becker was responsible for the major part of the photographic documentation, with additional photographs provided in particular by Fornäs and, at one point in the project, by several of our informants. We had permission to photograph on the condition that the head of Solna Centre could see and approve any pictures we wished to publish, which he did without reservation.

65. Benjamin (1936/1999: 230).

CHAPTER 2   CONSUMPTION AND COMMUNICATION

1. For example Appadurai (1986), Bowlby (1993), Douglas and Isherwood (1979/1996), Falk (1994), Lash and Urry (1994), Lunt and Livingstone (1992), Lury (1996), McCracken (1988/1990), Miller (1987, 1995 and 1998), Miller *et al.* (1998), Nava (1992) and Slater (1997).

2. Baudrillard (1972/1988) is one often cited example of the problematic tendency mentioned.

3. See for example McQuail (1983/1994: 49ff), Fiske (1982: 12ff), Wilden (1987), Carey (1989/1992) and Hannerz (1990).

4. 'Technology' should here be understood in a broad sense. See McLuhan (1964/1987), Williams (1974/1994), Kittler (1985/1990) and Thompson (1995).

5. Fornäs (2007).

6. See Williams (1974/1994) for a classical argument against technological determinism and the model of base and superstructure.

7. Changes might be both extensions of symbolic communication to new material substrata (e.g. electric current, radio waves and electromagnetism), but also reductions as some material substrata (e.g. stone and fire) have gradually been abandoned as means of communication.

8. The multimodality of symbolic modes is emphasized by Kress and van Leeuwen (1996) and Lehtonen (2000).

9. Bolter and Grusin (1999). For an analysis of the continuously emerging media in terms of metaphors like transparent 'windows' versus reflective 'mirrors', with 'frames' as a middle term, see Bolter and Gromala (2003).

10. Bolter and Gromala (2003: 6, 26 and 42).

11. Bolter and Grusin (1999: 45); McLuhan (1964/1987: 8).

12. See Livingstone (2005a) and Dayan (2005), as well as the overview of lingustic terms in Livingstone (2005c: 213ff).

13. This common-sense approach refers to the classical formulae from antiquity to Lasswell (1948) and later theories of communication and cybernetics. Its implications for issues of power will be further

discussed in the last chapter.

14. Drotner *et al.* (1996: 301ff).

15. The media mostly used by the Swedish population (aged nine to seventy-nine) on an average day in 2004 were television (85 per cent), radio (73 per cent), morning papers (71 per cent), books (37 per cent), CD (35 per cent) and Internet (35 per cent), followed by evening papers (31 per cent), weeklies (28 per cent), text-TV (26 per cent), specialist magazines (16 per cent), videos/DVDs (14 per cent), audio cassettes (5 per cent) and cinema (1 per cent), according to *Nordicom-Sveriges Mediebarometer 2004* (2005). In average daily use time, radio wins with 124 minutes, followed by television's 102 minutes. Then came daily papers (29': morning 21' + evening 8'), Internet (25'), CD (22'), books (20'), magazines (14': weekly 10' + specialist 4'), video/DVD (11'), text-TV (2') and audio cassettes (2'). Total media time was 351 minutes, i.e. almost 6 hours (not adjusting for double media use), divided into 42 per cent sound media, 33 per cent moving images, 18 per cent print media and 7 per cent Internet.

16. Marx (1858/1993: 11ff).

17. Cf. Thompson (1990: 317).

18. Radway (1984: 213).

19. Morley (1992: 133, 165).

20. Morley (1992: 40).

21. Appadurai (1988).

22. Robertson (1995); Straubhaar (1996/1997: 284).

23. Ricoeur (1976: 45).

24. Ricoeur (1981: 143).

25. The term 'structure of feeling' derives from Raymond Williams (1961/1965).

26. Lasswell (1948); Shannon and Weaver (1949).

27. Jakobson (1958/1960). For literary reception theories of reading, see Warning (1975), Eco (1979), Bürger (1979), Fish (1980), Brooks (1984), Iser (1984/1991) and Radway (1984). For media reception studies, see Moores (1993), Ang (1996), Abercrombie and Longhurst (1998), Alasuutari (1999), Bird (2003), Schrøder *et al.* (2003) and Livingstone (2005c).

28. Carey (1989/1992) is one of many proponents for a cultural or 'ritual' view of communication, as opposed to a transmission view.

29. Hall (1980: 130).

30. Williams (1961/1965).

31. Nick Crossley is one of the very few who have made a cross-reading of Bourdieu and Habermas, for instance in Crossley and Roberts (2004).

32. Polanyi (1944/1957). See also Therborn (1995) on different trajectories of modernity, with the European one as a special case.

33. Horkheimer and Adorno (1944/1972) and Habermas (1962/1989).

34. Thompson (1990: 248ff); Anderson (1991: 43ff).

35. These branches differ in terms of cultural capital (Bourdieu 1980/1990: 124ff). Bourdieu (1996/1998; see also 1979/1984: 33f, 1992/1996: 347 and 1994/1998: 40ff) emphasizes how the media have become a growing threat to the autonomy of the established fields of cultural production, but without producing a specific form of cultural capital of its own that deserves to be labelled 'media capital'.

36. Bourdieu (1992/1996, 1993); Habermas (1981/1984, 1981/1987 and 1992/1996). The model is partly inspired by John B. Thompson (1995: 12ff). Cf. also Fornäs (1995a: 72) and Couldry (2000a).

37. Habermas (1992/1996: 147ff).

38. Habermas (1992/1996: 151ff).

39. Bourdieu (1980/1990: 124ff and 1997/2000: 172ff).

40. Bourdieu (1989/1996: xii and 1997/2000: 172ff).

41. Habermas (1981/1984); Austin (1962); Searle (1968).

42. Foucault (1976/1990: 94f).

43. Foucault (1976/1990: 95f).

44. Foucault (1997/2003: 265f).

45. Willis (1977).

46. Fornäs (1995a: 123–33) develops a multidimensional model of resistance along these lines. Scott (1990: 198) presents another model, differentiating in one dimension between 'the open, declared forms of resistance, which attract most attention, and the disguised, low-profile, undeclared resistance that constitutes the domain of infrapolitics', and in another between material, status and ideological resistance.

47. Hall (1980: 136ff); see also Hall (1994).

48. Fiske (1987: 316; see also 1989 and 1993).

49. For external and internal criticisms of populism in cultural studies, see Curran (1990), McGuigan (1992), Ferguson and Golding (1997), McRobbie (1997) and Grossberg (1998 and 2004). For general overviews of trends in cultural studies, see Turner (1990/2003), Tudor (1999), Couldry (2000b) and Storey (2003).

50. Williams (1958/1968).

51. Adorno (1966/1990: 93 and 294; see also 1963/1991 and 1970/1984).

52. Habermas (1981/1987: 391ff). Drawing on cultural studies and media reception research, Habermas problematized his own earlier views as well as those of Adorno and Horkheimer.

53. Habermas (1992: 444f). See also Calhoun (1992) and Crossley and Roberts (2004).

CHAPTER 3   PRINT MEDIA

1. See also the statistics in Chapter 2 note 14 above. The figures for papers and for magazines do not add up evenly since some people read both morning (71 per cent) and evening (31 per cent) papers, and some consume both weeklies (28 per cent) and specialist magazines (16 per cent).

2. All information about newspapers, periodicals and books in the shopping centre is taken from articles of Camauër (2002), Ganetz and Lövgren (2002) and Ganetz (2002).

3. USK (2000: 8).

4. For an historical account, see Radway (1984 and 1997).

5. Both these book spaces are important to satisfy people's love for reading: in 2004, 19 per cent of those who had read a book in the preceding week had borrowed it from a public library, while 35 per cent had bought it in a bookshop, 14 per cent had received it as a gift, and 10 per cent had borrowed it from a friend or relative. The remaining modes of acquisition were through a book club (7 per cent), in a kiosk or department store (4 per cent), via an Internet bookstore (2 per cent), at an antiquarian bookshop (1 per cent), through a reading circle (1 per cent) and by other means (7 per cent). Adding

up then, 49 per cent circulated as commodities, 20 per cent as more or less public, collectively owned utilities, while 24 per cent circulated in a more intimate private sphere (10 per cent as loans and 14 per cent as gifts). The figures are applicable to the Swedish population between the ages of nine and seventy-nine and are taken from *Nordicom-Sveriges mediebarometer 2004* (2005).

6. UNESCO has defined books as 'a non-periodical printed publication consisting of at least 49 pages, excluding covers'. This definition may be questioned, since for instance many children's books have less than 49 pages, but even though magazines may well extend beyond that size, their periodicity definitively rules them out.

7. Clifford (1994 & 1997); Cohen (1987 and 1997/1999); Naficy (1993 and 1999a); Safran (1991); Tölöylan (1991 and 1996).

8. Since a taxonomy of the different migratory communities would lead away from the focus of this chapter, we here use the term 'migrants' to refer both to people who have moved from another country or culture and people who have migrated within Sweden.

9. In 2001, about 2,000 people visited the library in the shopping centre on weekdays and 1,200 on Saturdays. According to a customer survey made during two weeks in April 2000, 11 per cent of the visitors said that they had come in order to read newspapers and 7 per cent to read magazines and journals. The survey also shows that the proportion of men who read newspapers there is twice as large as women.

10. Twenty of our informants were interviewed within the scope of this study about their use of foreign and provincial papers in the two reading rooms in the library. See Camauër (2002).

11. According to the media researcher Michael Schudson (1984: 142) one-fifth of all books purchased are gifts. Statistics show the importance of book gifts for reading: 46 per cent of the Swedish population had read at least one book in 1997 that they had received as a gift (*SOU* 1997: 49).

12. According to Paccagnella (1997), cyberethnographic study means participatory observation (online), interviews and Internet text analysis (in a wide sense). See also Fornäs *et al.* (2002).

13. It is very common to lend books to, or borrow books from family, friends or acquaintances. This way of getting access to books is actually the fourth most common way, after buying them from a bookshop, borrowing them from a library and receiving them as gifts, according to *Nordicom-Sveriges mediebarometer 2004* (2005); see note 5 above.

14. Benjamin (1931/1999: 69).

15. Gabriel and Lang (1995).

16. Thomas (1991: 204).

17. Nor does Mauss place the gift in a power perspective, for example linked to gender (cf. Strathern 1988).

18. Miller (1998: 148).

19. Mauss argues that westerners live in a society where there is a sharp distinction between things and people, but that we still have echoes in our culture from a time when people and things were indistinguishable, when things were charged with the powers and magic of the owner, which could then be transferred together with the thing, transformed into a gift, to its new owner (cf. Mauss 1925/1990: 47 and 65).

20. Mauss (1925/1990: 39ff).

21. In this spirit, Ricoeur (2000/2004: 481ff) links gift and forgiveness, acknowledging their moments of symmetric reciprocity (an exchange of giving and receiving), but also of unconditional love.

22. Miller (1998: 40ff). Miller does not analyse gifts, however, but studies everyday shopping, mostly of foodstuffs.

CHAPTER 4   MEDIA IMAGES

1. Goffman (1959/1972).
2. Debord (1966).
3. For an overview of reflexivity concepts, see Fornäs (1995a: 210ff, but also 1994a, 1994b and 1995b). For institutional reflexivity, see Beck (1986/1992).
4. Bolter and Grusin (1999).
5. Becker (2002), Göthlund (2002).
6. For a fascinating discussion of the history of store window display see Leach (1993).
7. For consumption perspectives on Disney, see Smoodin (1994), The Project on Disney (1995), Wasko (2001), Wasko *et al.* (2001) and Drotner (2003 and 2004).
8. Cf. Hirdman (2002).
9. 'Foto-gänget' may be translated as 'the Photo Guys' or 'the Photo Crew', but 'the Photo Gang' seems best to catch the informal and vernacular character of the Swedish name.
10. Becker *et al.* (2002).
11. Benjamin (1936/1999).
12. Although digital photography has become more common, at the time of this study (2001) many consumers still preferred the tactile experience of the print. As one of them said, 'I really want to hold the paper prints in my hands, to *feel* them is part of the experience.'
13. Stewart (1993: 138).

CHAPTER 5   SOUND AND MOTION

1. See statistics in Chapter 2, note 14 above.
2. Both Mix Records and Video 48 Hours belong to chains operating in the Stockholm area. The name of Mix Records alludes to its varied mixture of genres and styles, though the overall emphasis is on mainstream pop, rock and dance music. The Video 48 Hours chain offers faithful customers various membership benefits and discounts. The name reflects that one may keep rented films for 48 hours, but get a 10 per cent discount off the price of the next rented film if one returns a rented film earlier. Since our ethnographic work in Solna Centre, both chains have been replaced by others with a more national coverage.
3. Sterne (1997) and Huss (2001: 222); Goffman (1959/1972).
4. Lövgren (2002).
5. See for instance Gray (1992), Morley (1995), Gripsrud (1999).
6. Bolin (1998).
7. Kopytoff (1986).
8. Huss (2002).
9. Huss (2002: 216).
10. Huss (2002: 217).
11. As explained in Chapter 2, the notions of immediacy and hypermediacy derive from Bolter and Grusin (1999). This is no entirely new phenomenon, but was discerned already in Paul Willis: *Profane Culture* (1978), which analysed how motorcycle boys and hippies preferred singles and LPs

respectively, homologously corresponding with the basic features of their cultures.

12. This is confirmed by the daily use and average time spent on different media in the Swedish population, according to *Nordicom-Sveriges mediebarometer 2004* (2005); see Chapter 2, note 14 above.

13. Wittgenstein (1953/2001: 27).

14. Many definitions of collecting and collections have been proposed in the theorizing about collecting, though most of them seem problematic and rarely stand up under scrutiny. One of the most elaborate definitions has been proposed by Belk (1995: 67), who states that 'collecting is the process of actively, selectively and passionately acquiring and possessing things removed from ordinary use and perceived as part of a set of non-identical objects or experiences'. This definition seems to work for most collecting practices, but not for all, since, for example, most record or book collectors do not remove their collectibles from 'ordinary use'.

15. Benjamin (1982/1999: 205).

16. Stewart (1993).

17. Stewart (1993: 135).

18. Stewart (1993: 151).

19. Asplund (1989).

20. Benjamin (1931/1999: 68).

21. Asplund (1989: 95ff).

22. Bourdieu (1980/1990: 133f and 1993: 39f)

23. Benjamin (1982/1999: 205)

24. Benjamin (1982/1999: 207)

25. http://www.bigwig.net/myrecords/ 2001-09-25.

26. Benjamin (1982/1999: 211).

27. See for example Belk (1995: 65ff).

CHAPTER 6 HARDWARE MACHINES

1. In a different sense, a model of a 'two-step flow of communication' and influence was developed for opinion campaigns by Katz and Lazarsfeld (1955). Their idea was that opinion campaigns had effects in two steps, first by influencing opinion leaders who were active media users and who then in turn talked to larger groups of people and spread that influence.

2. When consumption is economically productive, i.e. used for producing new commodities, the differences between the two parts of double media may appear as differences between fixed and mobile capital, which in industrial production is the economic aspect of machines and tools versus raw materials, reflected in routines for depreciation etc. But if the embodiments of media texts are called software, they may in some instances be actually very 'hard' and durable – even more so than many machines – so that the analogies between material, functional and economic forms do not really fit.

3. McLuhan (1964/1987), Sloterdijk (1981), Virilio (1990/2000 and 1995), Haraway (1991), Landow (1992), Turkle (1995/1996) and Hayles (1999 and 2002).

4. Media effects on time and space are discussed by McLuhan (1964/1987), Meyrowitz (1985), Harvey (1990), Giddens (1990) and Thompson (1995).

5. Expert originated in the mid 1950s, when some Swedish photo shops started a joint lab venture, Linkopia. In 1962, a number of radio and TV dealers started a parallel venture called Samex, which

soon changed its name to Expert and fused with the photo chain in 1975. By the mid-1960s, the Swedish Expert chain had already taken the initiative to form Expert International together with five other European chains, and soon chains from many other countries were associated. In 2003, Expert International was the world's largest chain for home electronics, photography and communication, with some 7,400 stores in twenty-two countries and a total turnover of almost US$20 billion (http://www.expert.se/).

6. The Technics Store (Teknikmagasinet) is a Swedish chain for 'exciting, fun products worth their price within the technique and hobby area'. It had thirty shops and post-order services. Its first store opened in 1989 in Skärholmen, a south Stockholm suburb (http://www.teknikmagasinet.se/).

7. Geab/The Phone House had more than fifty stores and was Sweden's largest independent mobile phone chain, dating back to 1983 and owned by the British Carphone Warehouse (http://www.geab.se/). Vodafone is the world's largest mobile network, found in almost thirty countries. It was established in 1991 and took the Vodafone name in 2002 (http://www.vodafone.se/400.jsp).

8. Bolin (2003) investigated the locations and functions of TV monitors for the project. For studies of television in public space, see Krotz and Eastman (1999) and McCarthy (2001).

9. 'Bananas in Pyjamas' is an entertainment business based in Australia, originating from a television programme some thirty years ago, but operating almost all over the world.

10. Jeancolas (2001: 35).

11. Uses of mobile phones and videos were studied by Lars Kaijser and Karin Lövgren respectively in Becker *et al.* (2002). See also Drotner (2005) on phones, mobility and publicness. Martina Ladendorf depicted centre visitors' media consumption in general in Becker *et al.* (2001). For other studies of domestic media use, see Silverstone and Hirsch (1992), Silverstone (1994), Ang (1996), MacKay (1997), Moores (2000) and Spigel (2001).

12. Communicative rights and cultural citizenship will be further discussed in the final chapter.

13. The following analysis summarizes findings by the project's economic historian Martin Gustavsson (2002).

14. Consumer activism is also discussed by Klein (2000).

15. Benjamin (1982/1999: 460).

CHAPTER 7 INTERMEDIAL CROSSINGS

1. Bjurström *et al.* (2000: 42ff and 143ff) and Fornäs (2001b and 2002a: 302ff). Cf. Douglas and Isherwood (1979/1996: xvi) and the dialectics of connecting 'bridges' and separating 'doors' in Simmel (1909/1994). Amin and Thrift (2002: 30) argue that places are best thought of 'not so much as enduring sites but as *moments of encounter*'.

2. Bolter and Grusin (1999). Bolter and Gromala (2003: 6) argue that 'every digital artefact oscillates between being transparent and reflective'.

3. Livingstone (2003) discusses relations between research on media use and media consumption.

4. Kittler (1997), Aarseth (1997), Peters (1999), Hörisch (2001) and Hayles (2002) have presented fascinating analyses of media history and of the material aspects of communication and culture, developing ideas from McLuhan, Foucault, Derrida, Deleuze and others.

5. Peters (1999). See also Williams (1962/1973), McLuhan (1964/1987), Winston (1998), Hörisch (2001) and Finnegan (2002) on historical and present forms of communication.

6. Fornäs (1995a); Jensen (1998); Fornäs (2001a); Fornäs *et al.* (2002).

7. Hertel (1996/1997: 212f). For further elaborations on intermediality, see Lehtonen (2000), Fornäs (2002a and b) and Rajewsky (2005).

8. Compare also the ideas of intertextuality developed by Julia Kristeva (1969/1986) and the forms of transtextuality proposed by Gérard Genette (1982/1997).

9. Bolter and Grusin (1999).

10. In a lecture in Norrköping in 2003, French cinema scholar Roger Odin explored the complex processes of remediation from (amateur and professional) photography to (home and feature) film and from there to television (also influenced by radio), to video and to computer-based digital disks. Odin differentiates between five levels of intermedial remediation: (1) contents, (2) stylistic traits, (3) narrative and discursive structure, (4) historical influences, and (5) the pragmatics and self-understanding of users and producers. On transformations of amateur film-making, see also Odin (1998 and 1999).

CHAPTER 8 LAYERS OF TIME

1. Ganetz (2001b).

2. Castells (1996: 375).

3. Benjamin (1982/1999: 880, 883 and 211).

4. Benjamin (1982/1999: 473).

5. Benjamin (1950/1999: 247).

6. Benjamin (1950/1999: 248).

7. Benjamin (1982/1999: 474).

8. Benjamin (1982/1999: 447).

9. Ricoeur (1983/1984, 1984/1985, 1985/1988 and 2000/2004: 238ff).

10. Benjamin (1936/1999: 227).

11. Kittler (1986/1999: 2ff).

12. Benjamin (1982/1999: 544).

13. Latour (1991/1993: 46 and 48).

14. Benjamin (1982/1999: 471).

15. Benjamin (1982/1999: 861).

16. Benjamin (1982/1999: 388ff and 13).

17. Benjamin (1982/1999: 392).

18. Benjamin (1982/1999: 392 and 1950/1999: 252f). See also Fornäs (1995a: 19f) on the relationship between modernity, the current period (in contrast to the distant past), the evasive present moment (versus long-term structures) and the new (in opposition to tenacious traditions).

19. Thompson (1995) and Miller (1998).

20. Ricoeur (1983/1984: 75).

21. Ricoeur (1983/1984: 54).

22. Ricoeur (1985/1988: 104ff). In a similar way Ricoeur (2000/2004: 131f) later discerns an intermediate level between individual and collective memory, consisting of the threefold attribution of memory to oneself, to one's close relations and to others, with which we enter into history.

23. Ricoeur (1985/1988: 109).

24. Ricoeur (1983/1984: 16).

25. Benjamin (1950/1999: 252f).
26. Benjamin (1982/1999: 476).
27. Benjamin (1982/1999: 407). The intention to look at the use of history in the present is expressed by Benjamin (1982/1999: 206): 'The true method of making things present is to represent them in our space (not to represent ourselves in their space).'
28. Williams (1974/1994: 86ff).
29. See e.g. Pine and Gilmour (1999: 27ff).
30. Benjamin (1982/1999: 154).
31. Benjamin (1982/1999: 476).
32. Cf. Appadurai (1996: 66ff).
33. The term 'invented tradition' derives from Hobsbawm and Ranger (1983).
34. Thompson (1995: 179ff).
35. Benjamin (1982/1999: 1137). This quote from *Das Passagen-Werk*, originating from a letter by Benjamin to Gershom Scholem, written in September 1935, is not included in the English translation of the work: 'den Versuch, das Bild der Geschichte in den unscheinbarsten Fixierungen des Daseins, seinen Abfällen gleichsam festzuhalten'.
36. Jameson (1991: 25).
37. Benjamin (1982/1999: 389). On memory, history and forgetting, see Ricoeur (2000/2004).
38. Benjamin (1982/1999: 388).
39. 'Diegetic' derives from the Greek *di égesis*: 'lead through'.
40. See Ricoeur (1985/1988: 170f) for a critique of the notion of an implied author and reader.
41. Bachtin (1981).
42. Lyotard (1979/1984).
43. See Ricoeur (2000/2004) on the dialectics of memory and historiography.
44. Walzer (1984) and Frye (1982).
45. Benjamin (1950/1999: 246 and 1955/1999: 87).
46. Latour (1991/1993: 10).
47. Ricoeur (1985/1988: 190).
48. Baudrillard (1981/1994 and 1988).
49. Ricoeur (1985/1988: 101).
50. Ricoeur (1985/1988: 159).

CHAPTER 9 TRANSLOCAL SPACES

1. Kroes (1996).
2. Murray (1997: 153f), Kowinski (1985).
3. Cf. Gottdiener (1997).
4. Hannerz (1996: 5f). See also Thörn (1999b).
5. Bachelard, Gaston (1958/1994), Lefebvre (1968/2002) and Certeau (1974/1988) would be useful for this purpose.
6. Ricoeur (2000/2004: 41f).
7. Ricoeur (2000/2004: 147f).
8. Ricoeur (2000/2004: 150). Henri Lefebvre (1974/1991: 33, 38f) distinguishes between 'spatial practice', 'representations of space' (the 'conceptualized space' of scientists and planners) and

'representational spaces' (or 'space as directly *lived* through its associated images and symbols' in everyday life, philosophy and the arts). This trichotomy has been much cited, but to us appears to be more difficult to operationalize, since it does not incorporate any developed understanding of the precise role of culture, communication and mediation.

9. Ricoeur (2000/2004: 150f).

10. Ricoeur (2000/2004: 153).

11. See also Fornäs (2004 and 2006).

12. Langer (1953) offers a fascinating theory of virtuality as the basis for cultural imagination (virtual space, time, powers, life, memory, history, etc.), long before the cybercultural inflation of the word; see Fornäs *et al.* (2002: 29ff).

13. Appadurai (1996: 33ff) proposes five dimensions of global cultural flows: ethnoscapes, mediascapes, technoscapes, financescapes and ideoscapes. The suffix '-scape' is supposed to acknowledge both the 'fluid, irregular shapes of these landscapes' and their character as being 'deeply perspectival constructs'.

14. Benjamin (1982/1999: 871).

15. Ganetz (2001a) makes a contextualizing reading of Solna Centre as a signifying material text.

16. Gottdiener (1995) distinguishes 'High-Tech Urban' from 'Olde Towne' style elements in shopping architecture.

17. Benjamin (1950/1999: 423 and 879).

18. Lefebvre (1974/1991: 331ff and 399) discusses the dialectic of urban centrality, implying simultaneity of contradictions in space. On city culture and city images, see Gottdiener and Lagopoulos (1986), Zukin (1995), Balshaw and Kennedy (2000), Blum (2003) and Johansson and Sernhede (2003).

19. Amin and Thrift (2002: 23).

20. Lash and Urry (1994: 280).

21. Appadurai (1996: 188f), Lash and Urry (1994: 307). See also Deleuze and Guattari (1972/1984).

22. Goffman (1959/1972).

23. Lövgren (2001); the controversy over the benches is also discussed in Chapter 1 above.

24. Gustavsson (2001).

25. Fornäs (2001c: 396ff).

26. Pine and Gilmour (1999) is an often-cited example of this ideology.

27. Becker (2004: 161ff), Fornäs (2002a: 331ff). A similar formulation appears on the shopping centre's home page, in the Retail Awards citation of Solna Centre as Sweden's 2001 Shopping Centre of the Year: 'This year's winner has developed from an ordinary, local town centre to a regional shopping centre of high international quality ... without losing its hometown atmosphere' (http://www.solnacentrum.se/info.asp 2004-11-03).

28. Rogoff (2000: 8) draws the critical distinction between considering cultural artefacts as reflective vs. constitutive.

29. See Drotner (2005) and Livingstone (2005b).

30. Bjurström (2001b).

31. Appadurai (1996: 181).

32. 'Tre nya biografer i nya filmstaden i Råsunda', http//www.sf.se/sf/rasundabilder 2004-11-05.

33. http://www.gamlafilmstaden.nu 2004-11-05.

34. Fornäs (2002a: 326-31).

35. Jeancolas (2001: 35). See also Friedberg (1993) for a discussion of relationships between film, consumption and urban life.

36. Canclini (1995/2001: 110f, 122), Fuller (2004), Corbett (2001: 26).

37. Sture Johansson, according to *DN På stan* (*Dagens Nyheter*'s weekend entertainment supplement) 28 December 2001. Niklas Wahllöf wrote a review of all of Stockholm's suburban cinemas in *DN På stan*, 1 March 2002.

38. Fuller (2004), Erickson (2000).

39. Couldry (2000a: 65ff); see also Lash and Urry (1994: 215f).

40. Cf. Lash and Urry (1994: 307).

41. Appadurai (1996).

42. Hannerz (2001).

43. Gemzöe (2004a).

44. Kaijser (2002).

45. Kaijser (2002: 187); Goffman (1959/1972).

46. Camauër (2002).

47. Camauër (2002: 71).

48. These periodicals accounted for the greater part of the library's media budget of two million crowns, or 10 per cent of the library's total budget. The library's selection is substantially broader than that of the shopping centre's newsagents. At the time of our study, Polish and Ethiopian news-papers were not available in the newsagents (Camauër 2002: 66f).

49. Camauër (2002: 72ff).

50. The 'local'/'cosmopolitan' binary derives from Merton (1968) and has been widely used, for instance by Thomson and Taylor (2005). See also how Morley (2001) discusses how media consumption relates to space, place and identity.

51. Ricoeur (2000/2004: 153).

52. Massey (2005: 183f).

53. Massey (2005: 9ff). In a similar vein, Amin and Thrift (2002: 30) argue that places are '*moments of encounter*', 'variable events; twists and fluxes of interrelation'.

54. This was highlighted in Chapter 1, with reference to Stallybrass and White (1986).

CHAPTER 10   COMMUNICATIVE POWER

1. Gustavsson (2001: 59ff).

2. Habermas (1981/1984: 285).

3. Bjurström (2001a: 120).

4. Livingstone (2005a: 20) mentions how space 'turns out to be ambiguous or shifting depending on its use', specifically in terms of the increasingly blurred public/private divide.

5. See also Jackson (1998).

6. USK (2000: 8).

7. 'Mediatheques' (or 'mediateques') are public places where people can interact with a wide range of different media. The term is formed in parallel to 'bibliotheques', i.e. the term for libraries in many non-English European languages (French, German, Scandinavian, etc.).

8. Collin (2003).

9. Benjamin (1950/1999).
10. The quotes are from Benjamin (1982/1999: 406 (compare also 839), 89 and 389).
11. Benjamin (1982/1999: 83).
12. Certeau (1974/1988: 95).
13. Certeau (1974/1988: 30).
14. Certeau (1974/1988: 174).
15. Foucault (1974/1979).
16. Benjamin (1982/1999: 541).
17. Gleber (1997: 67).
18. Benjamin (1982/1999: 10).
19. Benjamin (1982/1999: 21).
20. Benjamin (1982/1999: 442). See also Donald (1999: 44f) on flânerie as both urban practice and critical method.
21. Massey (2005: 45ff; 48).
22. Fiske (1993); Hardt and Negri (2000).
23. Hall (1992).
24. Wolff (1985, 1990, 1993); Gilloch (1999); Parsons (1999).
25. Petro (1989 and 1997); Friedberg (1993); Gleber (1997); Wilson (1992); Nava (1996 and 1997).
26. Husz (2004); Lancaster (1995: 182).
27. Nava (1996 and 1997).
28. *CentrumProfil 98*.
29. Miller (1998) found 68.4 and 71.7 per cent of women in two British shopping centres and reports that less than 5 per cent of all shopping was done by families, while single-person shopping accounted for 65 and 68 per cent in the two centres.
30. Reekie (1992); Ganetz (2005).
31. The remainder of this section is based on Gustavsson (2002), who refers to official documents from the Swedish state and Solna City.
32. Trägårdh (1999: 17, 35); Thörn (1999b: 432f, 441, 450, 455, 461).
33. Benjamin (1936/1999).
34. Klein (2000: 284).
35. Marshall (1950/1992); Murdock (1996 and 1999).
36. Williams (1958/1968: 301ff). The concept of 'common culture' became a buzzword in classical cultural studies and was for instance applied to youth culture by Paul Willis (1990).
37. Williams (1958/1968: 319). Williams (1958/1968: 320) stresses that every 'culture, while it is being lived, is always in part unknown, in part unrealized'. This has clear affinities to the idea of horizons of expectation and the lifeworld by Gadamer, Schütz and Habermas.
38. Williams (1962/1973: 120-3).
39. Williams (1962/1973: 127ff).
40. Williams (1962/1973: 138).
41. Habermas (1962/1989). The parallels between Habermas and Williams are analysed by Nieminen (1997).
42. See for instance Turner (1994 and 2001), Donald (1999: 97ff), Amnå and Johannesson (1999), Ilczuk (2001), Stevenson (2001), Couldry (2006) and Dahlgren (2006).

43. Foucault (1997/2003).
44. Williams (1958/1968: 18).
45. Williams (1981: 12f and 207ff).
46. In a partly similar spirit, George Yúdice (2003: 21ff) sees cultural citizenship as a way to democratically include 'communities of difference', based on the collective character of social identity. To him, cultural rights therefore include the freedom to engage in cultural activity, to speak and teach one's language of choice, to identify with any cultural community, to discover world heritage and to have an education.
47. Bhabha (1994: xxii).
48. Fraser (1999, 2000 and 2001).
49. Canclini (1995/2001: 13, 76 and 151; see also 127ff and 137ff).
50. In fact, all resources are socially organized. Material resources of the kinds discussed above are not natural resources but rather cultural and technological ones that ultimately belong to the social sphere. Still, they can be differentiated from the social settings by a certain artefactual object character. At the other extreme, the embodied and mental capacities of human beings are similarly identified as a subject dimension, even though subjects as well as texts are products of social interaction.
51. Williams (1962/1973: 152f) suggested a double task for society: (1) to guarantee personal ownership of means of communication when that is possible, and to ensure that distribution facilities are adequate; (2) when these means are too expensive or bulky to be privately owned, to hold them in trust for citizens and let them freely use them.
52. In the 1970s and 1980s, Habermas in several works diagnosticized a multiplied complexity and opacity in society, generating new crises of integration. On complexity theory, see Urry (2005).

REFERENCES

Aarseth, Espen J. (1997): *Cybertext: Perspectives on Ergodic Literature*, Baltimore/London: The Johns Hopkins University Press.

Abercrombie, Nicholas and Longhurst, Brian (1998): *Audiences: A Sociological Theory of Performance and Imagination*, London: Sage.

Adorno, Theodor W. (1963/1991): 'Culture Industry Reconsidered', *The Culture Industry: Selected Essays on Mass Culture*, London: Routledge.

Adorno, Theodor W. (1966/1990): *Negative Dialectics*, London: Routledge.

Adorno, Theodor W. (1970/1984): *Aesthetic Theory*, London: Routledge & Kegan Paul.

Alasuutari, Pertti (ed.) (1999): *Rethinking the Media Audience: The New Agenda*, London: Sage.

Althusser, Louis (1971): *Lenin and Philosophy*, New York: Monthly Review Press.

Amin, Ash and Thrift, Nigel (2002): *Cities: Reimagining the Urban*, Cambridge: Polity.

Amnå, Erik (ed.) (1999): *Civilsamhället. Demokratiutredningens forskarvolym VIII*, Stockholm: Fakta Info Direkt (SOU 1999: 84).

Amnå, Erik and Johannesson, Lena (eds) (1999): *Demokratins estetik. Demokratiutredningens forskarvolym IV*, Stockholm: Fakta Info Direkt (SOU 1999: 129).

Anderson, Benedict (1991): *Imagined Communities: Reflections on the Origin and Spread of Nationalism*, London: Verso.

Ang, Ien (1996): *Living Room Wars: Rethinking Media Audiences for a Postmodern World*, London & New York: Routledge.

Ankum, Katharina von (ed.) (1997): *Women in the Metropolis: Gender and Modernity in Weimar Culture*, Berkeley: University of California Press.

Appadurai, Arjun (1988): 'Putting Hierarchy in Its Place', *Cultural Anthropology*, 3:1.

Appadurai, Arjun (1991): 'Global Ethnoscapes: Notes and Queries for a Transnational Anthropology', Richard Fox (ed.): *Recapturing Anthropology*, Santa Fe: School of American Research Press.

Appadurai, Arjun (1996): *Modernity at Large: Cultural Dimensions of Globalization*, Minneapolis & London: University of Minnesota Press.

Appadurai, Arjun (ed.) (1986): *The Social Life of Things: Commodities in Cultural Perspective*, Cambridge: Cambridge University Press.

Asplund, Johan (1989): *Rivaler och syndabockar*, Göteborg: Korpen.

Austin, J.L. (1962): *How to Do Things with Words*, Oxford: Oxford University Press.

Bachelard, Gaston (1958/1994): *The Poetics of Space*, Boston: Beacon Press.

Bakhtin, Mikhail (1981): *The Dialogic Imagination: Four Essays*, Austin: University of Texas Press.

Balshaw, Maria and Kennedy, Liam (eds) (2000): *Urban Space and Representation*, London: Pluto Press.

Baudrillard, Jean (1972/1988): 'For a Critique of the Political Economy of the Sign', *Selected Writings*, Cambridge: Polity Press.

Baudrillard, Jean (1981/1994): *Simulacra and Simulation*, Ann Arbor: The University of Michigan Press.

Baudrillard, Jean (1988): *Selected Writings*, Cambridge: Polity Press.

Bauman, Zygmunt (2000): *Liquid Modernity*, Cambridge: Polity Press.

Beck, Ulrich (1986/1992): *Risk Society: Towards a New Modernity*, London: Sage.

Becker, Karin (2001): 'Bara titta – Solna Centrum som visuell arena', in Becker *et al.* (2001).

Becker, Karin (2002): 'Fotografier: Lagrade bildminnen', in Becker *et al.* (2002).

Becker, Karin (2004), 'Att synliggöra fältet. Fotografi och reflexiv etnografi', Gemzöe (2004a).

Becker, Karin, Bjurström, Erling, Fornäs, Johan and Ganetz, Hillevi (eds) (2001): *Passager. Medier och kultur i ett köpcentrum*, Nora: Nya Doxa.

Becker, Karin, Bjurström, Erling, Fornäs, Johan and Ganetz, Hillevi (eds) (2002): *Medier och människor i konsumtionsrummet*, Nora: Nya Doxa.

Belk, Russell W. (1995): *Collecting in a Consumer Society*, London & New York: Routledge.

Benjamin, Walter (1931/1999): 'Unpacking My Library: A Talk about Book Collecting', in Benjamin (1969/1999).

Benjamin, Walter (1936/1999): 'The Work of Art in the Age of Mechanical Reproduction', in Benjamin (1969/1999).

Benjamin, Walter (1950/1999): 'Theses on the Philosophy of History', in Benjamin (1969/1999).

Benjamin, Walter (1950/2002): 'Berlin Childhood around 1900', *Selected Writings. Vol. 3*, Cambridge MA/London UK: The Belknap Press of Harvard University Press.

Benjamin, Walter (1955/1997): *One-Way Street and Other Writings*, London: Verso.

Benjamin, Walter (1955/1999): 'The Storyteller', in Benjamin (1969/1999).

Benjamin, Walter (1969/1999): *Illuminations*, London: Pimlico.

Benjamin, Walter (1982/1999): *The Arcades Project*, Cambridge MA/London UK: The Belknap Press of Harvard University Press.

Bhabha, Homi K. (1994): *The Location of Culture*, London/New York: Routledge.

Bird, S. Elizabeth (2003): *The Audience in Everyday Life: Living in a Media World*, London: Routledge.

Bjurström, Erling (2001a): 'Bakom köpcentrumets kulisser', in Becker *et al.* (2001).

Bjurström, Erling (2001b), 'Hemmalagets plats', in Becker *et al.* (2001).

Bjurström, Erling (2002): 'Samlarkretsar: I mediekonsumtionens marginaler', in Becker *et al.* (2002).

Bjurström, Erling, Fornäs, Johan and Ganetz, Hillevi (2000): *Det kommunikativa handlandet. Kulturella perspektiv på medier och konsumtion*, Nora: Nya Doxa.

Blum, Alan (2003): *The Imaginative Structure of the City*, Montreal & Kingston/London/ Ithaca, NY: McGill-Queen's University Press.

Bolin, Göran (1998): *Filmbytare. Videovåld, kulturell produktion och unga män*, Umeå: Boréa.

Bolin, Göran (2001): 'Konsumentflöden', in Becker *et al.* (2001).

Bolin, Göran (2003): 'Spaces of Television: The Structuring of Consumers in a Swedish Shopping Mall', Nick Couldry and Anna McCarthy (eds): *Media/Space: Place, Scale and Culture in a Media Age*, London/New York: Routledge.

Bolter, Jay David and Grusin, Richard (1999): *Remediation: Understanding New Media*, Cambridge, MA/London: MIT Press.

Bolter, Jay David and Gromala, Diane (2003): *Windows and Mirrors: Interaction Design, Digital Art, and the Myth of Transparency*, Cambridge, MA/London: MIT Press.

Bourdieu, Pierre (1979/1984): *Distinction: A Social Critique of the Judgement of Taste*, Cambridge, MA: Harvard University Press.

Bourdieu, Pierre (1980/1990): *The Logic of Practice*, Cambridge: Polity Press.

Bourdieu, Pierre (1989/1996): *The State Nobility: Elite Schools in the Field of Power*, Cambridge: Polity Press.

Bourdieu, Pierre (1992/1996): *The Rules of Art: Genesis and Structure of the Literary Field*, Cambridge: Polity Press.

Bourdieu, Pierre (1993): *The Field of Cultural Production: Essays on Art and Literature*, Cambridge: Polity Press.

Bourdieu, Pierre (1994/1998): *Practical Reason: On the Theory of Action*, Cambridge: Polity Press.

Bourdieu, Pierre (1996/1998): *On Television*, New York: New Press.

Bourdieu, Pierre (1997/2000): *Pascalian Meditations*, Cambridge: Polity Press.

Bowlby, Rachel (1987): 'Modes of Shopping: Mallarmé at the Bon Marché', Nancy Armstrong and Leonard Tennenhouse (eds): *The Ideology of Conduct*, New York: Methuen.

Bowlby, Rachel (1993): *Shopping with Freud*, London & New York: Routledge.

Brooks, Peter (1984): *Reading for the Plot: Design and Intention in Narrative*, Oxford: Oxford University Press.

Buck-Morss, Susan (1989): *The Dialectics of Seeing: Walter Benjamin and the Arcades Project*, Cambridge, MA/London: The MIT Press.

Bürger, Peter (1979): *Vermittlung – Rezeption – Funktion. Ästhetische Theorie und Methodologie der Literaturwissenschaft*, Frankfurt am Main: Suhrkamp.

Calhoun, Craig (ed.) (1992): *Habermas and the Public Sphere*, Cambridge, MA/London: MIT Press.

Camauër, Leonor (2002): 'Tidningar och tidskrifter: Transnationella förbindelser', Becker *et al.* (2002).

Campbell, Colin (1997): 'When the Meaning is Not a Message: A Critique of the Consumption as Communication Thesis', Mica Nava, Andrew Blake, Iain MacRury and Barry Richards (eds): *Buy this Book: Studies in Advertising and Consumption*, London & New York: Routledge.

Canclini, Néstor García (1995/2001): *Consumers and Citizens: Globalization and Multicultural Conflicts*, Minneapolis/London: University of Minnesota Press.

Carey, James W. (1989/1992): *Communication as Culture: Essays on Media and Society*, New York/London: Routledge.

Castells, Manuel (1996): *The Information Age: Economy, Society and Culture. Volume 1: The Rise of the Network Society*, Oxford: Blackwell.

Caygill, Howard (1998): *Walter Benjamin: The Colour Experience*, London/New York: Routledge.

Certeau, Michel de (1974/1988): *The Practice of Everyday Life*, Berkeley: University of California Press.

Clifford, James (1994): 'Diasporas', *Cultural Anthropology*, 9:3.

Clifford, James (1997): *Routes: Travel and Translation in the Late Twentieth Century*, Cambridge, MA: Harvard University Press.

Clifford, James, and Marcus, George (eds) (1986): *Writing Culture: The Poetics and Politics of Ethnography*, Berkeley: University of California Press.

Cohen, Robin (1987): *The New Helots: Migrants in the International Division of Labour*, Aldershot: Gower.

Cohen, Robin (1997/1999): *Global Diasporas: An Introduction*, London: Routledge.

Collin, Marienette (2003): *Kista Galleria som en galleria med 'citykomplex'*, Journalism and Multimedia paper, Flemingsberg: Södertörns högskola (http://jmm.sh.se/exjobb/2003vt/gallerian/kista_galleria.html).

Corbett, Kevin J. (2001), 'The Big Picture: Theatrical Moviegoing, Digital Television, and Beyond the Substitution Effect', *Cinema Journal*, 40:2.

Couldry, Nick (2000a): *The Place of Media Power: Pilgrims and Witnesses of the Media Age*, London/New York: Routledge.

Couldry, Nick (2000b): *Inside Culture: Re-imagining the Method of Cultural Studies*, London: Sage.

Couldry, Nick (2006): 'Culture and Citizenship: The Missing Link?', *European Journal of Cultural Studies*, 9:3.

Couldry, Nick and McCarthy, Anna (2004): *MediaSpace: Place, Scale and Culture in a Media Age*, London: Routledge.

Crossley, Nick and Roberts, John Michael (eds) (2004): *After Habermas: New Perspectives on the Public Sphere*, Oxford/Malden, MA: Blackwell.

Curran, James (1990): 'The New Revisionism in Mass Communication Research – A Reappraisal', *European Journal of Communication*, 5:2–3.

Dahlgren, Peter (2006): 'Doing Citizenship: The Cultural Origins of Civic Agency in the Public Sphere', *European Journal of Cultural Studies*, 9:3.

Dayan, Daniel (2005): 'Mothers, Midwives and Abortionists: Genealogy, Obstetrics, Audiences and Publics', in Livingstone (2005c).

Debord, Guy (1966): *The Society of the Spectacle*, Detroit: Black and Red.

Deleuze, Gilles and Guattari, Félix (1972/1984): *Anti-Oedipus: Capitalism and Schizophrenia*, London: Athlone Press.

Donald, James (1999): *Imagining the Modern City*, London: The Athlone Press.

Douglas, Mary and Isherwood, Baron (1979/1996): *The World of Goods: Towards an Anthropology of Consumption*, London/New York: Routledge.

Drotner, Kirsten (1996) 'Less Is More: Media Ethnography and its Limits', Peter I. Crawford and Sigurjob B. Hafsteinsson (eds): *The Construction of the Viewer*, Århus. Intervention Press.

Drotner, Kirsten (2003): *Disney i Danmark. At vokse op med en global mediegigant*, Copenhagen: Høst & søn.

Drotner, Kirsten (2004): 'Disney Discourses, or Mundane Globalization', Ib Bondebjerg and Peter Golding (eds): *European Culture and the Media*, Bristol: Intellect Books.

Drotner, Kirsten, Jensen, Klaus Bruhn, Poulsen, Ib and Schrøder, Kim (1997): *Medier og kultur: En grundbog i medieanalyse og medieteori*, Copenhagen: Borgen.

Drotner, Kirsten (2005): 'Media on the Move: Personalised Media and the Transformation of Publicness', in Livingstone (2005c).

Eco, Umberto (1979): *The Role of the Reader: Explorations in the Semiotics of Texts*, Bloomington: Indiana University Press.

Erickson, Steve (2000): 'Permanent Ghosts: Cinephilia in the Age of the Internet and Video', *Senses of Cinema*, 4.

Falk, Pasi (1994): *The Consuming Body*, London: Sage.

Falk, Pasi and Campbell, Colin (eds) (1997): *The Shopping Experience*, London: Sage.

Falkheimer, Jesper and Jansson, André (eds) (2006): *Geographies of Communication*, Gothenburg: Nordicom.

Ferguson, Marjorie and Golding, Peter (eds) (1997): *Cultural Studies in Question*, London: Sage.

Finnegan, Ruth (2002): *Communicating: The Multiple Modes of Human Interconnection*, London/New York: Routledge.

Fish, Stanley (1980): *Is There a Text in this Class? The Authority of Interpretive Communities*, Cambridge, MA: Harvard University Press.

Fiske, John (1982): *Introduction to Communication Studies*, London: Methuen.

Fiske, John (1987): *Television Culture*, London: Methuen.

Fiske, John (1989): *Understanding Popular Culture*, Boston: Unwin Hyman.

Fiske, John (1993): *Power Plays, Power Works*, London/New York: Verso.

Fornäs, Johan (1994a): 'Listen to Your Voice! Authenticity and Reflexivity in Rock, Rap and Techno Music', *New Formations*, 24.

Fornäs, Johan (1994b): 'Mirroring Meetings, Mirroring Media: The Microphysics of Reflexivity', *Cultural Studies*, 8:2.

Fornäs, Johan (1995a): *Cultural Theory and Late Modernity*, London: Sage

Fornäs, Johan (1995b): 'Do You See Yourself? Reflected Subjectivities in Youthful Song Texts', *Young: Nordic Journal of Youth Research*, 3:2.

Fornäs, Johan (2001a): 'Trassliga informationsnät', in Becker *et al.* (2001).

Fornäs, Johan (2001b): 'Passager och möten', in Becker *et al.* (2001).

Fornäs, Johan (2001c): 'Upplevelseproduktion i händelsernas centrum', in Becker *et al.* (2001).

Fornäs, Johan (2002a), 'Mediesamspel i tid och rum', in Becker *et al.* (2002).

Fornäs, Johan (2002b): 'Passages Across Thresholds: Into the Borderlands of Mediation', *Convergence: The Journal of Research into New Media Technologies*, 8:4.

Fornäs, Johan (2004): 'Intermedial Passages in Time and Space: Contexts, Currents and Circuits of Media Consumption', *Nordicom Review*, 25:1–2.

Fornäs, Johan (2006): 'Media Passages in Urban Spaces of Consumption', in Falkheimer and Jansson (2006).

Fornäs, Johan (2007): 'Reading the Euro: Money as a Medium of Transnational Identification', Norrköping: Tema Q, Linköping University (Report 2007: 1).

Fornäs, Johan, Klein, Kajsa, Ladendorf, Martina, Sundén, Jenny and Sveningsson, Malin (2002): *Digital Borderlands: Cultural Studies of Identity and Interactivity on the Internet*, New York: Peter Lang Publishing.

Foucault, Michel (1974/1979): *Discipline and Punish: The Birth of the Prison*, Harmondsworth: Penguin.

Foucault, Michel (1976/1990): *The History of Sexuality. Volume One: An Introduction*, London: Penguin.

Foucault, Michel (1997/2003): *'Society Must be Defended': Lectures at the Collège de France, 1975–76*, London: Penguin.

Fraser, Nancy (1999): 'Social Justice in the Age of Identity Politics: Redistribution, Recognition, and Participation', Larry Ray and Andrew Sayer (eds): *Culture and Economy after the Cultural Turn*, London: Sage, 25–52.

Fraser, Nancy (2000): 'Rethinking Recognition', *New Left Review*, 3.

Fraser, Nancy (2001): 'Recognition Without Ethics', *Theory, Culture & Society*, 18:2–3.

Friedberg, Anne (1993): *Window Shopping: Cinema and the Postmodern*, Berkeley: University of California Press.

Frye, Northrop (1982): *The Great Code: The Bible and Literature*, New York: Harcourt Brace Jovanovich.

Fuller, Glen (2004): 'On the Status of the Sequel', unpublished manuscript, Norrköping: ACSIS.

Fyfe, Nicholas R. (ed.) (1998): *Images of the Street: Planning, Identity and Control in Public Space*, London/New York: Routledge.

Gabriel, Yiannis and Lang, Tim (1995): *The Unmanageable Consumer: Contemporary Consumption and its Fragmentations*, London: Sage.

Ganetz, Hillevi (2001a): 'Hemligheter och lögner i köpcentrumet', in Becker *et al.* (2001).

Ganetz, Hillevi (2001b): 'Med julen i centrum', in Becker *et al.* (2001).

Ganetz, Hillevi (2002): 'Böcker: Lån och gåvor', in Becker *et al.* (2002).

Ganetz, Hillevi (2005): 'Damernas Paradis? En historia om varuhus och köpcentrum', Tora Friberg, Carina Listerborn, Birgitta Andersson and Christina Scholten (eds): *Speglingar av rum. Om könskodade platser och sammanhang*, Stockholm/Stehag: Symposion.

Ganetz, Hillevi and Ladendorf, Martina (2001): 'Kommers och karneval i cyberrymden', in Becker *et al.* (2001).

Ganetz, Hillevi and Lövgren, Karin (2002): 'Böcker: Urvalsprocesser i bokhandeln', in Becker *et al.* (2002).

Gemzöe, Lena (ed.) (2004a): *Nutida etnografi. Reflektioner från mediekonsumtionens fält*, Nora: Nya Doxa.

Gemzöe, Lena (2004b): 'Var finns medieconsumtionens fält? Centrifugalt och centripetalt kunskapssökande', Gemzöe (2004a).

Genette, Gérard (1982/1997): *Palimpsests: Literature in the Second Degree*, Lincoln, NE: University of Nebraska Press.

Giddens, Anthony (1990): *The Consequences of Modernity*, Cambridge: Polity Press.

Gilloch, Graeme (1999): 'The Return of the *Flaneur*: The Afterlife of an Allegory', *New Formations*, 38.

Gilroy, Paul (1997): 'Diaspora and the Detours of Identity', Kathryn Woodward (ed.): *Identity and Difference*, London/Milton Keynes: Sage/The Open University.

Ginsburg, Faye D., Abu-Lughod, Lila and Larkin, Brian (eds) (2002): *Media Worlds: Anthropology on New Terrain*, Berkeley: University of California Press.

Gleber, Anke (1997): 'Female Flanerie and the *Symphony of the City*', in Ankum (1997).

Goffman, Erving (1959/1972): *The Presentation of Self in Everyday Life*, London: Penguin.

Goffman, Erving (1979): *Gender Advertisements*, Cambridge, MA: Harvard University Press.

Goss, Jon (1993): 'The "Magic of the Mall": An Analysis of Form, Function, and Meaning in the Contemporary Retail Built Environment', *Annals of the Association of American Geographers*, 83:1.

Göthlund, Anette (2002): 'Affischer och kort: Bildgenrer i bruk', in Becker *et al.* (2002).

Gottdiener, Mark (1995): *Postmodern Semiotics: Material Culture and the Forms of Postmodern Life*, Oxford/Cambridge: Blackwell.

Gottdiener, Mark (1997): *The Theming of America: Dreams, Visions and Commercial Spaces.* Boulder, CO: Westview Press.

Gottdiener, Mark and Lagopoulos, Alexandros Ph. (eds) (1986): *The City and the Sign: An Introduction to Urban Semiotics*, New York: Columbia Universty Press.

Gray, Ann (1992): *Video Playtime: The Gendering of a Leisure Technology*, London/New York: Routledge.

Gripsrud, Jostein (1999): *Mediekultur, mediesamhälle*, Gothenburg: Daidalos.

Grossberg, Lawrence (1998): 'The Cultural Studies' Crossroads Blues', *European Journal of Cultural Studies*, 1:1.

Grossberg, Lawrence (2004): 'Cultural studies: The life of a project, the times of its formations', opening keynote at the 5th Crossroads in Cultural Studies international conference, Urbana-Champaigne.

Gupta, Akhil and Ferguson, James (eds) (1997): *Anthropological Locations. Boundaries and Grounds of a Field Science*, Berkeley: University of California Press.

Gustavsson, Martin (2001), 'Markägare och mötesplatser', in Becker *et al.* (2001).

Gustavsson, Martin (2002): 'Mediemaskiner: Kommunikationens hårdvaror', in Becker *et al.* (2002).

Habermas, Jürgen (1962/1989): *The Structural Transformation of the Public Sphere: An Inquiry into a Category of Bourgeois Society*, Cambridge: Polity Press.

Habermas, Jürgen (1981/1984): *The Theory of Communicative Action. Volume One: Reason and the Rationalization of Society*, Cambridge: Polity Press.

Habermas, Jürgen (1981/1987): *The Theory of Communicative Action. Volume Two: The Critique of Functionalist Reason*, Cambridge: Polity Press.

Habermas, Jürgen (1992): 'Further Reflections on the Public Sphere', in Calhoun (1992).

Habermas, Jürgen (1992/1996): *Between Facts and Norms: Contributions to a Discourse Theory of Law and Democracy*, Cambridge, MA: MIT Press.

Hall, Stuart (1980): 'Encoding/Decoding', Stuart Hall, Dorothy Hobson, Andrew Lowe and Paul Willis (eds): *Culture, Media, Language*, London: Hutchinson.

Hall, Stuart (1992): 'The West and the Rest: Discourse and Power', Stuart Hall and Bram Gieben (eds): *Formations of Modernity*, Cambridge/Milton Keynes: Polity Press/The Open University.

Hall, Stuart (1994): 'Reflections upon the Encoding/Decoding Model: An Interview with Stuart Hall', Jon Cruz and Justin Lewis (eds): *Viewing, Reading, Listening: Audiences and Cultural Reception*, Boulder, CO/Oxford: Westview Press.

Hannerz, Ulf (ed.) (1990): *Medier och kulturer*, Stockholm: Carlssons.

Hannerz, Ulf (1996): *Transnational Connections*, London: Routledge.

Hannerz, Ulf (ed.) (2001a): *Flera fält i ett: Socialantropologer om translokala fältstudier*, Stockholm: Carlssons.

Hannerz, Ulf (2001b): 'Introduction: När fältet blir translokalt', Hannerz (2001a).

Hannerz, Ulf (2004): *Foreign News: Exploring the World of Foreign Correspondents*, Chicago: University of Chicago Press.

Haraway, Donna J. (1991): *Simians, Cyborgs, and Women*, London: Free Association Books.

Hardt, Michael and Negri, Antonio (2000): *Empire*, Cambridge, MA/London: Harvard University Press.

Harvey, David (1990): *The Condition of Postmodernity*, Oxford/Cambridge, MA: Basil Blackwell.

Hayles, N. Katherine (1999): *How We Became Posthuman: Virtual Bodies in Cybernetics, Literature, and Informatics*, Chicago/London: The University of Chicago Press.

Hayles, N. Katherine (2002): *Writing Machines*, Cambridge, MA/London: The MIT Press.

Hertel, Hans (1996/1997): "Boken i mediesymbiosens tid", Lars Furuland and Johan Svedjedal (eds): *Litteratursociologi. Texter om litteratur och samhälle*, Lund: Studentlitteratur.

Hewison, S. (1989): *The Heritage Industry*, London: Methuen.

Hirdman, Anja (2002): *Tilltalande bilder*, Stockholm: Atlas.

Hobsbawm, Eric J. and Ranger, Terence (1983): *The Invention of Tradition*, Cambridge: Cambridge University Press.

Hörisch, Jochen (2001): *Der Sinn und die Sinne. Eine Geschichte der Medien*, Frankfurt am Main: Eichborn Verlag.

Horkheimer, Max and Adorno, Theodor W. (1944/1972): *Dialectic of Enlightenment*, New York: Herder & Herder.

HUI (2001): *Branschfakta 2000. Bok- och pappershandel*, Stockholm: AB Handelns Utredningsinstitut (HUI).

Huss, Hasse (2001): 'Passagernas ton', in Becker *et al.* (2001).

Huss, Hasse (2002): 'Musik: Egna ljudspår', in Becker *et al.* (2002).

Husz, Orsi (2004): *Drömmars värde, varuhus och lotteri i svensk konsumtionskultur 1897–1939*, Stockholm: Gidlunds.

Ilczuk, Dorota (2001): *Cultural Citizenship: Civil Society and Cultural Policy in Europe*, Amsterdam: Boekmanstudies.

Iser, Wolfgang (1984/1991): *The Act of Reading: A Theory of Aesthetic Response*, Baltimore, MD: Johns Hopkins University Press.

Jackson, Peter (1998): 'Domesticating the Street: The Contested Spaces of the High Street and the Mall', in Fyfe (1998).

Jakobson, Roman (1958/1960): 'Closing Statement: Linguistics and Poetics', T.A. Seboek (ed.): *Style and Language*, Cambridge, MA: MIT Press

Jameson, Fredric (1991): *Postmodernism or, The Cultural Logic of Late Capitalism*, London/New York: Verso.

Jeancolas, Jean-Pierre (2001): 'Naissance et développement de la salle de cinéma', Gérard Cladel, Kristian Feigelson, Jean-Michel Gévaudan, Christian Landais and Daniel Sauvaget (eds): *Le cinéma dans la cité*, Paris: Éditions du Félin.

Jencks, Christopher (1987): *The Language of Post-modern Architecture*, Harmondsworth: Penguin.

Jensen, Jens F. (1998): '"Interactivity": Tracking a New Concept in Media and Communication Studies', *Nordicom Review*, 19:1.

Jervis, John (1998): *Exploring the Modern: Patterns of Western Culture and Civilization*, Oxford: Blackwell.

Johansson, Thomas and Sernhede, Ove (eds) (2003): *Urbanitetens omvandlingar, Kultur och identitet i den postindustriella staden*, Göteborg: Daidalos.

Kaijser, Lars (1999): *Lanthandlare. En etnologisk undersökning av en ekonomisk verksamhet*, Stockholm: Akademitryck.

Kaijser, Lars (2002): 'Telefoni: Mobila gränser', in Becker *et al. (*2002).

Katz, Elihu and Lazarsfeld, Paul F. (1955): *Personal Influence: The Part Played by People in the Flow of Mass Communication*, Glencoe, IL: Free Press.

Kittler, Friedrich A. (1985/1990): *Discourse Networks 1800/1900*, Stanford, CA: Stanford University Press.

Kittler, Friedrich A. (1986/1999): *Gramophone, Film, Typewriter*, Stanford, CA: Stanford University Press.

Kittler, Friedrich A. (1997): *Literature, Media, Information Systems: Essays*, Amsterdam: G+B Arts International/OPA.

Klein, Naomi (2000): *No Logo*, London: Flamingo.

Kopytoff, Igor (1986): 'The Cultural Biography of Things: Commodization as a Process', in Appadurai (1986).

Kowinski, W. (1985). *The Malling of America: An Inside Look at the Great Consumer Paradise*, New York: William Murrow.

Kress, Gunther and van Leeuwen, Theo (1996): *Reading Images: The Grammar of Visual Design*, London/New York: Routledge.

Kristeva, Julia (1969/1986): 'Word, Dialogue and Novel', Toril Moi (ed.): *The Kristeva Reader*, Oxford: Basil Blackwell.

Kroes, Rob (1996): *If You've Seen One, You've Seen the Mall: Europeans and American Mass Culture*, Urbana/Chicago: University of Illinois Press.

Krotz, Friedrich and Eastman, Susan Tyler (1999): 'Orientations Toward Television Outside the Home', *Journal of Communication*, 49:1.

Ladendorf, Martina (2001): 'Köpcentrumet som vardagsrum', in Becker *et al.* (2001).

Lancaster, Bill (1995): *The Department Store: A Social History*, London/New York: Leicester University Press.

Landow, George P. (1992): *Hypertext: The Convergence of Contemporary Critical Theory and Technology*, Baltimore, MD/London: Johns Hopkins University Press.

Lash, Scott and Urry, John (1994): *Economies of Signs and Space*, London: Sage.

Lasswell, Harold (1948): 'The Structure and Function of Communication in Society', Lyman Bryson (ed.): *The Communication of Ideas: A Series of Addresses*, New York: Harper.

Latour, Bruno (1991/1993): *We Have Never Been Modern*, Cambridge, MA: Harvard University Press.

Leach, William (1993): *Land of Desire: Merchants, Power and the Rise of a New American Culture*, New York: Random House/Vintage Books.

Lees, Loretta (1998): 'Urban Renaissance and the Street: Spaces of Control and Contestation', in Fyfe (1998).

Lefebvre, Henri (1968/2002): *Everyday Life in the Modern World*, London: Continuum.

Lefebvre, Henri (1974/1991): *The Production of Space*, Oxford: Blackwell.

Lehtonen, Mikko (2000): 'On No Man's Land: Theses on Intermediality', *Nordicom-Information*, 22:3–4.

Livingstone, Sonia (2003): 'The Changing Nature of Audiences: From the Mass Audience to the Interactive Media User', Angharad N. Valdivia (ed.): *A Companion to Media Studies*, Oxford: Blackwell.

Livingstone, Sonia (2005a): 'In Defence of Privacy: Mediating the Public/Private Boundary at Home', in Livingstone (2005c).

Livingstone, Sonia (2005b): 'On the Relation between Audiences and Publics', in Livingstone (2005c).

Livingstone, Sonia (ed.) (2005c): *Audiences and Publics: When Cultural Engagement Matters for the Public Sphere*, Bristol: Intellect Books.

Lövgren, Karin (2001): 'Batonger och bänkar', Becker *et al.* (2001).

Lövgren, Karin (2002): 'Video: Brukets tider och platser', in Becker *et al.* (2002).

Lunt, Peter K. and Livingstone, Sonia M. (1992): *Mass Consumption and Personal Identity*, Buckingham/Philadelphia: Open University Press.

Lury, Celia (1996): *Consumer Culture*, Cambridge: Polity.

Lyotard, Jean-François (1979/1984): *The Postmodern Condition: A Report on Knowledge*, Manchester: Manchester University Press.

Mackay, Hugh (1997): 'Consuming Communication Technologies at Home', Hugh Mackay (ed.): *Consumption and Everyday Life*, London/Milton Keynes: Sage/The Open University.

Marcus, George (1986): 'Contemporary Problems of Ethnography in the Modern World System', in Clifford and Marcus (1986).

Marcus, George E. and Myers, Fred R. (eds) (1995): *The Traffic in Culture*, Berkeley: University of California Press.

Marshall, Thomas Humphrey (1950/1992): *Citizenship and Social Class*, London: Pluto.

Marx, Karl (1858/1993): *Grundrisse: Foundations of the Critique of Political Economy (rough draft)*, London: Penguin.

Massey, Doreen (1994): *Space, Place and Gender*, Cambridge: Polity Press.

Massey, Doreen (2005): *For Space*, London: Sage.

Mauss, Marcel (1925/1990): *The Gift: The Form and Reason for Exchange in Archaic Societies*, London: Routledge.

McCarthy, Anna (2001): *Ambient Television: Visual Culture and Public Space*, Durham, NC/London: Duke University Press.

McCracken, Grant (1988/1990): *Culture and Consumption: New Approaches to the Symbolic Character of Consumer Goods and Activities*, Bloomington/Indianapolis: Indiana University Press.

McGuigan, Jim (1992): *Cultural Populism*, London/New York: Routledge.

McLuhan, Marshall (1964/1987): *Understanding Media: The Extensions of Man*, London/New York: Ark/Routledge.

McQuail, Denis (1983/1994): *Mass Communication Theory: An Introduction*, 3rd edition, London: Sage.

McRobbie, Angela (ed.) (1997): *Back to Reality? Social Experience and Cultural Studies*, Manchester/New York: Manchester University Press.

Merton, Robert King (1968): *Social Theory and Social Structure*, New York: Free Press.

Meyrowitz, Joshua (1985): *No Sense of Place: The Impact of Electronic Media on Social Behavior*, Oxford: Oxford University Press.

Miles, Malcolm (1997): *Art, Space and The City: Public Art and Urban Futures*, London/New York: Routledge.

Miller, Daniel (1987): *Mass Consumption and Material Culture*, Oxford: Blackwell.

Miller, Daniel (ed.) (1995): *Acknowledging Consumption: A Review of New Studies*, London/New York: Routledge.

Miller, Daniel (1998): *A Theory of Shopping*, Cambridge: Polity Press.

Miller, Daniel, Jackson, Peter, Thrift, Nigel, Holbrook, Beverly and Rowlands, Michael (1998): *Shopping, Place and Identity*, London/New York: Routledge.

Moores, Shaun (1993): *Interpreting Audiences: The Ethnography of Media Consumption*, London: Sage.

Moores, Shaun (2000): *Media and Everyday Life in Modern Society*, Edinburgh: Edinburgh University Press.

Morley, David (1992): *Television, Audiences and Cultural Studies*, London/New York: Routledge.

Morley, David (1995): 'Theories of Consumpion in Media Studies', in Miller (1995).

Morley, David (2001): 'Belongings: Place, Space and Identity in a Mediated World', *European Journal of Cultural Studies*, 4:4.

Murdock, Graham (1996): 'Rights and Representations: Public Discourse and Cultural Citizenship', Jostein Gripsrud (ed.): *Media and Knowledge: The Role of Television*, Bergen: Department of Media Studies (Working Papers Rhetoric – Knowledge – Mediation 2/96).

Murdock, Graham (1999): 'Corporate Dynamics and Broadcasting Futures', Hugh Mackay and Tim O'Sullivan (eds): *The Media Reader: Continuity and Transformation*, London: Sage.

Murray, Sally-Ann (1997), 'An Academic Milling Around "the Mall": (De)Constructing Cultural Knowledge', *Critical Arts*, 11:1-2.

Naficy, Hamid (1993): *The Making of Exile Cultures: Iranian Television in Los Angeles*, Minneapolis: University of Minnesota Press.

Naficy, Hamid (ed.) (1999a): *Home, Exile, Homeland: Film, Media, and the Politics of Place*, London/New York: Routledge.

Naficy, Hamid (1999b): 'Introduction: Framing Exile from Homeland to Homepage', in Naficy (1999a).

Nava, Mica (1992): *Changing Cultures: Feminism, Youth and Consumerism*, London: Sage.

Nava, Mica (1996): 'Modernity's Disavowal: Women, the City and the Department Store', Mica Nava and Alan O'Shea (eds): *Modern Times: Reflections on a Century of English Modernity*, London/New York: Routledge.

Nava, Mica (1997): 'Women, the City and the Department Store', in Falk and Campbell (1997).

Nava, Mica (1998): 'The Cosmopolitanism of Commerce and the Allure of Difference: Selfridges, the Russian Ballet and the Tango 1911–1914", *International Journal of Cultural Studies*, 1:2.

Nava, Mica (2002): 'Cosmopolitan Modernity: Everyday Imaginaries and the Register of Difference', *Theory, Culture & Society*, 19:1–2.

Nieminen, Hannu (1997): *Communication and Democracy: Habermas, Williams and the British Case*, Helsinki: The Finnish Academy of Science and Letters.

Nordicom-Sveriges Mediebarometer 2004 (2005), Gothenburg: Nordicom-Sverige (Medienotiser 1/2005).

Odin, Roger (1998): 'From Home Movies to "TV Home Productions" and "*I* Home Productions": A Semio-Pragmatic Approach', *Assaph*, 1/1998.

Odin, Roger (1999): 'La question de l'amateur', *Communications*, 68.

Olofsson, Anna (1995): 'Butiken ett kvinnligt rum', *Kvinnovetenskaplig Tidskrift*, 16:2–3.

Paccagnella, Luciano (1997): 'Getting the Seats of Your Pants Dirty: Strategies for Ethnographic Research on Virtual Communities', *Journal of Computer Mediated Communication*, 3: 1.

Parsons, Deborah (1999): '*Flaneur* or *Flaneuse*?: Mythologies of Modernity', *New Formations*, 38.

Peters, John Durham (1997): 'Seeing Bifocally: Media, Place, Culture', in Gupta and Ferguson (1997).

Peters, John Durham (1999): 'Exile, Nomadism, and Diaspora: The Stakes of Mobility', in Naficy (1999a).

Petro, Patrice (1989): *Joyless Streets: Women and Melodramatic Representation in Weimar Germany*, Princeton, NJ: Princeton University Press.

Petro, Patrice (1997): 'Perceptions of Difference: Woman as Spectator and Spectacle', in Ankum (1997).

Pine, B. Joseph II and Gilmore, James H. (1999): *The Experience Economy: Work is Theatre, Every Business a Stage*, Boston, MA: Harvard Business School Press.

Polanyi, Karl (1944/1957): *The Great Transformation: The Political and Economic Origins of Our Time*, Boston: Beacon Hill Press.

Project on Disney, The (1995): *Inside the Mouse: Work and Play at Disney World*, Durham: Duke University Press.

Radway, Janice (1984): *Reading the Romance: Women, Patriarchy, and Popular Literature*, Chapel Hill/London: University of North Carolina Press.

Radway, Janice (1984/1991): 'Interpretive Communities and Variable Literacies: The Function of Romance Reading', Chandra Mukerji and Michael Schudson (eds): *Rethinking Popular Culture:*

Contemporary Perspectives in Cultural Studies, Berkeley: University of California Press.

Radway, Janice (1997): *A Feeling for Books: The Book-of-the-Month Club, Literary Taste, and Middle-Class Desire*, Chapel Hill/London: University of North Carolina Press.

Rajewsky, Irina O. (2005): 'Intermediality, Intertextuality, and Remediation: A Literary Perspective on Intermediality', *Intermédialités*, 6.

Reekie, Gail (1992): 'Changes in the Adamless Eden: The Spatial and Sexual Transformation of a Brisbane Department Store 1930–90', Rob Shields (ed.): *Lifestyle Shopping: The Subject of Consumption*, London/New York: Routledge.

Ricoeur, Paul (1976): *Interpretation Theory: Discourse and the Surplus of Meaning*, Fort Worth, TX: Texas Christian University Press.

Ricoeur, Paul (1981): *Hermeneutics and the Human Sciences: Essays on Language, Action and Interpretation*, Cambridge: Cambridge University Press.

Ricoeur, Paul (1983/1984): *Time and Narrative. Volume 1*, Chicago/London: The University of Chicago Press.

Ricoeur, Paul (1984/1985): *Time and Narrative. Volume 2*, Chicago/London: The University of Chicago Press.

Ricoeur, Paul (1985/1988): *Time and Narrative. Volume 3*, Chicago/London: The University of Chicago Press.

Ricoeur, Paul (2000/2004): *Memory, History, Forgetting*, Chicago/London: The University of Chicago Press.

Robertson, Roland (1995): 'Glocalization: Time-Space and Homogeneity-Heterogeneity', Mike Featherstone, Scott Lash and Roland Robertson (eds): *Global Modernities*, London: Sage.

Rogoff, Irit (2000): *Terra Infirma: Geography's Visual Culture*, London/New York: Routledge.

Safran, William (1991): 'Diasporas in Modern Societies: Myths of Homeland and Return', *Diaspora*, 1:1.

Schrøder, Kim, Drotner, Kirsten, Kline, Stephen and Murray, Catherine (2003): *Researching Audiences*, London: Arnold.

Schudson, Michael (1984): *Advertising, the Uneasy Persuasion: Its Dubious Impact on American Society*, New York: Basic Books, Publishers.

Scott, James C. (ed.) (1990): *Domination and the Arts of Resistance: Hidden Transcripts*, New Haven, CT/London: Yale University Press.

Searle, John R. (1968): *Speech Acts*, Cambridge: Cambridge University Press.

Shannon, Claude E. and Weaver, Warren (1949): *The Mathematical Theory of Communication*, Urbana, IL: University of Illinois Press.

Sheller, Mimi and Urry, John (2003): 'Mobile Transformations of "Public" and "Private" Life', *Theory, Culture & Society*, 20:3.

Silverstone, Roger (1994): *Television and Everyday Life*, London/New York: Routledge.

Silverstone, Roger and Hirsch, Eric (eds) (1992): *Consuming Technologies: Media and Information in Domestic Spaces*, London/New York: Routledge.

Simmel, Georg (1909/1994): 'Bridge and door', *Theory, Culture & Society*, 11:1.

Slater, Don (1997): *Consumer Culture and Modernity*, Cambridge: Polity Press.

Sloterdijk, Peter (1981): *Kritik der zynischen Vernunft*, 2 vols, Frankfurt am Main: Suhrkamp.

Smoodin, Eric (ed.) (1994): *Disney Discourse: Producing the Magic Kingdom*, New York/London: Routledge.

SOU (1997): *Boken i tiden: Betänkande från utredningen om boken och kulturtidskriften*, Stockholm: Regeringskansliet (Statens Offentliga Utredningar 1997: 141).

Spigel, Lynn (2001): 'Media Homes: Then and Now', *International Journal of Cultural Studies*, 4:4.

Stallybrass, Peter and White, Allon (1986): *The Politics and Poetics of Transgression*, Ithaca, NY: Cornell University Press.

Sterne, Jonathan (1997): 'Sounds Like the Mall of America: Programmed Music and the Architectonics of Commercial Space', *Ethnomusicology*, 41:1.

Stevenson, Nick (ed.) (2001): *Culture and Citizenship*, London: Sage.

Stewart, Susan (1993): *On Longing: Narratives of the Miniature, the Gigantic, the Souvenir, the Collection*, Durham, NC: Duke University Press.

Storey, John (2003): *Inventing Popular Culture: From Folklore to Globalization*, Oxford: Blackwell.

Strathern, Marilyn (1988): *The Gender of the Gift: Problems with Women and Problems with Society in Melanesia*, Berkeley: University of California Press.

Straubhaar, Joseph D. (1996/1997): 'Distinguishing the Global, Regional and National Levels of World Television', Annabelle Sreberny-Mohammadi, Dwayne Winseck, Jim McKenna and Oliver Boyd-Barret (eds.): *Media in Global Context: A Reader*, London: Arnold.

Therborn, Göran (1995): *European Modernity and Beyond: The Trajectory of European Societies 1945–2000*, London: Sage.

Thomas, Nicholas (1991): *Entangled Objects: Exchange, Material Culture, and Colonialism in the Pacific*, Cambridge, MA/London: Harvard University Press.

Thompson, John B. (1990): *Ideology and Modern Culture: Critical Social Theory in the Era of Mass Communication*, Cambridge: Polity Press.

Thompson, John B. (1995): *The Media and Modernity: A Social Theory of the Media*, Cambridge: Polity Press.

Thomson, Rachel and Taylor, Rebecca (2005): 'Between Cosmopolitanism and the Locals: Mobility as a Resource in the Transition to Adulthood', *Young: Nordic Journal of Youth Research*, 13:4.

Thörn, Håkan ((1999a): 'Nya sociala rörelser och politikens globalisering. Demokrati utanför parlamentet?' Amnå (1999).

Thörn, Håkan ((1999b): 'Vad är globalisering? Sociologin utmanad', *Sociologisk forskning*, 4/1999.

Tölölyan, Khachig (1991): 'The National State and Its Others: In Lieu of a Preface', *Diaspora*, 1:1.

Tölölyan, Khachig (1996): 'Rethinking Diaspora(s): Stateless Power in the Transnational Moment', *Diaspora*, 5:1.

Trägårdh, Lars (1999): 'Det civila samhället som analytisk begrepp och politisk slogan', Amnå (1999).

Tudor, Andrew (1999): *Decoding Culture: Theory and Method in Cultural Studies*, London: Sage.

Turkle, Sherry (1995/1996): *Life on the Screen: Identity in the Age of the Internet*, London: Weidenfeld & Nicolson.

Turner, Bryan S. (1994): 'Postmodern Culture/Modern Citizens', Bart van Steenbergen (ed.): *The Condition of Citizenship*, London: Sage.

Turner, Bryan S. (2001): 'Outline of a General Theory of Cultural Citizenship', in Stevenson (2001).

Turner, Graeme (1990/2003): *British Cultural Studies: An Introduction*, 3rd edition, New York/London: Routledge.

Urry, John (1995): *Consuming Places*, London/New York: Routledge.

Urry, John (2005): 'The Complexity Turn', *Theory, Culture & Society*, 22:5.

USK (2000): *Besökarna bedömer kvaliteten på Biblioteken i Solna Centrum, Bergshamra och Huvudsta*, Stockholm: Utrednings- och statistikkontoret i Stockholm.

Virilio, Paul (1990/2000): *Polar Inertia*, London: Sage.

Virilio, Paul (1995): *The Art of the Motor*, Minneapolis: The University Press of Minnesota.

Walzer, Michael (1984): *Exodus and Revolution*, New York: Basic Books.

Warning, Rainer (ed.) (1975): *Rezeptionsästhetik. Theorie und Praxis*, Munich: Wilhelm Fink Verlag.

Wasko, Janet (2001): *Understanding Disney: The Manufacture of Fantasy*, Cambridge: Polity Press.

Wasko, Janet, Phillips, Mark and Meehan, Eileen R. (eds) (2001): *Dazzled by Disney: The Global Disney Audiences Project*, London: Leicester University Press.

Wilden, Anthony (1987): *The Rules Are No Game: The Strategy of Communication*, London/New York: Routledge.

Williams, Raymond (1958/1968): *Culture and Society 1780–1950*, Harmondsworth: Penguin.

Williams, Raymond (1961/1965): *The Long Revolution*, Harmondsworth: Penguin.

Williams, Raymond (1962/1973): *Communications*, Harmondsworth: Penguin.

Williams, Raymond (1974/1994): *Television: Technology and Cultural Form*, London/New York: Routledge.

Williams, Raymond (1981): *Culture*, London: Fontana Press.

Willis, Paul (1977): *Learning to Labour: How Working Class Kids get Working Class Jobs*, Aldershot: Gower Publishing.

Willis, Paul (1978): *Profane Culture*, London: Routledge & Kegan Paul.

Willis, Paul (1990): *Common Culture: Symbolic Work at Play in the Everyday Cultures of the Young*, Milton Keynes: Open University Press.

Wilson, Elizabeth (1992): 'The Invisible Flâneur', *New Left Review*, 191.

Winston, Brian (1998): *Media Technology and Society. A History: From the Telegraph to the Internet*, London/New York: Routledge.

Wittgenstein, Ludwig (1953/2001): *Philosophical Investigations*, London: Blackwell.

Wolff, Janet (1985): 'The Invisible Flâneuse: Women and the Literature of Modernity', *Theory, Culture & Society*, 2:3.

Wolff, Janet (1990): *Feminine Sentences: Essays on Women and Culture*, Cambridge: Polity Press.

Wolff, Janet (1993): 'Memoirs and Micrologies: Walter Benjamin, Feminism and Cultural Analysis', *New Formations*, 20.

Yúdice, George (2003): *The Expediency of Culture: Uses of Culture in the Global Era*, Durham, NC/London: Duke University Press.

Zukin, Sharon (1995): *The Cultures of Cities*, Malden, MA/Oxford: Blackwell.

INDEX